AN OLD TESTAMENT T
OF THE SPIRIT OF GOD

An Old Testament Theology of the Spirit of God

WILF HILDEBRANDT

HENDRICKSON
PUBLISHERS

P. O. Box 3473
Peabody, Massachusetts 01961–3473

Printed in the United States of America

ISBN 1–56563–051–3

First printing — October 1995

Library of Congress Cataloging-in-Publication Data

Hildebrandt, Wilf.
An Old Testament Theology of the Spirit of God / Wilf Hildebrandt.
Includes bibliographical references and index.
ISBN 1–56563–051–3 (pbk.)
1. Holy Spirit—Biblical teaching. 2. Bible. O.T.—Theology. I. Title
BS1199.S69H55 1994
231′.3—dc20 95–2442
CIP

This book is dedicated to the
Faculty, Staff, Students, and Boards
of Pan Africa Christian College
who helped me to apply many of the teachings
pertaining to the Spirit of God,
in ministry.

Table of Contents

Acknowledgments

During the research and writing of this book I have experienced the inspiration, motivation, direction, and teaching of the Spirit of God, for which I am grateful. The encouragement of Lillian and our parents has greatly helped me in this project. I am also indebted to many anointed teachers who have assisted me in both academic and practical ways during the research phase of this book. These include David Lim and Roger Stronstad of Western Pentecostal Bible College, William Dumbrell, Elmer Dyck, Gordon D. Fee, Sven Soderlund, and Bruce K. Waltke of Regent College. I learned many theological insights from them. I also appreciate my colleagues Gordon Bergman and Douglas Whitelaw at Pan Africa Christian College who proofread the manuscript and made valuable suggestions. Special thanks goes to Roger Stronstad for his friendship and for submitting my thesis to Hendrickson Publishers.

Abbreviations

AB	Anchor Bible
AJSL	*American Journal of Semitic Languages and Literature*
ANET	*Ancient Near Eastern Texts*, ed. J. B. Pritchard
BA	*The Biblical Archaeologist*
BARev	*Biblical Archaeology Review*
BDB	Brown, F., S. R. Driver, and C. A. Briggs, *Hebrew and English Lexicon of the Old Testament*
Bib	*Biblica*
BSac	*Bibliotheca Sacra*
BibTheoBul	*Biblical Theology Bulletin*
BT	*The Bible Translator*
BZAW	Beihefte zur *ZAW*
CBQ	*Catholic Biblical Quarterly*
ConB	Coniectanea biblica
EvQ	*Evangelical Quarterly*
EvTh	*Evangelishe Theologie*
HTR	*Harvard Theological Review*
HUCA	*Hebrew Union College Annual*
ICC	International Critical Commentary
IDB	*Interpreter's Dictionary of the Bible*, ed. G. A. Buttrick
IJT	*The Indian Journal of Theology*
Int	*Interpretation*
ISBE	*International Standard Bible Encyclopedia*, ed. G. W. Bromiley
JBL	*Journal of Biblical Literature*

JNWSL	*Journal for Northwest Semitic Languages*
JQR	*Jewish Quarterly Review*
JSOT	*Journal for the Study of the Old Testament*
JTS	*Journal of Theological Studies*
NCBC	New Century Bible Commentary
NICNT	New International Commentary on the New Testament
NICOT	New International Commentary on the Old Testament
NIDNTT	*New International Dictionary of New Testament Theology*, ed. C. Brown
NIGTC	New International Greek Testament Commentary
NTS	*New Testament Studies*
OTL	Old Testament Library
RTR	*Reformed Theological Review*
SBT	Studies in Biblical Theology
TDNT	*Theological Dictionary of the New Testament*, ed. G. Kittel and G. Friedrich
TDOT	*Theological Dictionary of the Old Testament*, ed. G. J. Botterweck and H. Ringgren
THAT	*Theologisches Handwörterbuch zum Alten Testament*, ed. E. Jenni and C. Westermann
TWAT	*Theologisches Wörterbuch zum Alten Testament*, ed. G. J. Botterweck and H. Ringgren
TWOT	*Theological Wordbook of the Old Testament*, ed. R. L. Harris, G. L. Archer, Jr., and B. Waltke
Tyn Bul	*Tyndale Bulletin*
WBC	Word Biblical Commentary
WEC	*Wycliffe Exegetical Commentary*
WTH	*Wesleyan Theological Journal*
WTJ	*Westminster Theological Journal*
VT	*Vetus Testamentum*
VTSup	Vetus Testamentum Supplements
ZAW	*Zeitschrift für die Alttestamentliche Wissenschaft*
ZTK	*Zeitschrift für Theologie und Kirche*

Preface

A cursory reading of the NT, particularly the gospels, will alert and intrigue the reader to the many references made concerning the Spirit of God and his activities. In the Gospel of Matthew, Mary conceives "through" the Holy Spirit (Matt 1:18–20). In the same gospel, as well as in Mark and in Luke, the Spirit of God descends like a dove on Jesus as he comes up out of the waters of baptism. Luke's gospel records that an angel informs Zachariah that his son "will be filled with the Holy Spirit even from birth" (1:15). It is prophetically stated that this son "will go on before the Lord in the spirit and power of Elijah" (1:17). Zachariah is then filled with the Holy Spirit and as a result prophesies in hymnic form the Benedictus (1:67ff.). After Jesus' baptism, he is "full" of the Holy Spirit and is then led by the Spirit into the desert, where he is tempted for forty days (4:1–2). At the end of this period of testing, he returns to Galilee "in the power of the Spirit" and commences his earthly ministry of preaching, teaching, delivering, and healing (4:14ff.). The book of Acts records the descent of the Holy Spirit on the expectant, prayerful people of God, who upon reception of the Spirit begin to speak in other tongues (Acts 2:4).

To these examples may be added many references to the Holy Spirit in the Johannine literature and Pauline epistles, as well as in other NT books. From an examination of such texts, a number of questions may arise. What is the source of this developed pneumatology, which the evangelists and apostles apparently assume the reader understands? What background does the terminology found in these references have? How was the NT pneumatology developed to the extent that Spirit-endowed gifts, Spirit-inspired prophecy, and guidance by the Spirit, among other phenomena, were viewed as normative in the early church?

Questions like these motivated me to research and write this book. In part, my interest in this subject has grown due to the interest in NT pneumatology as is evidenced by the amount of literature written on the subject in recent decades. Scholars have presented a rich theology of the Spirit's vital work, both in the believer and in the church community. But, the OT background to the NT pneumatology is often neglected or only briefly surveyed. For instance, F. D. Brunner's *A Theology of the Holy Spirit* (Grand Rapids: Eerdmans, 1970) makes scant reference to OT background material on the subject. S. M. Horton surveys the OT material in three chapters in, *What the Bible Says About the Holy Spirit* (Springfield: Gospel, 1976).

A survey of the principal OT texts from a Catholic perspective is presented by G. T. Montague in *The Holy Spirit: Growth of a Biblical Tradition* ([1976] Peabody, Mass.: Hendrickson, 1994). More recently, J. Rea published a commentary which also surveys the OT passages, *The Holy Spirit in the Bible: All the Major Passages About the Spirit* (Florida: Creation House, 1990).

Many of the books that deal specifically with OT pneumatology are out of print or are inaccessible to most readers. Two of the more recent contributions are L. Neve, *The Spirit of God in the Old Testament* (Tokyo: Seibunsha, 1972), and L. J. Wood, *The Holy Spirit in the Old Testament* (Grand Rapids: Zondervan, 1976). Neve's book is very readable and he has significantly contributed to my understanding of the Spirit's work in the OT. Two other studies are by P. Volz, *Der Geist Gottes* (Tübingen: J. C. B. Mohr, 1910) and D. Lys, *Rûach: Le Souffle dans l'Ancien Testament* (Paris: Presses Universitaires de France, 1962). Most other recent contributions deal with the New Testament material and are systematic theological approaches to the subject.

In addition to the above observations, the principles applied to the interpretation of pneumatological texts are often subjective and speculative. Many popular approaches to OT material referring to the work of the Spirit of God are examples of spiritualizing and allegorizing—methods that diminish the authority of some passages. Books selected at random from sections on pneumatology illustrate this point, such as F. E. Marsh,

Emblems of the Holy Spirit (Grand Rapids: Kregel, 1957–76); and A. W. Ness, *The Holy Spirit* (2 vols.; Christian Centre Publications, 1979). This hermeneutical problem is partially due to the nature of OT language where images, symbols, anthropomorphisms, and figurative language are employed. However, even these forms have their contexts and referents that one must carefully consider.

Unfortunately, by spiritualizing texts to make them mean something that was not intended, authors undermine the authority of their teaching. For example, one author refers to three kinds of anointings that he claims indicate a progression of the touch and influence of the Spirit in the believer's life. Frequently, the hermeneutical principles employed do not support the conclusions reached. The main conclusions some writers make might be supported from other texts, but the ones employed are often subjectively applied. Too often, spiritualizing, allegorizing, and proof-texting have led to abuses and wrong emphases in our practices that mislead believers and teach them methods of interpretation that are harmful.

In light of this state of affairs, we propose to add to the discussion of the Spirit of God in the OT. I endeavour to consider relevant pneumatological passages within their contexts in order to bring forth their plain teaching and instruction. Research for this book took place primarily during graduate studies at Regent College and culminated in a thesis called, "An Investigation of *rûaḥ* as the Spirit of God in the Hebrew Canon (1989)." The thesis has been completely revised and widened in scope from mainly an investigation into specific lexical references to the Spirit of God. It now includes material on symbols, allusions, and figures of speech that also refer to the Spirit of God. I trust that the material provides a comprehensive understanding of some of the background to NT pneumatology.

The format and structure of the book have arisen in part from a canonical investigation of the lexical term *rûaḥ*. The order in which I proceed is the order in which the Hebrew canon is presented, the Law, the Prophets (Former and Latter Prophets), and the Writings. For those unfamiliar with this order, it is as follows. The Torah (Law) consists of the first five books, Genesis through Deuteronomy. The Former Prophets include Joshua, Judges, 1 and 2 Samuel, and 1 and 2 Kings. The Latter Prophets consist of Isaiah, Jeremiah, Ezekiel, and the book of the Twelve (the Minor Prophets). The Writings include Psalms, Proverbs,

Job, Song of Solomon, Ruth, Lamentations, Ecclesiastes, Esther, Daniel, Ezra-Nehemiah, and 1 and 2 Chronicles, in that order. My reason for this approach is mainly that Israel organized and presented its faith and beliefs according to the threefold canon of the Law, the Former and Latter Prophets, and the Writings. This structure is the final form of the OT Scriptures that the people of God recognized and accepted as their constitutive canon and that bears witness to Israel's faith.

Wilf Hildebrandt

1

*The Semantic Range of **rûaḥ** in the Hebrew Canon*

The wind blows wherever it pleases. You hear its sound, but you cannot tell where it comes from or where it is going. So it is with everyone born of the Spirit. (John 3:8)

It is almost as difficult to trace the source of the winds that sweep across the universe as it is to pinpoint the origins of "spirit" notions in the ancient Near East. Nearly as complex is the tracing of the background to Israel's pneumatology as presented in the OT. The OT literature presents a variety of concepts in regard to the Israelites' perceptions of the spirit. References to the Spirit of God in the OT are mainly with the term *rûaḥ*. The Hebrew OT has three hundred and eighty-nine occurrences of this term.[1] Of these references, approximately one hundred and seven refer to the activity of God in the world of nature and in the life of humankind. In these passages, *rûaḥ* is translated "Spirit" and indicates the work and activity of the Spirit of God. Other meanings of the term are "wind," in its plain sense of moving air, and "breath." The majority of the references to *rûaḥ*, however, have an anthropological meaning that may point to the emotions and dispositions of humankind. In addition, *rûaḥ*

[1] A. Even-Shoshan, ed., *A New Concordance of the Old Testament* (Jerusalem: Kiryat Sepher, 1983), 1063–66. Eleven of these references occur in the Aramaic portions of Daniel. Refer also to R. Albertz and C. Westermann, *"rûaḥ, Geist," THAT,* 2.727; S. Tengström, *"rûaḥ," TWAT,* 6.389.

is used to express the animating principle of life in both humankind and beast. Because of its various meanings, it is crucial for the interpreter to analyze the specific context in which the word occurs.

An overview of the distribution of occurrences of *rûaḥ* in the Hebrew canon is informative. In the Pentateuch, it occurs thirty-eight times, with no occurrences in Leviticus. Forty-seven appearances of the word are in the Former Prophets, with one hundred and fifty-four in the Latter Prophets. The majority of occurrences in the prophetic literature are from the exilic period and after. Ezekiel and Isaiah use the word most frequently. Jeremiah uses it only eighteen times in reference to wind as an instrument of God. The Writings record the word one hundred and thirty-nine times, with an additional eleven references in the Aramaic portion of Daniel. Books not employing the term *rûaḥ* at all are Leviticus, Obadiah, Nahum, Ruth, Song of Solomon, and Esther. Some OT books resort to other phrases, imagery, and symbols to convey the work of the Spirit, such as "the hand of the Lord."

In order to understand the concept of *rûaḥ* as the Spirit of God, I will survey the OT references to *rûaḥ* in this chapter. I will briefly summarize the various translations of *rûaḥ* to provide the background and range of its uses in the OT. An overview of texts that use *rûaḥ* in the sense of "wind," various emotions and dispositions, and "breath," provides a helpful context in which to understand the passages referring specifically to the Spirit of God. Limiting this study to the lexical term *rûaḥ,* however, would be inadequate for a comprehensive understanding of the Spirit's activity in the OT. Numerous allusions, emblems, symbols, images, and figurative expressions denote the work and movement of the Spirit of God in the Hebrew canon. This range of allusions to the Spirit is dealt with in subsequent chapters in conjunction with specific texts. Significant aspects are the symbolism of water, the anointing oil, the hand of the Lord, the blessing, and the presence of God. Specific facets of OT theology in which the Spirit of God is featured, such as ecstasy and restoration, will also be examined.

The main purpose of this study is to provide some foundational biblical insights into the OT teaching regarding the Spirit of God. In doing so, I consider the chronology and development of the theological understanding of the Spirit's work. I have sought to avoid spiritualizing and allegorizing material so that clear biblical and contextual applications may be drawn that can then be applied to contemporary practice. Also, OT pneumatology is understood to be the main background material for NT pneumatology. We should, therefore, discover many theological tenets in the OT that help to clarify the NT experience of the Spirit and the NT literature on this subject.

Origins and Comparisons

The origin and development of meaning for the term *rûaḥ* remain shrouded in history. In the OT, Genesis 1:2 is the first reference to the word. There the *rûaḥ* is present over the chaotic, uninhabitable earth. As we read this passage, it is not immediately apparent what the background and etymology of the term are. It is left to the reader to determine what the lexical term and context convey. A survey of translations for Genesis 1:2 shows that translators differ on how the term *rûaḥ* should be rendered. This example demonstrates that it is crucial for the reader to recognize the ancient Near Eastern context and background to this OT concept. Therefore, the understanding of *rûaḥ* as "spirit" must be sought in the context of how the relationship between god and humanity is conceived and presented in the ancient Near East. Rather than reading back into the OT literature our NT views and pneumatology, we must come to the material afresh, with an OT perspective if possible. This is the cultural context of the biblical characters and the perspective that we will seek to reflect as we discuss various OT passages on the subject. How did the ancients perceive the influence of the gods in their experience? How did they view the mode and method in which the godly power of life was transferred to humankind? What was it that animated life and brought about fertility and strength for existence?[2] These are some of the questions that no doubt interested the ancient world and led to their formulations of their respective worldviews. In order to answer some of these queries, we look to literature from biblical times to discover how Israel's neighbors convey the work of the *rûaḥ*, if in fact they do.

---

[2] J. Hehn, "Zum Problem des Geistes im Alten Orient und im Alten Testament," *ZAW* 43 (1925) 212ff.

Life in the Ancient Near East

J. Hehn provides evidence that in the Egyptian culture, the gods, particularly Amon, affect life-giving breath in a manner similar to that found in some OT texts (cf. Gen 2:7; Job 33:4). Breath as the symbol of life and the longing for the *lebenatem* ("life-breath") is strongly expressed in Egyptian texts, where life is attributed to the breath of Amon and Horus.[3] The Egyptians believed that life was received from the gods. Particularly the king is believed to be formed and given life-breath by the gods. Hehn makes it clear, however, that the concept of the spirit as developed by the OT is unique to Israel. No texts in the Egyptian literature attribute the life-breath to the "spirit of the gods." Hehn is therefore correct in claiming that the differences in the expressions for wind, spirit, and life are without a doubt due to the particular national, cultural, and religious views of the West Semites. Whereas an Egyptian model may be used for some cultural aspects, the content pertaining to the Spirit is unique to OT literature.

Wind, Air, and Breath in the Ancient Near East

In the West Semitic literature, particularly at Ugarit, the term *rḥ* is the equivalent of the OT term *rûaḥ*. Although diverse opinions concerning the ancient Near Eastern background to the term *rûaḥ* abound, some lexical data suggest that the West Semitic languages attributed the following meanings to the *rḥ* root.[4] In Ugaritic, *rḥ* means "wind, breath, fragrance," and in Aramaic, *rwḥ* is "wind, spirit." The Arabic form makes a distinction between *ruḥ*, "life-breath," and *riḥ*, "wind." When *rḥ* occurs in the Ugaritic poems of Baal, it refers generally to the atmospheric phenomena that accompany his movements. The epithet of Baal is typically "the rider of the clouds." Lightning, rain, and stormy conditions are claimed to be in his control (cf. Pss 18:10 [11 MT]; 104:3).

---

[3] Hehn, "Problem," 216–18; Also see H. Kleinknecht, "*pneuma, pneumatikos*," *TDNT*, 6.339–42.

[4] The *rḥ* root occurs in all Semitic languages except for the eastern branch. See A. R. Johnson, *The Vitality of the Individual in the Thought of Ancient Israel* (2d ed.; Cardiff: University of Wales Press, 1964) 23.

Akkadian literature exhibits beliefs regarding wind and life-breath similar to those in the OT, but the East Semitic languages do not employ the *rḥ* root using instead the word *šāru* for "wind, breath."[5] The Akkadian term *šāru* is more similar to the Hebrew word for storm (*śaʿar*) than to *rûaḥ*.[6] In ancient Near Eastern texts, the term *rûaḥ* is never used in the sense of the *rûaḥ* of God, but at times, the *rûaḥ* as wind is viewed as the instrument of the gods. Thus, the elements of breath, air, wind, or atmosphere in relation to gods like Enlil are similar to some OT concepts, but the lexical terms are different. Other than in Egyptian texts, the creation myths do not speak of gods giving life-breath to humankind. In fact, the gods praise Marduk for his "good breath" that he breathes into the gods, not into humans. Marduk is also viewed as the god who reserves control over some atmospheric conditions, which includes the bringing of catastrophe and sickness.[7] In the Akkadian literature calamities are often attributed to the seven storm demons.

In short, the West Semitic usage of the root *rḥ* is similar to the OT translation of "wind" and "breath," but there is no evidence that the root has the meaning "spirit" or "Spirit," in the OT sense, outside of the Hebrew canon. Ancient Near Eastern texts do not use *rûaḥ* to indicate that gods have spirits or that the *rûaḥ* is an extension of a god. Nor does the term refer to aspects of the human spirit. Therefore, although Israel has many similarities with the cultural environment of the ancient Near East, the term *rûaḥ* has a unique development of its lexical range of meanings in the OT. The OT is the only ancient literature that develops this term to portray a people's experience with their God.

Chronological Development

The chronological development of meaning for the term *rûaḥ* is also difficult to ascertain. According to W. R. Schoemaker, who based his views on subjective dating of the earliest references to *rûaḥ* from 900 to 700 BC, *rûaḥ* initially had only the two

[5] See Albertz and Westermann, "*rûaḥ, Geist*," 726–27.
[6] See Hehn, "Problem," 210–25.
[7] Tengström, "*rûaḥ*," 390–93.

general meanings of "wind" and "spirit."[8] He dismissed the view that the Hebrews conceived of wind as "air in motion" and preferred the two main connotations of "energy" and "invisibility" for the term. Schoemaker understood the connection between wind and spirit in the influence noted when God by his unseen spirit acted on human beings just as the invisible wind acted on natural objects.[9] Furthermore, he claimed that when the term *rûaḥ* referred to a person's physical strength, courage, and anger, it indicated the association between God's activity in moving human beings and the subsequent changes of disposition within them.[10]

I agree that the connection between "wind" and "spirit" is found in the correspondences between the invisibility and powerful activity of the *rûaḥ*. But, the important connotation of "air in motion" is also evident in many passages, particularly where *rûaḥ* refers to wind. The same verdict concerns the view that the translation "breath" for *rûaḥ* prior to the exile is impossible. The main problem with this opinion is the subjective dating of OT documents that fails to recognize the early provenance of some passages of Scripture such as Exodus 15:8 and 2 Samuel 22:16, which use the term *rûaḥ*. F. M. Cross provides evidence of an early provenance for these passages.[11] Even some Ugaritic texts use the *rḥ* root in the sense of "vital breath." On this basis, P. van Imschoot concludes that the primary sense of *rûaḥ* is probably "breath."[12] From this sense, the meaning was probably extended to signify wind or moving air. This development may explain the mysterious and powerful effect that the *rûaḥ* has on both nature and humanity. Probably the change of respiration when affected by the emotions and by circumstances led to a variety of anthropological meanings. In the West Semitic literature the term *rûaḥ* is primarily associated with "breathing" and with "feeling," which

---

[8] W. R. Schoemaker, "The Use of *rûaḥ* in the Old Testament and of *pneuma* in the New Testament," *JBL* 23 (1904) 13f.

[9] Schoemaker, "The Use of *rûaḥ*," 14.

[10] Schoemaker, "The Use of *rûaḥ*," 19; cf. L. Neve, *The Spirit of God in the Old Testament* (Tokyo: Seibusha, 1972) 1.

[11] F. M. Cross and D. N. Freedman, "A Royal Song of Thanksgiving: 2 Samuel 22 and Psalm 18," *JBL* 72 (1953) 15–34.

[12] P. van Imschoot, *Theology of the Old Testament* (trans. K. Sullivan and F. Buck; Rome: Desclée Company, 1954) 1.173. See also, D. Hill, *Greek Words and Hebrew Meanings* (Cambridge: Cambridge University Press, 1967) 205–6.

changes according to the fluctuations in respiration and disposition.[13] The term also refers to that which is living and vibrant.

Pneuma in the Septuagint and Greek Literature

Although not directly related to the background of the OT development of meaning for *rûaḥ,* the translation of *rûaḥ* in the LXX and in Greek literature is informative. The verb *pneō,* from which *pneuma* is derived, means "to blow" or "to breathe" (wind or air).[14] The LXX translates *rûaḥ* by *anemos* instead of *pneuma* when the meaning "wind" is clearly intended (52 times). The usual translation of *rûaḥ* is *pneuma* (277 times). *Pneuma* not only refers to wind and life breath in the LXX, but to superhuman power, spiritual ability, resolve of the will, the constitution of the soul, an eschatological gift and the principle of life in man.[15]

In classical Greek literature the term *pneuma* is classified in two main ways. For the most part, pneuma is "wind," which ranges from a gentle breeze to a violent blast. Second, *pneuma* is breathed out in the sense of respiration, which indicates the breath of life. The externally recognizable feature of life for the ancients is respiration. As long as a beast or human breathes in and out, life is clearly present, and without consistent respiration, life is considered to be absent. In this connotation, breath becomes the symbol of life and is associated with moving air. Although distinctly invisible, it still affects physical matter in a manner that is visibly seen. Therefore, the term *rûaḥ* has always "retained the meaning 'wind' denoting the movement of air both outside Man in Nature, and inside him, his own breath."[16] In addition to the translation of *rûaḥ* by *pneuma* for wind and the breath of life, Greek literature uses the term in reference to soul, mental and spiritual realities, inspiration, something divine, and as a cosmic and universal power.[17] From his survey of Greek literature, Kleinknecht follows W. Porzig and concludes that the verbal noun *pneuma* "means the elemental natural and vital force

[13] Tengström, *"rûaḥ,"* 389.

[14] H. G. Liddell and R. Scott, *"pneuma," A Greek-English Lexicon,* reprinted ed., Revised by H. S. Jones (Oxford: Clarendon, 1978) 1424.

[15] See W. Bieder, *"pneuma, pneumatikōs," TDNT,* 6.368–72.

[16] W. Eichrodt, *Theology of the Old Testament* (trans. J. A. Baker; Philadelphia: Westminster, 1967) 2.46.

[17] See Kleinknecht, *"pneuma,"* 336–39.

which, matter and process in one, acts as a stream of air in the blowing of the wind and the inhaling and exhaling of breath, and hence transferred as the breath of the spirit which, in a way which may be detected both outwardly and inwardly, fills with inspiration and grips with enthusiasm."[18]

In the light of these observations, we conclude that the word *rûaḥ,* translated *pneuma,* has to do with moving air and is therefore associated mainly with breathing and wind. The association with breath and respiration, which indicates the presence of life, gives rise to the concept of the unseen living spirit. External factors that may influence the spirit would in turn cause changes in the "spirit" of humankind that affect dispositions and emotions. Spirit, therefore, becomes the ideal word to indicate God's omnipotence in affecting both nature and humanity. In nature, the invisible winds sent by God can effect calamities and atmospheric disturbances. In relation to humankind, God's actions, that begin with the provision of the breath of life, may cause a change in disposition, in respiration, and in action. This term becomes the best one for Israel to communicate God's invisible presence through which God effectively brought the world into existence. The invisible *rûaḥ* is, therefore, behind all of God's designs and actions which bring about dramatic changes in the physical world.

Rûaḥ as Wind in the Law, the Prophets, and the Writings

Although scholars disagree on the exact number of times *rûaḥ* is to be rendered "wind" in the OT, the majority agree on a figure between one hundred and thirteen and one hundred and seventeen times. Differences occur depending on the context and whether passages are considered to be figurative, literal, or

---

[18] Kleinknecht, *"pneuma,"* 334–35. Regarding the development of meaning Kleinknecht notes, "In the metaphorical speech of poetry in particular, concrete natural processes such as the blowing of the wind or breathing express corresponding experiences of mental or spiritual reality. *pneuma* is more or less strongly spiritualized and takes on the transferred sense of any kind of breath or spirit which blows in interpersonal relations or from the invisible world of the divine," 336.

metaphorical.[19] In a variety of contexts, the translation "wind" belongs to the realm of cosmology and meteorology.

In the OT, *rûaḥ* as "wind" is often used as an instrument in the hands of Yahweh to accomplish the divine purpose. The first occurrence as "wind" is in Genesis 3:8, where the translation should be either "in the cool of the day" or "in the evening breeze." It describes the period of the day when the wind brings its relieving breezes. The *rûaḥ* sent by God over the earth caused the floodwaters to recede (Gen 8:1). In the religious conflict between Yahweh and Pharaoh, God employed the wind from the east to bring the plague of locusts over the land of Egypt (Exod 10:13). When Pharaoh petitioned for the plague to be removed, the Lord used a strong west wind to carry the locusts into the sea. The great exodus event was made possible by the Lord's parting of the Reed Sea with a strong east wind (Exod 14:21). To satisfy the appetites of the Israelites in the wilderness, the Lord used a wind from the west to drive in quail from the sea (Num 11:31). The wind from the east is often a hot sirocco while the west wind is a relief-bringing sea breeze (Exod 10:19). When used metaphorically in these and other texts, judgment is usually viewed as coming with the east wind while deliverance comes from the west (cf. Jer 18:17; Ezek 17:10; 19:12). The verbs used with *rûaḥ* as wind are verbs of movement and action that stress that the wind is set in motion by the volition of Yahweh. Yahweh can cause the wind to "go out" (Num 11:31) and drive the quail inland. When Yahweh uses the wind to do his bidding in salvation history, the wind is an instrument of God, whether to deliver (Exod 14:21) or to punish people (Num 11:31).

The prophets employ the common understanding of wind with modifiers such as "destructive," "powerful," "blustering," and "mighty." Often, the wind refers simply to that which brings with it rain, hail, or dark skies (1 Kgs 18:45; 19:11; cf. 2 Kgs 3:17). Wind may also be used in a metaphorical sense as in Isaiah 7:2, where hearts are shaken as trees by the wind, or in judgment, where individuals are blown as chaff before the wind (Isa 17:13). The metaphorical expression of wind coming

[19] H. W. Wolff, *Anthropology of the Old Testament* (trans. M. Kohl; Philadelphia: Fortress, 1974) 32; H. W. Robinson, *Inspiration and Revelation in the Old Testament* (Oxford: Clarendon, 1946) 74; C. A. Briggs, "The Use of *rûaḥ* in the Old Testament," *JBL* 19 (1900) 133–34.

from the "four corners of the heavens" presents the extent of God's judgment on Elam (Jer 49:36). Ezekiel also uses the expression "the four winds" to point figuratively to the origins of "breath" that will animate the "bones" in order to give them life (Ezek 37:9–10). In this text, the term *rûaḥ* is used five times and is translated mainly in the anthropological sense of the life-breath.

God's control over the winds is noted in the metaphor of the wind being brought out of God's "storehouses" (Jer 10:13). Other references summarize the origins of "every wind" to be with God (Jer 49:32; Ezek 5:10, 12; 12:14; 17:21). Indeed, God is the creator of the wind (Amos 4:13). In the prophets, the use of wind as an instrument predominates. As protectors of God's covenant, the prophets respond to threats of covenant breach with judgment oracles. In Hosea, those who break the covenant "sow to the wind" (Hos 8:7). Israel's idolatrous worship reaps them a harvest of judgment that is likened to the hot easterly wind that comes in the form of the Assyrian army (Hos 13:15; cf. 12:1 [2 MT]). The imagery of wind is used to convey the coming judgment of God, who directs the wind for purposes of punishment. Whereas the wind may blow from the west, it most often comes from the east (Jer 18:17; Ezek 17:10; 19:12; Jonah 1:4; 4:8). In these contexts of proclaimed judgment, the hot easterly winds, which wither crops and torment people, illustrate the nature of the events to come. God in wrath will unleash a violent wind (Ezek 13:11).

The insignificance of idols is emphasized by the ease with which they are swept away: "The wind *[rûaḥ]* will carry all of them off, a mere breath will blow them away" (Isa 57:13). "See, they are all false! Their deeds amount to nothing; their images are but wind *[rûaḥ]* and confusion" (41:29). The wind will pick up men like chaff on the threshing floor (Jer 4:11–12; cf. Isa 41:16) and drive the false shepherds away (Jer 22:22). Also, the words of false prophets are like the wind. They are devoid of God's truth and revelation (Jer 5:13; cf. Mic 2:11). Before God's wind, human beings are like grass and will wither away (Isa 40:7). Just as the wind sweeps over the earth, so also will a person's sins sweep him or her away (64:6).

For the most part, the Writings employ the translation "wind" and its variants in a similar manner to the way the Pentateuch and the Prophets do. The wind may come from a variety of directions as a breeze or as a violent storm.[20] But, Yahweh also rides "the wings of the wind," which are his messengers. They do his bidding and accomplish the will of their powerful creator (Pss 18:10 [11 MT]; 104:4; 148:8).

The Wisdom literature often compares the wind to the emptiness and vanity of life, which is as fleeting as "chasing after the wind" and is therefore folly (Eccl 1:14, 17; 2:11, 17, 26; 4:4, 6, 16; 6:9). Wind is metaphorically used of the illusory aspects of life such as an empty inheritance and toil without reward (Prov 11:29; 25:4; 27:16; Eccl 5:16 [15 MT]). In addition, words and speeches devoid of wisdom, substance, and truth are likened to a blustering wind (Job 6:26; 8:2; 16:3).

In short, the term *rûaḥ* in many contexts is to be rendered "wind." God is the creator of the wind, which he releases from storehouses at his discretion. Wind functions in the normal course of nature to bring clouds, seasonal rains, and storms. But, the winds are also instruments and messengers in God's hands through which the divine purposes are accomplished. In times of judgment they may bring about plagues and drought. Moreover, a wide range of metaphorical uses indicates the nature of wind to blow away chaff, sweep away dust, shake trees, and wither crops. Like the elusive and invisible wind, words may also be devoid of content and the circumstances of life may be viewed as meaningless.

The *rûaḥ* in Relation to Humankind in the Law, the Prophets, and the Writings

When *rûaḥ* is used in relation to humankind, it is an anthropological and psychological term. It is used in the majority of cases in this sense, with a great variety of meanings. These meanings may be categorized from simple physical breath to a range of psychological and emotional dispositions. One must carefully consider the particular context of a passage in order to determine the right connotation of the word. Moreover, a variety of biblical terms are used to present the anthropological nature and human existence in addition to the term *rûaḥ*.

---

[20] Cf. Pss 1:4; 11:6; 18:42 [43 MT]; 35:5; 48:7; 83:13 [14 MT]; 103:16; 107:25; 135:7; Job 1:19; 15:2, 30; 21:18; 28:25; 30:15, 22; 37:21; 41:16 [8 MT]; Prov 30:4; Eccl 1:6; 11:4–5; Dan 2:35; 7:2; 8:8; 11:4.

R. G. Bratcher captures the OT perspective that places the word in its proper anthropological context:

> The biblical writers, as a rule, view man as a whole, a unit which cannot be divided into separate parts, each with its own separate existence. This is especially true in the OT books. Man is not simply the sum of physical (flesh, body), spiritual (spirit, soul), and intellectual and emotional (mind, heart) parts. He can be described by any one of these qualities, but this does not imply that the others are separate entities. And in a given context a person's will, or intellect, or instinct, or desire, or passion, or any other emotion may be described as localized in the heart, the bowels, the spleen, the genital organs, the spirit, or the soul.[21]

With this context in mind we will observe the various uses of *rûaḥ* in relation to humankind.

The Creation of Humankind and Beasts

Perhaps the most important connotation of *rûaḥ* in relation to humankind is its reference to the animating principle of life. With this meaning, it is often found in synonymous parallelism with the term *nep̱eš,* which is usually translated "soul, life, life-breath" (cf. Isa 26:9).[22] The *rûaḥ* is the gift of God, who forms human beings and breathes life into them. It usually indicates the inner person. Similarly, when God breathes into the nostrils of man, *nep̱eš* constitutes a living, breathing human being (Gen 2:7). A distinction is evident between the terms in that the *nep̱eš* may represent the whole person (Isa 19:3, 14; 26:9; 63:11; Ezek 11:19; Hos 5:4; Zech 12:1; Ps 51:12). H. W. Wolff concludes, "*nep̱eš*

---

[21] R. G. Bratcher, "Biblical Words Describing Man: Breath, Life, Spirit," *BT* 34 (April 1983) 201.

[22] When signifying the spirit of the living, breathing being, dwelling in the flesh (*bāśār*) of humans and of animals, the terms *nep̱eš* and *rûaḥ* are parallel about 25 times. Cf. Briggs, "Use of *rûaḥ,*" 137. Concerning the distinction between the terms, L. Kohler's view, that the soul comes into being when God breathes the spirit of life into humankind, indicates their relationship to one another. "Soul is therefore, the (individualized) spirit, delimited by its connexion with a body, which animates the body." *Old Testament Theology* (trans. A. S. Todd; Philadelphia: Westminster, 1957) 145. Albertz and Westermann make the distinction between *rûaḥ* and *nᵉšāmāh* in that the latter pertains more to the normal aspect of breath, indicating the presence of life, while *rûaḥ* is the special respiration in which the dynamic vitality of humankind is seen. "*rûaḥ, Geist,*" 734–35.

is designed to be seen together with the whole form of man, and especially with his breath; moreover man does not have *nep̱eš*, he is *nep̱eš*, he lives as *nep̱eš*."[23] The hunger and thirst of man, including spiritual hunger for God, is often referred to as a need of the *nep̱eš* or of the *rûaḥ:* "My soul finds rest in God alone; my salvation comes from him" (Pss 62:1 [2 MT]; cf. 104:9, 29; 139:7).[24]

The deluge on the earth was God's judgment and plan to extinguish the life-breath of both humankind and animals. "I am going to bring floodwaters on the earth to destroy all life under the heavens, every creature that has the breath *[rûaḥ]* of life in it" (Gen 6:17; cf. 7:15, 22). Thus, both humankind and beasts are living creatures by virtue of the *rûaḥ ḥayyîm* that God breathes into them. These terms, when appearing together, indicate the life-breath bestowed on creatures that distinguishes them from the dead. Yahweh gives his *rûaḥ* in order to provide life. As bestower of life by the *rûaḥ,* God is not only the creator but also the owner of all flesh. In the context of a transition in leadership, Moses requests, "May the Lord, the God of the spirits of all mankind, appoint a man over this community" (Num 27:16). By implication, because of the God-given vitality of life and the ongoing care of God for creatures, they in turn are to be subject to God's rule alone.[25]

In the Prophets, Yahweh is identified as the one who forms the human *rûaḥ* within a person (Zech 12:1). As the principle of life, *rûaḥ* often parallels *nep̱eš* where God gives living breath (*n*^{e}*šāmāh*) to humankind (Isa 42:5). Subsequent to Hezekiah's prayer, his *rûaḥ* was restored to life (Isa 38:16). In Ezekiel's vision, the bones are animated by the *rûaḥ* of God (Ezek 37:5–10). The term may also refer to breath in the sense of simple respiration (Jer 10:14; 51:17). The metaphoric use of *rûaḥ* is apparent in the context of judgment where the *rûaḥ* goes forth to punish the wicked (Isa 11:4). As the animating principle of life, one may render *rûaḥ* "breath" or "spirit" in the Writings. Thus, the length of life depends on the *rûaḥ* remaining in a person (Job 27:3). In Yahweh's hand lies the life and breath of every creature (Job 12:10; cf. Lam 4:20), over which

[23] Wolff, *Anthropology,* 10.

[24] Tengström, *"rûaḥ,"* 396–97; cf. J. Scharbert, *"nep̱eš," TWAT,* 5.538; N. H. Snaith, *The Distinctive Ideas of the Old Testament* (New York: Schocken, 1964) 146ff.

[25] Eichrodt, *Theology,* 2.48.

he providentially watches (Job 10:12). God knows the frail nature of humans who are but flesh and a "breeze" *[rûaḥ]* that passes away with no return (Ps 78:39).

The pessimistic preacher sees the fate of humankind and animals in similar terms—both have the same *rûaḥ* and therefore return to dust from which they were formed (Eccl 3:19; cf. Ps 146:4). Where the *rûaḥ* goes after death remains a mystery to the preacher (Eccl 3:21), but the epilogue of Ecclesiastes affirms that the *rûaḥ* returns to God who gave it (12:7). Death is the result of being without breath or *rûaḥ* (Ps 104:29). Just as human beings have no power over the wind, they are powerless to determine the day of their death (Eccl 8:8; 11:5). Their only recourse is to commit the *rûaḥ* into the hands of Yahweh (Ps 31:5 [6 MT]). When Job suffers from illness, it is noted that he needs the *rûaḥ* for recovery, for without it his life would be cut short and ready for the grave (Job 9:18; 17:1; 19:17).[26]

Human Dispositions

A rich field of meaning ranging from the physical to the psychological and emotional aspects is attributed to *rûaḥ* in relation to humankind. The translation often derives from the immediate context of the word. The emotions are understood to come forth out of the *rûaḥ* and affect both disposition and behavior. In this way, *rûaḥ* is at times similar to or parallel to *lēḇ* (heart). A distinction between them is that the *rûaḥ* is God's gift of life to humankind but what proceeds from a person's own will comes out of that person's heart (cf. Jer 23:16; Ezek 13:2–3). The human spirit is the location of God's activity in an individual. W. Eichrodt states, "It is therefore understandable that Yahweh's direct influence on a man is aimed especially at the *rûaḥ* as the organ of higher psychic activity; he awakens or stirs it up to decisive action, but he may also harden it, and so inflict punishment."[27]

The *rûaḥ* may be said to be filled with grief, discontent, or bitterness (Gen 26:35). It may be troubled, as in the case of the pharaoh of whom it is said, "In the morning his mind *[rûaḥ]* was

[26] See J. Moltmann's perceptive views on the human spirit in *God in Creation: An Ecological Doctrine of Creation* (trans. M. Kohl; London: SCM, 1985) 262ff.

[27] Eichrodt, *Theology,* 2.133.

troubled" (41:8). Or the *rûaḥ* may be revived, as in the case of Jacob when he received good news (45:27). It may also refer to the general feeling of a people as a group. When Moses tried to help the Israelites out of bondage, their *rûaḥ* was discouraged or in anguish (Exod 6:9). At times, the *rûaḥ* of the people could be moved to generosity and cooperation (35:21). The *rûaḥ* of Caleb is said to have been different from that of the others in that he responded in a spirit of faith and courage (Num 14:24; cf. 12:30). In a negative sense, the *rûaḥ* may be moved to jealousy (5:14, 30), or in the case of Sihon, king of Heshbon, the spirit and heart may become hardened and obstinate (Deut 2:30).

It is in the *rûaḥ* of humankind that fear or loss of courage is noted. The *rûaḥ* of those who oppose God's rule will eventually be broken in defeat (Ps 76:12 [13 MT]). In the light of adverse circumstances, the psalmist in need of assistance grows faint in *rûaḥ* (Pss 77:3 [4 MT]; 142:4; 143:4, 7). The human *rûaḥ* that is strong will sustain a person in illness, but a weak, pessimistic, or crushed *rûaḥ* is hard to bear (Prov 15:4, 13).

The *rûaḥ* is also the place where emotions are controlled. *Rûaḥ* is often rendered "temper" or "rage." Control over the spirit is necessary or a person may lose one's temper (Prov 16:32), and thus be rendered a fool (29:11). The sage advises that one should not be quickly provoked in one's *rûaḥ* (Eccl 7:9), for a person without self-control (*rûaḥ*) is like a broken-down city (Prov 25:28; cf. Job 15:13; Eccl 10:4). In contrast to the quick tempered person is the patient one (Prov 14:29). Job, whose spirit seems to be the target of God's poison arrows (Job 6:4), claims the right to be "impatient" (21:4) and thus is compelled by his *rûaḥ* to speak (32:18).

Nebuchadnezzar is "troubled" in *rûaḥ* by the dreams he has and desires to know the interpretation of them in his "mind" (*rûaḥ*) (Dan 2:1, 3; cf. Gen 41:8). In the same sense, Job also wants an understanding "mind" (*rûaḥ*) so that he can reply (Job 20:3). The *rûaḥ* is parallel to *lēḇ* ("heart") where decisions are made and understanding is gained. The *rûaḥ* may "think" or "muse" about something (Ps 77:6 [7 MT]). A willing or obedient spirit is also a desire of the psalmist (51:10, 12 [12, 14 MT]), an expression often synonymous with *lēḇ* (57:8; 112:7).

The character of an individual is at times reflected by the state of a person's *rûaḥ*. Yahweh desires the one with a "broken" or "crushed" *rûaḥ* (Pss 34:18 [19 MT]; 51:17 [19 MT]). The opposite of a broken spirit is one that is "haughty and proud" (Prov

16:18; Eccl 7:8). Unfaithful "spirits" and disloyal hearts are grievous to Yahweh, but blessed is the person with a "trustworthy" *rûaḥ* (Prov 11:13), and a *rûaḥ* without deceit (Ps 32:2). The one lowly in *rûaḥ* brings honor (Prov 29:23).

Human Emotions

It is predominately in the Prophets that changes in the emotions, or the *rûaḥ,* of humankind are noted. Circumstances or common experiences may affect the human *rûaḥ* changing one's disposition from calmness to excitement or depression. When the queen of Sheba surveys the splendor of Solomon's court, her *rûaḥ* is "overwhelmed" (1 Kgs 10:5; 2 Chron 9:4). Ahab's *rûaḥ* is depressed when he does not receive Naboth's vineyard (1 Kgs 21:5). Food and drink may also revive the famished person physically, which in turn revives the spirit (Judg 15:19; 1 Sam 30:12).

In the midst of adverse circumstances, the *rûaḥ* may also lose "courage," as in the case where the enemies of Israel were faced with the conquest activities (Josh 2:11; 5:1; Isa 19:3). The loss of courage at times parallels a "sinking heart." However, Yahweh may "stir up" the *rûaḥ* and provide the courage necessary for the individual to accomplish God's purposes (Jer 51:11). This "stirring up" of the *rûaḥ* is also the motivating factor in encouraging the exiles to fulfill their task. "So the LORD stirred up the spirit *[rûaḥ]* of Zerubbabel son of Shealtiel, governor of Judah, and the spirit *[rûaḥ]* of Joshua son of Jehozadak, the high priest, and the spirit *[rûaḥ]* of the whole remnant of the people" (Hag 1:14; cf. 1 Chron 5:26; 2 Chron 21:16; 36:22). Resentment can also afflict the *rûaḥ* (Judg 9:23), as well as bitterness due to the distressing situations of life (Isa 54:6; Ezek 3:14). Hannah is "distressed" in her *rûaḥ* at the prospect of remaining barren (1 Sam 1:10). Despair is another result of misfortune or judgment (Ezek 21:12), but a reversal of circumstances brings an end to despair (Isa 61:3).

Other passages add to the variety of affects that the *rûaḥ* may experience. By putting a particular "spirit" in the field commander of the Assyrians, Yahweh caused him to change his plans (2 Kgs 19:7; Isa 37:7). A "spirit" of prostitution captivated the hearts of the people and proceeded to lead them astray (Hos 4:12; 5:4). Malachi warned the people concerning their marital relationships, saying: "Has not the LORD made them one? In flesh and spirit *[rûaḥ]* they are his. And why one? Because he was seeking godly offspring. So guard yourself in your spirit *[rûaḥ]*, and do not break faith with the wife of your youth" (Mal 2:15–16; cf. Isa 54:6). For the remnant, Yahweh would be a "spirit *[rûaḥ]* of justice to him who sits in judgment (Isa 28:6)."

Miscellaneous

The *rûaḥ* of Elijah the prophet is considered exemplary by the prophetic bands of his day. At the prospect of Elijah leaving the band, Elisha requests from Elijah a "double portion" of his *rûaḥ* (2 Kgs 2:9). The request is granted and the prophets recognize the spirit's presence on Elisha (2 Kgs 2:15). False prophets are also recognized in various ways. They are usually characterized by lying or by prophesying of their own accord rather than receiving a revelation from Yahweh (Ezek 13:3; cf. 13:7). Their lies are the result of an impure "spirit" (Zech 13:2). Their spirits may also be insensible or unresponsive, as are some of the inhabitants of Jerusalem who are in a "deep sleep" spiritually. "The LORD has brought over you a [spirit *[rûaḥ]* of] deep sleep" (Isa 29:10). These passages refer to the human *rûaḥ* rather than the Spirit of God. But as indicated in chapter 5, the Spirit of God is very much active in the whole range of prophetic activity.

In a number of passages, *rûaḥ* is similar to *lēḇ*, which may signify the seat of understanding. "Those who are wayward in spirit *[rûaḥ]* will gain understanding" (Isa 29:24). The *rûaḥ* may therefore receive instruction much like the mind does. In fact, Yahweh is capable of reading the *rûaḥ* ["mind"] and of knowing people's thoughts (Ezek 20:32).

As we have seen, the human *rûaḥ* is capable of experiencing many emotions, dispositions, and tendencies, both negative and positive. Yahweh has a preference for some dispositions, mainly for the *rûaḥ* that is humble and contrite in nature (Isa 66:2; 57:15–16). Those without this *rûaḥ* are exhorted to rid themselves of offenses and to exhibit anguish for sins in the light of the coming judgment (Ezek 18:31; Isa 65:14). God's response to such action would be the giving of an "undivided heart" and a "new spirit" which would be devoted and obedient to Yahweh (Ezek 11:19; 36:26).

Rûaḥ as the Spirit of God

This section is an overview of the key texts employing the term *rûaḥ* that refer specifically to the Spirit of God and his actions in the OT. In retrospect of an analysis of the whole OT, four major thematic categories emerged under which we may now group the relevant texts and content. The passages are briefly presented here in a thematic overview with a more in-depth exegetical analysis presented in the chapters to follow. In the OT, the term *rûaḥ* is applied to God in approximately one hundred and seven instances. Of this number, the phrase *rûaḥ* *ᵓᵉlōhîm* ["Spirit of God"] occurs fifteen times in Hebrew and its equivalent five times in Aramaic, while the phrase *rûaḥ yhwh* ["Spirit of the Lord"] occurs about twenty-seven times.

OT theology textbooks usually place the subject matter relating to the Spirit of God in the context of the manner and method in which God accomplishes the divine will in the world. When Israel thought about the source of the forces that they saw affecting and influencing humankind in creation and in nature, they often pointed to the activity of the *rûaḥ*. This was the way Israel answered the question of how God brought about creation. It was also the way they understood their experience of deliverance, salvation, guidance, and the presence of God. When experiencing various leadership role models in their midst, they attributed many of the externally observable manifestations to the *rûaḥ*, whose internal influence they noted in the lives of various leaders. In addition, the prophetic era is one in which the *rûaḥ* of God was influential in many ways. The texts mentioned in this section help to survey the development of Israel's understanding concerning the reality that God revealed himself and his power in Israel through the *rûaḥ*.

The Spirit and Creation

The first occurrence of *rûaḥ* in the Hebrew canon is in Genesis 1:2, where the phrase "and the Spirit of God *[rûaḥ ᵓᵉlōhîm]* was hovering over the waters" indicates the presence of God in the creation activities. The interpretation of this text is debated regarding the nature of the activity of *rûaḥ* in this context. Does *rûaḥ* mean "wind," which indicates a further chaotic description of the world's state before creation? Does *rûaḥ ᵓᵉlōhîm* point to the presence of God, who brings creation into existence by the divine word and creative power through the Spirit? The Spirit's role as the creative power and presence of God in creation is too often overlooked. J. Moltmann's comment is a refreshing affirmation of the Spirit's role: "The whole creation is a fabric woven by the Spirit, and is therefore a reality to which the Spirit gives form."[28] The issues surrounding this difficult passage and the role of the Spirit in creation are discussed in chapter 2.

In the Prophets, the incomparability and transcendence of Yahweh are highlighted in connection with God's work as creator. Isaiah asks, "Who has understood the mind of the Lord [*rûaḥ yhwh*], or instructed him as his counselor?" (Isa 40:13). In this reference Yahweh is the creator who planned and implemented the design for creation by the *rûaḥ*. The importance of this reference is indicated by its position at the beginning of a major division in Isaiah. The prophet alludes to and speaks about the creation theme more than any other prophet. This reference, therefore, is a précis to the creation theme as developed in Isaiah 40–66.

Some passages in the Writings are commentaries and reflections on God's creative work. Although specific examples of the activity and presence of *rûaḥ* in creation are limited, a number of texts do affirm the *rûaḥ* as an agent of creation. Psalm 33:6 is a reflection on Genesis 1 and asserts that the creation event was a result of the spoken word of God brought into reality by his *rûaḥ*. The context of the passage affirms that order and existence come about as a result of Yahweh's work through the agency of the *rûaḥ*.

The divine activity in creation continues as God renews and sustains the cyclical patterns that bring life and fertility to each generation of humankind. God's creatures look to him for sustenance and provision. When he sends his *rûaḥ* "they are created," said the psalmist (Pss 104:30; 147:18). Job 26:13 alludes to the creation event as a battle between God and a dragon. God's victory over Rahab the serpent is asserted. By the *rûaḥ,* God was victor over all opposing forces of nature. Elihu voices an understanding of the creation of humankind claiming that the Spirit of God gives both the breath of life and insight by the

[28] Moltmann, *God in Creation,* 99.

rûaḥ (32:8). Life is given by the *rûaḥ ʾēl,* who made man (33:4). Loss of *rûaḥ* results in death, indicating humankind's dependency on God for all of life (34:14).

In the various texts indicating the work of the *rûaḥ* in creation, the OT presents the efficacy of the Spirit's activity. All living creatures, as well as the physical world, are brought into reality through the Spirit's work and are sustained through the same. Moltmann summarizes: "Everything that is, exists and lives in the unceasing inflow of the energies and potentialities of the cosmic Spirit. This means that we have to understand every created reality in terms of energy, grasping it as the realized potentiality of the divine Spirit. Through the energies and potentialities of the Spirit, the Creator is himself present in his creation. He does not merely confront it in his transcendence; entering into it, he is also immanent in it."[29]

The nature of God's creative and sustaining work is examined in greater detail in chapter 2. Consideration of the earth and humankind as a sacred sanctuary is also discussed there.

The Spirit and the People of God

The exodus account of Israel's deliverance from Egypt is recorded in both narrative (Exod 14), and poetic form, called the Song of the Sea (15). The Reed Sea was driven back by a strong east wind (*rûaḥ*), which provided Israel with the way of deliverance from their period of bondage (14:21f.). The Song of the Sea attributes Yahweh's intervention to "the blast *[rûaḥ]* of your nostrils" (15:8), and says of Yahweh, "you blew with your *rûaḥ*" (15:10). In this passage, the active agent in bringing about Israel's deliverance was the *rûaḥ* that came from Yahweh himself.

One should note that this reference to the *rûaḥ* is more than figurative. A distinction must be made between the wind simply as a cosmological force and the breath of Yahweh, which is at times equated with the *rûaḥ ʾelōhîm* (Job 33:4; 34:14). The power of Yahweh is here dynamically at work to punish Egypt and yet to deliver Israel. The Hebrews are thus set free to worship God at Sinai, where they are established as a nation through their covenant with Yahweh. The exodus deliverance then becomes

[29] Moltmann, *God in Creation,* 9.

the ultimate paradigm of deliverance for Israel in the Hebrew canon that from the beginning is associated with the *rûaḥ*.

Once established as God's people through the agency of the *rûaḥ*, Israel experienced God's preservation, judgment, and restoration by the *rûaḥ yhwh*. The preservation of the king by the *rûaḥ* is also evident after David is established upon his throne through the deliverance effected by the *rûaḥ* (2 Sam 22:16; Ps 18:15 [16 MT]). The king then attributed the victories he experienced to the direct intervention of Yahweh by the *rûaḥ*.

Just as the king found deliverance and salvation in Yahweh, so also did Yahweh care for and preserve Israel. However, the nation was called to trust in Yahweh for guidance. It is often the lack of trust in Yahweh's leadership that brings judgment on Israel. Rather than looking to Yahweh for guidance by his *rûaḥ*, the nation turned to foreign powers. The foolishness of this tendency is made clear in the statement, "But the Egyptians are men and not God; their horses are flesh and not spirit *[rûaḥ]* (Isa 31:3)." Therefore, it is by the *rûaḥ* that Yahweh guides and preserves the nation just as Yahweh did during the wilderness wanderings (cf. 63:7–14).

As God's covenant people, Israel is subject to particular obligations. When the covenant is threatened, the prophets warn of imminent punishment. The day of cleansing that is promised is associated with the *rûaḥ* of "judgment" *[mišpāṭ]* and the *rûaḥ* of fire (Isa 4:4). The judgment of Yahweh is also expressed figuratively. The enemy could be slain with the *rûaḥ* of "God's lips" or by a scorching wind (Isa 11:15; 27:8; 30:28; cf. Hos 13:15). His "breath" can cause humankind to wither like grass (Isa 40:7). A vivid illustration of punishment is recorded in Isaiah. During the wilderness wanderings, Yahweh judges Israel. Because of Israel's rebellion, the *rûaḥ* is grieved (Isa 63:10), and God turns against the people in order to bring about repentance in the nation.

Judgment is not the last word, however, for the presence of God's *rûaḥ* also brings restoration. The faithful remnant could expect Yahweh's blessing on them (Isa 59:21). The *rûaḥ* brings fruitfulness (32:15), fertility (44:3; cf. 34:16; 40:7), and transformation in the nation. Ezekiel indicates that the *rûaḥ* will be placed in the people to motivate a positive new response to Yahweh (Ezek 36:27; cf. 37:1, 5–6, 8–10, 14; 39:29). This response will be effected when the *rûaḥ* is "poured out" on the exiles (Joel 2:28, 29 [3:1, 2 MT]). Also, the presence of Yahweh will be with the exiles in order to motivate them in the rebuilding of the temple (Hag 2:5). This project will be accomplished only by the *rûaḥ* of Yahweh (Zech 4:6; cf. 6:8), who is actively involved in motivating the people in the process of restoration.

The continued presence of God with his people and with the individual is also asserted in the Writings (Ps 18:15–19). Providential care and guidance is given by the ever-present *rûaḥ* (33:4–9; 139:7; 143:10). In the Psalter, the petitioner acknowledges the presence of Yahweh and trusts in the Deity to protect, guide, and deliver (51:11 [13 MT]).

The Spirit and Leadership

Even before Israel is established as a nation, the gift of the *rûaḥ* for leadership is evident (Gen 41:38). The pharaoh recognizes a special endowment of wisdom in Joseph, who also has the ability to interpret dreams. Although the utterance that attributes Joseph's unique ability to the *rûaḥ ᵓᵉlōhîm* comes from a pagan ruler, we must note that Joseph has previously informed the pharaoh that the ability to answer his request is dependent on the source of his wisdom and ability, *ᵓᵉlōhîm* (41:16). The presence of the *rûaḥ ᵓᵉlōhîm* earns Joseph the promotion to a greater leadership position as vizier of Egypt.

Once Israel is established as the people of God, the need for rulers or leaders becomes evident. In this context, the majority of references in the Pentateuch to *rûaḥ* as Spirit deal with some kind of leadership ability given by the *rûaḥ* for a particular task. Although the book of Exodus does not specifically indicate that Moses' leadership is a result of being endowed with the *rûaḥ*, there are indications that he is so endowed. Moses rather reluctantly accepts the call to leadership (Exod 3), which is then certified and confirmed by numerous signs and by his ability to lead Israel in the midst of adverse circumstances. But when the need for assistance in leading Israel becomes evident, Moses is directed by Yahweh to call seventy officials and leaders together who then have the *rûaḥ* put on them (Num 11:16–17, 24–26). The *rûaḥ* that is understood to be on Moses is now distributed among the seventy elders. In this context Moses expresses the programmatic desire that Yahweh place the *rûaḥ* on all God's people (11:29).

Once delivered and established as God's people, Israel is called to worship Yahweh in accordance with divine revelation.

Israel is commissioned to construct the tabernacle for worship where the presence of God will dwell (Exod 25–28). Those involved in the tabernacle construction and the making of sacred garments are given the *rûaḥ ḥok̲māh,* which gives them the skills for their tasks (28:3). Specifically, Bezalel is "filled" *(mālēʾ)* with the *rûaḥ ʾᵉlōhîm* (31:3; 35:31), which not only provides the ability and knowledge for work in all kinds of crafts but also gives Bezalel and Oholiab the ability to teach others their skills (35:34; cf. 36:1ff). This example highlights the practical aspect of leadership given by the *rûaḥ.*

Two references in the Pentateuch underline Joshua's qualification for leadership. Yahweh points to the fact that the *rûaḥ* is in Joshua. Moses is publicly to commission Joshua, who was also among the seventy who experienced Spirit-reception and prophetic utterance, to receive the *rûaḥ* (Num 11) for his leadership responsibility (27:18ff.). Deuteronomy 34:9 implies that Joshua was filled with the *rûaḥ ḥok̲māh* for leadership because Moses placed his hands on him. By the *rûaḥ,* Joshua was enabled to lead Israel in the conquest of Canaan. In short, the connection between leadership and *rûaḥ* is asserted in the Pentateuch, especially at key transition points.

Isaiah attributes the leadership of Israel in the wilderness wanderings to the *rûaḥ yhwh.* Moses' leadership and the signs and miracles accomplished through him are credited to the presence of the "Holy Spirit" (*rûaḥ qod̲ᵉšô;* Isa 63:11). The result of his successful leadership in the face of much adversity is Israel's ultimate rest in the land brought about by the *rûaḥ* (63:14). Therefore, Isaiah affirms explicitly that Moses led the nation by the *rûaḥ.*

Once settled in the land, Israel no longer submits to one leader over the twelve tribes. The period of the judges is a time when many forsake Yahwism (Judg 2:6–12). The title "judge" *(šōp̄ēṭ)* refers to a leader or deliverer who in the period of the judges is raised up by Yahweh to deliver the people of God. In the cycle of apostasy noted in the book of Judges, where the people are punished by oppressors, God answers Israel's cry by raising up deliverers to defeat the enemy and bring about rest for the nation. In this cycle, the abilities exhibited by a judge are often attributed to the coming of the *rûaḥ* that makes the judge "charismatic" and gives the judge power to mediate Yahweh's deliverance.

Not all the judges are said to receive the *rûaḥ*, but we are dealing with selective history. Othniel is the first judge to have the "Spirit of Yahweh" come on him (Judg 3:10). Gideon (6:34), Jepthah (11:29), and Samson (13:25; 14:6, 19; 15:14, 19) are the others who explicitly receive the *rûaḥ* that gives them extraordinary powers for their tasks. Through these figures Yahweh preserves the nation of Israel in the midst of severe circumstances.

From the period of the judges to the era of the monarchy, the activity of the *rûaḥ* continues to be evident. In 1 Samuel, the coming of the *rûaḥ* on Saul is evidenced by a two fold consequence. First, Saul prophesies when the *rûaḥ yhwh* rushes on him (cf. 1 Sam 10:6, 10; 11:6; 19:20, 23; Judg 14:6, 19; 15:14); second, Saul is changed by the *rûaḥ* (10:6). This change may include the giving of courage for his leadership duties. With the *rûaḥ* on him, Saul becomes a "deliverer" who is successful until the *rûaḥ* departs from him (16:14), an event that seriously diminishes his ability to lead the nation. The *rûaḥ yhwh* is then transferred to David (16:13). At this key transition period in the history of Israel, the *rûaḥ* is present to equip kings for their roles.

With the growing disillusionment in the nation during the monarchy period, the prophets not only rebuke and exhort various kings but they begin to cast their hopes for an ideal ruler far into the future. When this ruler appears, the *rûaḥ yhwh* will rest on him and provide him with the abilities required for the kind of leadership Yahweh intended from the beginning. Wisdom, understanding, counsel, power, knowledge, and the fear of the Lord will be on him (Isa 11:2). The *rûaḥ* on the "servant" of the Lord will equip him to bring justice *[mišpāṭ]* to the nations (42:1). Perhaps also to be included in the "Servant Songs" is Isaiah 61:1, where the servant, like a king, is anointed for a specific ministry of deliverance. These passages and their contexts present the far-reaching results of the messianic servant. Israel's future existence and hope depends on the coming ruler whom Yahweh would send, anoint, and place his *rûaḥ* upon for the purpose of establishing a righteous rule.

Not only does God raise up an anointed messianic ruler, but he also employs pagan kings on occasion as instruments of judgment and restoration. Such is the case in the experience of Cyrus, whom Yahweh anoints for the purpose of effecting a new policy of repatriation (Isa 45:1ff.; Ezra 1:1ff.). In addition, Yahweh uses Artaxerxes I to effect his plan among the exiles. This ruler will be "driven along by the *rûaḥ*" in order to accomplish

God's purposes (Isa 59:19). Through his work, the nation would know Yahweh's presence among them (59:21).

The prophetic office came into prominence with the rise of the monarchy. Much of what is known about the monarchy comes to us from the prophetic perspective. Numerous passages indicate the role of the *rûaḥ* in enabling the prophets for their specific tasks within the nation. Because of the *rûaḥ,* the two prominent figures of Elijah and Elisha were able to stem the tide of apostasy during the Omride dynasty. Their ministries are characterized by supernatural feats. It is no surprise that the *rûaḥ* is associated with their prophetic office (2 Kgs 2:9, 15).

Prophets are conscious of inspiration by the *rûaḥ*. They are sure that Yahweh will not only give his word through them but will also bring his word to fulfillment in history (Isa 48:16c; 59:21). But the people's perception of the prophets is less than honorable. They refer to Hosea as an inspired fool or one who is out of control (Hos 9:7), even though the prophet cares deeply for the nation. Micah shows his concern by speaking to the leaders who abuse their authority. In contrast to them, Micah is inspired by the *rûaḥ* to stand for what is right, and he boldly declares Yahweh's word (Mic 3:8). Zechariah summarizes the rebellious nature of the people. The nation hardens their hearts against the word Yahweh gives by the *rûaḥ* through the prophets (Zech 7:12). Although the reception of the prophets is not favorable, they are still able to lead the faithful and foster faith among the remnant. During the exile, the remnant is encouraged in their rebuilding project by the *rûaḥ,* who was present to accomplish the task at hand through gifted men (4:6).

References to the activity of the *rûaḥ* are limited in the Writings, although a few allusions are evident in some passages. David's request in Psalm 51:11 [13 MT] for God not to take his Holy Spirit from him may be connected to the fear that loss of the *rûaḥ* could mean the loss of kingship (cf. 1 Sam 10:6–11:6; ch. 16). Another leader who has the *rûaḥ ᵓᵉlōhîm* in him is Daniel. He is given extraordinary abilities for administrative and interpretive responsibilities. His gift is recognized by others to be the result of the *rûaḥ ᵓᵉlōhîm* within him (Dan 4:8, 9, [4:5–6 MT]; 5:11, 14). Daniel is promoted, much like Joseph is (Gen 41:38), to the position of a high-ranking official because the *rûaḥ* of the "holy gods" is in him. Intelligence, wisdom, insight, and the ability to interpret dreams are credited to the presence of the *rûaḥ*. The leadership of *rûaḥ* is also indicated in Nehemiah 9:20–30, which refers to Moses' instruction as well as that of the prophets in general. Throughout Israel's history, God admonishes his people through the prophets and by the *rûaḥ*.

Prophecy and the Spirit

Although limited, a number of instances in the Pentateuch clearly connect prophecy and *rûaḥ*. The office of prophet is already known in the Pentateuch. The term *nāḇîʾ* ["prophet"] appears fourteen times in the Pentateuch and refers to Abraham (Gen 20:7), Aaron (Exod 7:1), and the paradigm of Moses as prophet (Deut 34:10–12).[30] When Yahweh puts the *rûaḥ* on the seventy elders, they begin to prophesy (Num 11:25). At the same time, Eldad and Medad prophesy as a result of the *rûaḥ* on them (11:26). It is clear that the prophesying of the elders is a temporary occurrence. This external manifestation indicates their reception of the *rûaḥ* publicly before the nation. In another instance, the coming of the *rûaḥ* on a person results in the activity of prophecy. Balaam has the *rûaḥ ʾᵉlōhîm* come on him and is inspired with two oracles (24:2ff.). The consequences of this experience indicate features normally associated with the prophets of Yahweh. Balaam gives inspired oracles that have extensive future implications for Israel.

In the Former and Latter Prophets the *rûaḥ* and prophecy are closely connected. Saul is enabled for leadership when the *rûaḥ* comes on him. Subsequently, Saul "prophesies" (1 Sam 10:6, 10; 11:6; 19:20, 23). The nature of this "ecstatic" outburst is examined in chapter 5, but the external manifestation of prophesying seems to serve as a public indicator that Saul receives the *rûaḥ* and is a designated leader.

As noted previously, the *rûaḥ yhwh* is shown to be active in the Elijah and Elisha narratives. Concerning Elijah, Obadiah queries where the *rûaḥ* may carry Elijah (1 Kgs 18:12; 2 Kgs 2:16). The question indicates the popular understanding that the prophetic leadership of Elijah was encompassed by the activity of the *rûaḥ* that could "transport" the prophet at will. A similar activity is ascribed to *rûaḥ* as the motivational guiding force behind the creatures of Ezekiel (cf. 1:12, 20–21; 10:17). The *rûaḥ* also "transports" and "raises" Ezekiel. Associated with this phe-

[30] W. Zimmerli, "Der Prophet im Pentateuch," *Studien zum Pentateuch* (ed. C. Westermann; Vienna: Herder, 1977) 197–211.

nomenon is the inspiration of the prophet (cf. 2:2; 3:12, 14, 24; 8:3; 11:1, 5, 24; 43:5).

Prophetic inspiration, whether visionary or auditory, is attributed to *rûaḥ*. Thus, David claims, "The Spirit of the LORD spoke through me, his word was on my tongue" (2 Sam 23:2). The nature of *rûaḥ* and the prophetic word is evaluated by determining whether prophecy is inspired by Yahweh or by a lying *rûaḥ* (1 Kgs 22:24; cf. Mic 2:7). The word of Yahweh is thus inspired and proclaimed to Israel by the prophets (Zech 7:12). In 1 and 2 Chronicles, the Levitical priests give prophetic leadership to the community. Inspired speech is often connected to the *rûaḥ* coming on the priests (1 Chron 12:18 [19 MT]). The Spirit of prophecy continues to be as vital in the exilic period as it was during the monarchy (2 Chron 15:1, 8; 18:23; 20:14; 24:20).

Through this survey of passages concerning the term *rûaḥ*, we have discovered four main classifications in which the term refers specifically to the Spirit of God's activity. The first is in relation to the creation of the universe and humankind. Second, the establishment of and subsequent provisions for the people of God are effected through the Spirit. Their judgment and restoration are also experiences that actively involve the *rûaḥ*. Third, the kingdom of God is established and promoted on earth through charismatic leadership. God effects the divine purposes and rule through Spirit-anointed individuals who are enabled and motivated for their tasks by the Spirit of God. From the patriarchal age into the Mosaic period, through the conquest, the period of the judges, during the monarchy and into the messianic age, the Spirit of God is the common denominator in making the rule of God effective through elected, anointed leadership. Lastly, the Spirit of God has a unique role in the leadership of the prophets. Through the Spirit, prophets are called, inspired, transported, motivated, and used by the *rûaḥ* to accomplish their difficult tasks within the nation. Throughout the OT, the Spirit of God is featured as the main mover in the Trinity to bring into reality the plans and purposes of God.

2

The Spirit of God in Creation

On the watery calm; his brooding wings the Spirit of God outspread, and vital virtue infus'd, and vital warmth, throughout the fluid mass. (Milton, Paradise Lost)

In this chapter we will examine the OT theological teaching concerning the role of the Spirit of God in creation. We discuss specifically the passages which indicate the activity of God in the creation of the universe and in the creation of humankind. The nature of the role of the *rûaḥ* in creating the universe is a disputed issue caused by frequent mistranslations of some verses. In addition, OT theology texts often emphasize the word of God as the agent of creation over the active involvement of the *rûaḥ*, or Spirit, which brings the spoken word into reality. My purpose is to present a more complete perspective of how the word and the *rûaḥ* function together in various OT texts that seek to make clearer the mystery of creation. Furthermore, the *rûaḥ* is also involved in the creation of humankind as the animating principle of life in relation to the initial creation and in the ongoing preservation of humanity. The nature of this sustaining activity is examined.

Genesis 1: The Context

Various creation accounts have been discovered during the past century. Some of these ancient cosmologies, such as the

Babylonian *Enuma elish* and components in Egyptian literature, have a bearing on the understanding of the scriptural creation account. Diverse categories of ancient Near Eastern accounts such as (1) creation by birth or succession of births; (2) creation through struggle; (3) creation as fashioning, making, or forming; and (4) creation through utterance, have some elements similar to a few biblical texts.[1] From Israel, however, comes a presentation of creation that differs significantly from the polytheistic accounts of the other nations.

Against Polytheism

Genesis 1 specifically takes on the belief systems of the ancient Near East and dismisses the pantheons of gods perceived to be responsible for creation. The importance of this polemical background to the creation account is emphasized by C. Hyers: "Each day of creation takes on two principal categories of divinity in the pantheons of the day, and declares that these are not gods at all, but creatures—creations of the one and true God who is the only one, without a second or third. Each day dismisses an additional cluster of deities, arranged in a cosmological and symmetrical order."[2] Therefore, an important day in the history of Israel, concerning its identity and constitution as a people, is the day of creation, when God by the *rûaḥ ʾelōhîm* brought all things into existence, including the people of God.

B. K. Waltke identifies the period of around 1400 BC, during Israel's wilderness wanderings, as the time when Moses revealed to the nation the creation account of Genesis 1:1–2:3, an account that many writers claim is a polemic against the Hymn of Aton (dated around 1350 BC). "The Genesis creation narrative gives the faithful a firm foundation for their covenant with God. Why have no other gods (Exod 20:3)? Because he alone is Maker of heaven and earth (Gen 1:1). Why not murder (Exod 20:13)? Because humans alone are created in his image (Gen 1:26–28). Why set apart a day for rest (Exod 20:8-11)? Because he set it

[1] C. Westermann, *Genesis 1–11: A Commentary* (trans. J. J. Scullion; Minneapolis: Augsburg, 1984) 97. The most noteworthy creation texts may be found in *ANET,* 3, 37–40, 60–70.

[2] C. Hyers, "Biblical Literalism: Constricting the Cosmic Dance," *Is God a Creationist? The Religious Case Against Creation-Science* (ed. R. M. Frye; New York: Charles Scribner's Sons, 1983) 101.

apart (Gen 2:2–3)."[3] Therefore, to Israel in the wilderness, Moses stresses that the same God who led them out of Egypt and through the Reed Sea by the divine *rûaḥ* (Exod 15:8–10), also singularly made the heavens and the earth by the *rûaḥ*. The power exhibited in the making of the universe is now at work in the deliverance and creation of the nation of Israel. The creation account also provides the foundational record that indicates to Israel God's lordship over all nations, including Egypt, since humankind descended from Adam.

Genesis 1:2: Philological and Syntactical Analysis

Scripture claims that in the beginning and out of the chaotic darkness of primeval times, the world as we know it was born. While scientific explanations of the beginning are avoided, theological implications are salient. The phrase "and the *rûaḥ* *ᵓᵉlōhîm* was hovering over the waters" forms an integral part of the main text which explains creation events. In order to expose the key intentions of this verse we must consider the structure and philological concerns of the text.

An observation of the structure of the first three verses of Genesis is crucial to the proper translation of the text. The view with the strongest support is called the "precreation chaos theory."[4] In this view, Genesis 1:1 is an independent clause (taking *bᵉrēšîṯ* in the absolute state): "In the beginning *[bᵉrēšîṯ]* God created the heavens and the earth." Thus, verse 1 is a summary statement or a principle sentence that is elaborated in the creation narrative.[5] The acts of creation are then presented, with the fitting conclusion, "Thus the heavens and the earth were completed in all their vast array" (2:1).

---

[3] B. K. Waltke, "The Literary Genre of Genesis, Chapter One," *Crux* 27 (1991) 3.

[4] B. K. Waltke, "The Creation Account in Genesis 1:1-3, Part III: The Initial Chaos Theory and the Precreation Chaos Theory," *BSac* 132 (1975) 221ff.

[5] Waltke, *BSac* 132 (1975) 225–27; G. von Rad, *Genesis: A Commentary* (OTL; trans. J. H. Marks; 1st ed. 1961; rev. ed. Philadelphia: Westminster, 1972) 49; Westermann, *Genesis 1–11*, 97. cf. Waltke, "Literary Genre," 3–4.

Genesis 1:2 consists of three nominal clauses: "Now the earth was formless and empty, darkness was over the surface of the deep, and the Spirit of God *[rûaḥ ʾᵉlōhîm]* was hovering over the waters." These clauses are circumstantial to the main clause in verse 3: "And God said, 'Let there be light,' and there was light." The fundamental exegetical issue is whether all three of these clauses describe the same situation of chaos or whether the third clause stands in contrast to the first two.

Chaos and Order

The situation of the earth in the beginning is referred to as *tōhû wāḇōhû*. The connotation of *tōhû* as a desert waste is implicit in a number of OT passages (Deut 32:10; Job 6:18; 12:24), and in others it threatens total devastation (Isa 24:10; 34:11; 40:23; Jer 4:23).[6] The theological application is that persistent disobedience in the nation will bring about a reversal in God's created order to a state of emptiness and chaos. The word may also denote a condition of "nothingness" (1 Sam 12:21; Isa 29:21; 40:17; 41:23; 44:9; 45:19; 59:4). However, the significance of the word must be found in the idiom in which it appears. U. Cassuto claims that the term refers to the unformed, unorganized, and lifeless state, which was present prior to creation.[7] This state was devoid of order and preceded the creative activity of God. In Deuteronomy 32:10, *tōhû* is also used to illustrate that just as God's presence was with Israel during the period of the wilderness wanderings, so God was present over the chaotic, unformed earth. This adjective now becomes the key for the literary structure of the narrative: the lack of form *[tōhû]* is overcome in the first three days, and the empty space *[wāḇōhû]* is filled up in the fourth to sixth days.[8]

The description of the chaotic state preceding creation includes the presence of darkness *[ḥōšeḵ]*, which is mentioned four times in Genesis 1 (1:2, 4, 5, 18). In each instance it is

[6] Westermann, *Genesis 1–11*, 102–03. In Jeremiah 4:23 and Isaiah 34:11, the terms *tōhû wāḇōhû* appear together in judgment oracles that threaten a reversal of creation back to the chaotic beginning.

[7] U. Cassuto, *A Commentary on the Book of Genesis*, Vol. 1 (trans. I. Abrahams; Jerusalem: Magnes, 1961) 23. Cf. von Rad, *Genesis*, 49.

[8] B. K. Waltke, "The Creation Account in Genesis 1:1–3, Part 5: The Theology of Genesis 1," *BSac* 133 (1976) 29.

subjugated to God's control. Darkness is separated from the created light (1:4; cf. Job 26:10; 39:19f); it is named night and is separated from the light by the heavenly bodies. However, the darkness mentioned in Genesis 1:2 is apparently independent of God's creation, and constitutes a further description of chaos before God's creative work begins.[9]

Through the influence of H. Gunkel, the term *t^ehôm* was initially compared with Tiamat, the Babylonian sea goddess of the *Enuma elish.* For numerous reasons, however, the word has been liberated from its association with mythical backgrounds and from the suggestion that it indicates a struggle between *ᵓ^elōhîm* and a chaotic force. A. Heidel shows convincingly that *t^ehôm* is never a monster in the OT but rather refers to the sea, ocean, or a large body of water.[10] Moreover, the fluctuation of gender in the OT usage of the word points to the probability of it being depersonalized and used predominately as a poetic term for a large body of water. As such, in Genesis 1:2 it refers to a deep, world ocean. It is purely a physical concept referring to matter and has no personality or autonomy. Theologically, *t^ehôm* is not anti God and has no mythical function. Outside Genesis 1:2 it belongs to the created world and is understood to be subject to God's control (cf. Ps 135:6).[11] This term stands in parallel with the waters over which the *rûaḥ ᵓ^elōhîm* moved.

Wind, Breath, or Spirit?

An analysis of the clause *w^erûaḥ ᵓ^elōhîm meraḥepeṯ ᶜal-penê hamayîm* is necessary at this juncture to determine if this third nominal clause of verse 2 continues to describe chaos or if it introduces the creative presence of God. The *waw* before *rûaḥ* is best understood as an adversative *waw,* as in Genesis 6:8 or 1 Kings 2:26. In this way it separates the description of the

---

[9] B. S. Childs, *Myth and Reality in the Old Testament* (SBT 1/27; London: SCM, 1960) 33; cf. H. Ringgren, "*ḥōšeḵ,*" *TDOT,* 5.248ff.

[10] A. Heidel, *The Babylonian Genesis: The Story of Creation* (Chicago: University of Chicago Press, 1942) 83–86.

[11] See M. K. Wakeman, *God's Battle with the Monster* (Leiden: Brill, 1973) 86–87, 89; J. Day, *God's Conflict with the Dragon and the Sea: Echoes of a Canaanite Myth in the Old Testament* (Cambridge: Cambridge University Press, 1985) 49–51. cf. also, Cassuto, *Genesis,* 84–85; G. F. Hasel, " The Polemic Nature of the Genesis Cosmogony," *EvQ* 46 (1974) 84–85; C. Westermann, "*t^ehôm,*" *THAT,* 2.1030–31.

chaotic situation from the plain meaning of *rûaḥ ʾ^e^lōhîm*.[12] However, there is considerable disagreement concerning this grammatical assertion. The key issue is the translation of *rûaḥ*. Some commentators accept the translation "wind" in this verse on the supposition that it fits into the context of the chaotic situation of verse 2 in a better sense than the term "Spirit." Thus, some versions translate the phrase, "a mighty wind from God."[13] The assumption accompanying this translation in some cases is that verse 2 corresponds to a demythologized parallel of ancient Near Eastern creation epics. While we have no doubt about a polemical purpose in the creation account, this background to the text should not influence the grammatical exegesis of the content. The rendering of *ʾ^e^lōhîm* as having superlative force and thus the translation "mighty" is inappropriate in this context, and is used sparingly in others.[14]

The translation of the Targum Onkelos, "and a wind from before the Lord was blowing on the face of the waters," is based on a similar understanding carried over by some rabbis. This rendering however, is influenced by differing textual data from

---

[12] M. R. Westfall, "The Scope of the Term 'Spirit of God' in the Old Testament," *IJT* 26 (1, 1977) 29–43. For critical views against the "Spirit" rendering, cf. H. M. Orlinsky, "The Plain Meaning of *rûach* in Genesis 1:2," *JQR* 48 (1957–58) 174–82.

[13] The phrase *rûaḥ ʾ^e^lōhîm meraḥepeṯ* is translated "a wind from God swept" (New Jewish Version, 1962; New Revised Standard Version, 1990), "a mighty wind swept" (New American Bible, 1970), "a mighty wind that swept (New English Bible, 1972), "the Spirit of God was hovering" (New International Version, 1973), "the Spirit of God moved" (King James Version, 1611), and "the Spirit of God was moving" (New American Standard Bible, 1960).

[14] See J. M. P. Smith, "The Syntax and Meaning of Genesis 1:1–3," *AJSL* 44 (1927–28) 108–15; J. M. P. Smith, "The Use of Divine Names as Superlatives," *AJSL* 45 (1928–29) 212–13. Smith's investigation depends on the presupposition that Genesis 1 is strongly influenced by the *Enuma Elish*. cf. J. M. P. Smith, "A Semotactical Approach to the Meaning of the Term *rûaḥ ʾ^e^lōhîm* in Genesis 1:2," *JNWSL* 81 (1920) 99–104. Coming from the presupposition that the wind of Baal motif is behind this verse, Day claims it is connected to the tradition of Yahweh driving the waters of the earth by the wind (cf. Job 26:13; Gen 8:1). Cf. Day, *God's Conflict*, 53. However, *ʾ^e^lōhîm* here is either possessive or adjectival in the sense of "awesome or divine," but not superlative in the sense of "mighty." Cf. E. A. Speiser, *Genesis*, AB. 8th ed. (New York: Doubleday, 1986) 5. For examples where divine epithets may indicate the superlative force, see D. W. Thomas, "A Consideration of Some Unusual Ways of Expressing the Superlative in Hebrew," *VT* 3 (1953) 214–24.

the MT. The Targum changes the name *ʾᵉlōhîm* to the tetragrammaton *YHWH,* thus "Lord," no doubt due to the tendency to avoid the anthropomorphism in reference to God. In addition, the MT term *mᵉraḥepeṯ* is changed in the Targum to *mʾnaḥḇṯ,* which is correctly translated "blowing."[15] A more fitting translation that takes into consideration the MT is by Rabbi M. Zlotowitz: "and the divine presence hovered upon the surface of the waters." He follows Rashi and explains that this phrase refers to "the Throne of Divine Glory,' which stood suspended in the air hovering above the surface of the waters by the 'breath' of the mouth of the Holy One, and by his command—as a dove hovers over its nest."[16]

The term *ʾᵉlōhîm* is translated "God" in all thirty-six occurrences in Genesis 1. In the OT, the phrase *rûaḥ ʾᵉlōhîm* occurs fifteen times in Hebrew and five times in Aramaic. It is never rendered "a mighty wind" or "a wind of God" in these occurrences. If the writer intended to convey "mighty wind," he would have used an adjective to make this clear (cf. Jonah 1:4; Job 1:19). The word *śaʿar* could have been employed to convey the turbulence of a storm or a raging tempest.[17] As in the Targum noted above, a specific term for "blowing" could also have been employed. It is therefore evident that this interpretation was foreign to the author's intention.

O. H. Stek argues that Genesis 1:2 presents the uninhabitable and unusable precreation situation of the earth, which is then made fit for humankind through the creative activity of God.[18] He questions what purpose a "wind" from God going back and forth over the deep waters would have, and concludes that *rûaḥ ʾᵉlōhîm* in this context is pregnant with meaning and must be

---

[15] M. Aberbach and B. Grossfeld, *Targum Onkelos to Genesis: A Critical Analysis Together with an English Translation of the Text* (New York, Ktav, 1982) 20. Cf. Hagigah 12a.

[16] Rabbi M. Zlotowitz, *Bereishis: Genesis—A Translation with a Commentary Anthologized from Talmudic, Midrashic, and Rabbinic Sources* (Brooklyn, N.Y.: Mesorah, 1986) 1.38.

[17] H. J. Fabry, "*śaʿar,*" *TWAT,* 5. 895ff.; cf. Day, *God's Conflict,* 53ff. The superlative force could have been expressed by *rûaḥ seʿārāh, rûaḥ seʿārōt,* or by *rûaḥ qādîm* (Pss 107:24; 148:8; 48:7 [8 MT]).

[18] O. H. Stek, *Der Schöpfungsbericht der Priesterschrift: Studien zur literarkritischen und überlieferungsgeschichtlichen Problematik von Genesis 1,1–2, 4a* (Göttingen: Vandenhöeck & Ruprecht, 1975) 231–32.

considered in its relationship to *wayyōʾmer ʾᵉlōhîm* ("and God said") in verse 3. When taken together, Stek claims that the "God said" of 1:3 is clearest if *rûaḥ* is translated "breath of God" (*Atem, Hauch Gottes*). In his view, the *rûaḥ ʾᵉlōhîm* is not creatively at work in 1:2c, but the presence of God as a creative principle is present. In this conception, the *rûaḥ* is the breath of God through which the spoken word in verse 3 sets the creative acts in effect.[19] Similarly, S. Tengström argues that in a metaphoric way, the breath which holds the active potential for creative activity becomes actualized through God's speaking and brings creation into reality.[20]

Both of these arguments show the fruitlessness of taking the rendering "wind" in this context to portray a further chaotic situation in the creation narrative. However, the translation "breath" is difficult to explain in its relationship to the active participle *mᵉraḥep̱eṯ*, which signifies significant movement (see below). Whereas we may agree with the basic conclusion that the presence of God is here involved in providing creative energy we understand that the writer intended more in this text and that the translation "breath" is insufficient to portray this intention. It is evident that the *rûaḥ ʾᵉlōhîm* is not only superintending the work of creation but in fact brings creation about through the word. The passage is emphasizing the actual, powerful presence of God, who brings the spoken word into reality by the Spirit. Thus, the Spirit and the word work together to present how the one God is responsible for all that is seen in the physical universe.[21] That which was invisible became the material, physical world through the creatively active Spirit.

---

[19] Stek, *Schöpfungsbericht*, 235–36.

[20] Tengström, "*rûaḥ*," 406. J. Moltmann's observation that "The masculine word *(dāḇar)* and the feminine life force *(rûaḥ)* necessarily complement each other" may also provide insight into the word/Spirit relationship in some contexts. See *The Spirit of Life: A Universal Affirmation* (trans. M. Kohl; London: SCM, 1992) 42.

[21] Significant discussions that reinforce this interpretation in various degrees may be found in A. S. Kapelrud, "Die Theologie der Schöpfung im Alten Testament," *ZAW* 91 (1979) 165–66; Neve, *Spirit of God*, 69; E. J. Young, "The Interpretation of Genesis 1:2," *WTJ* 23 (1960–61) 173; A. R. Johnson, *The Vitality of the Individual in the Thought of Ancient Israel*, 2d ed. (Cardiff: University of Wales Press, 1964) 33.

Hovering or Blowing?

The interpretation of the active participle *m^{e}raḥepet* which modifies *rûaḥ *$^{\supset e}$*lōhîm,* has also been controversial. Gunkel promoted the theory that the term incorporated the idea of "brooding," which in Genesis 1:2 could refer to the theory of the world egg associated with ancient Near Eastern cosmogonies. However, many commentators reject this theory in favor of the analogy of an eagle's wing action while teaching her young to fly.[22] The phrase "like an eagle that stirs up its nest and hovers over its young," appears in a context of care and protection, which illustrates God's care for Israel (Deut 32:11). The piel participle indicates that action of some kind is here involved, and therefore the notion of "flap, shake, flutter, hover" is signified.[23] In Jeremiah 23:9, the word denotes the knocking together of bones in terror. Thus, vigorous motion is indicated by the term, but the verb *rāḥap* is not used in the context of wind or a storm in the OT. The writer could have selected other verbs to indicate a chaotic situation with a blowing wind.

In short, the *rûaḥ *$^{\supset e}$*lōhîm* is not the wind of God in Genesis 1 (cf. Amos 4:13), but a vibrant presence awaiting the proper time to actively begin the creation process.[24] Neve summarizes: "Just as Yahweh, likened to a mother eagle in Deut 32:10–11, cares for the infant Israel, 'the work of his hands,' so Yahweh, directly through his own spirit, transforms the as yet unformed cosmos from chaos, darkness, and formlessness."[25] Also, in the context of this passage, the verb indicates the divine activity of guidance. God led Israel through the wilderness as an eagle leads her young. At Sinai, God reminds Israel, "You yourselves have seen what I did to Egypt, and how I carried you on eagles' wings and brought you to myself" (Exod 19:4).

Another allusion to the eagle's activity, but associated mainly with the cherubim, is developed later in Scripture and may be reflected here. The concept of the heavenly council with

---

[22] J. P. Peters, "The Wind of God," *JBL* 30 (1911) 45ff.

[23] Childs, *Myth and Reality,* 33–34; Westermann, *Genesis 1–11,* 107.

[24] Cf. V. P. Hamilton, *The Book of Genesis: Chapters 1–17* (NICOT; Grand Rapids: Eerdmans, 1990) 111–15.

[25] Neve, *The Spirit of God,* 70; cf. H. Blocher, *In the Beginning: The Opening Chapters of Genesis* (trans. D. G. Preston; Downers Grove, Ill.: InterVarsity, 1984) 68.

God on the throne surrounded by angelic beings is conceived in Ezekiel's vision as a portable throne directed and moved by beings with wings (Ezek 1; cf. 1 Kgs 22:19–22; Isa 6; Job 1:6–12). Based on such passages, M. G. Kline states, "Reflecting on Genesis 1:2, Psalm 104 envisages the Creator Spirit (*rûaḥ*) as the one who makes the clouds his chariot and moves on the wings of the wind *[rûaḥ]*, making the winds his angel-messengers and flames his servants (vv. 3f.)."[26] The plural references in the creation text are typical of "heavenly council" contexts. Here the creator addresses his council and informs them of his decisions. In particular, each creative day's work is prefaced with the decision, "Let there be. . . . " In the deliberation on the creation of man God said, "Let us make man. . . . " Concerning the former, the presence of God with his heavenly council is conceived as a theophanic cloud from which God brings about creative acts. Further allusions to this conception occur throughout passages in the Psalter.

The above evidence illustrates the nature and way the acts of creation were brought into existence. When we consider the pattern of the creation narrative where God both announces and fulfills his word, we believe the "missing-link" in the pattern between the word and fulfillment is the activity of the Spirit. Therefore, the following pattern noted by B. W. Anderson should have an additional descriptive note under point 3. The pattern, (1) a declarative formula, (2) a command, (3) the execution of the command, and (4) the approbation formula, is more complete if we note that the execution of the command is carried out by the *rûaḥ ʾelōhîm*.[27] The word and its fulfillment are brought to fruition through the powerful, active force of the Spirit of God.

The Dove as a Symbol of the Spirit

The symbol of the dove has traditionally been associated with the Holy Spirit, but the origins of the imagery seem to arise specifically from the NT evidence. However, many

---

[26] M.G. Kline, *Images of the Spirit* (Grand Rapids: Baker, 1980) 15.

[27] B. W. Anderson, "A Stylistic Study of the Priestly Creation Story," *Canon and Authority*, ed. G. W. Coats and B. O. Long (Philadelphia: Fortress, 1977) 151–155.

commentators have noted the allusion to a bird in Genesis 1:2, either an eagle or a dove. Attempts to find allusions are probably motivated by the search for the NT background to the dove that alights on Jesus at his baptism. It is appropriate at this point to present some material which may contribute to the NT background. I have already noted that the main correspondence between the bird allusion and the creation account lies in the active participle, *m^e^raḥep̱eṯ*. In context, it indicates the movement of wings, especially when considered with Deuteronomy 32:11. It is the action of "hovering" to which the NT writers evidently refer.

The first reference to a dove in the OT appears in Genesis 8:8–12. Noah sends out a raven and then a dove to determine whether the chaotic flood waters have receded enough to allow the passengers to disembark from the ark. The significance of this passage is the context of the re-creation that is brought about by God after the deluge. A new beginning is inaugurated for humankind at this juncture, and some commentators view the dove as symbolic of God's Spirit presence at the initial creation. However, in the Song of Moses, the leadership of God up to the period of the conquest is compared to that of an eagle and her young (Deut 32). This includes the symbolic "baptism" through the Reed Sea, and the subsequent new beginning for Israel as a nation. Thus, the bird imagery is indeed significant in re-creation events, especially in the NT Gospels. But is it a dove or an eagle?

The question arises whether the dove imagery is more significant than that of an eagle. It does seem that the dove is one of the most important birds in the OT. The turtledove has a cultic role (Lev 1:14; 5:7, 11; 12:6, 8), and as a migratory bird (Jer 8:7) is the harbinger of springtime.[28] The emphasis on the activity of "hovering" as done by the dove rather than by the eagle comes surprisingly from the later references made in rabbinic literature. This may have to do with the dove of Genesis 8. Two key texts refer to Genesis 1:2 and the presence of a dove. The first, as noted above but here quoted from a different source, comes from rabbi Rashi: "The Spirit of God was moving: the Throne of glory was standing in the air and moving on the face of the waters by the Spirit of the mouth of the Holy One, blessed be he, and by his Word like a dove which

[28] G. F. Hasel, "Dove," *ISBE* (1979) 1.987–89.

broods on the nest."[29] Rashi probably adopted the simile of a dove from Ben Zoma, whose view is recorded in the Babylonian Talmud (Hagigah 15a):

> Rabbi Joshua the son of Hananiah was standing on an ascent on the Temple Mount, and Ben Zoma saw him but did not stand before him. He said to him: Whence comest thou and whither go thy thoughts, Ben Zoma? He replied: I was considering the space between the upper waters and the lower waters, and there is only between them a mere three fingers' breadth, as it is said, And the Spirit of God was brooding on the face of the waters like a dove which broods over the young but does not touch them.[30]

In rabbinic literature, the choice of a dove over an eagle seems to be arbitrary but it is the more popular one. A recent discovery in the new Dead Sea Scroll substantiates this.[31] Apart from this background, the OT does not seem to attribute any special significance in the symbolic nature between the dove and the Spirit of God. Nor does it develop the differences between the dove and the eagle. The emphasis is on the similarities between the actions of the bird and of the *rûaḥ* in "hovering" and "protecting." When characteristics of the dove are extolled and compared to the work of the Spirit, they arise not from OT texts but from conjecture. However, in the OT the dove may be a symbol of love (Song Sol 2:14; 5:2; 6:9). A NT connection to this concept is that love is a fruit of the Spirit.

The Creator in Isaiah 40:13

Isaiah's court life and prophetic ministry occurred during the momentous events from Uzziah's death, through the reigns of Jotham, Ahaz, and Hezekiah (from around 745 BC), and perhaps even into the reign of Manasseh, according to tradition. The themes of salvation and redemption from captivity are featured in Isaiah 40–66 (41:14; 43:14), with an emphasis on Yahweh as supreme ruler over all the nations (40:11, 13–17). Isaiah 40 opens with the glad announcement of comfort to the

[29] Quoted in I. Abrahams, *Studies in Pharisaism and the Gospels* (Cambridge: University Press, 1924) 47–50.

[30] b. Hag., 15a.

[31] D. C. Allison, Jr., "The Baptism of Jesus and a New Dead Sea Scroll," *BARev* 18 (2, 1992) 58–60.

exiles. To the disheartened people of God is given the message that Yahweh, who created the universe, will again intervene in the lives of his people.

The context of verse 13, which asks the rhetorical question "Who has understood the mind of the LORD *[rûaḥ yhwh]*, or instructed him as his counsellor?" highlights the incomparability and transcendence of Yahweh. On the one hand he has power over human beings, who are like the grass—when the *rûaḥ* blows on them, they wither (40:6–7). On the other hand, he is a caring shepherd for his flock (v. 11). The major theme of chapter 40, however, is Yahweh as Creator. Whereas, humankind may fashion idols for themselves (vv. 18–20), Yahweh created the universe (vv. 26, 28). It is likely that this passage counters the salvation traditions that claimed that counselor gods informed Marduk on how to create the world.[32] But the prophet clarifies that Yahweh is sufficient in himself to create all things without assistance (Isa 40:12–14).

The translation of *rûaḥ yhwh* in verse 13 is literally "the Spirit of Yahweh." However, Whybray correctly translates verses 13–14 in this context: "Who has understood the mind of Yahweh, or who was his counsellor, who instructed him? Whom did he consult for his guidance, and who taught him the way to achieve order, and showed him how to exercise creative skill?"[33] The LXX translates *rûaḥ* with *noûs* (mind), which is followed by the NT writers (1 Cor 2:16; Rom 11:34). The translation *noûs* is usually associated with the volitional and rational capacities of humankind. The context of Isaiah 40:12–14 includes terms such as "understand," "instruct," "enlighten," "taught," and "knowledge"—words normally associated with the mind. With this in view it is evident that the passage asserts the ability of Yahweh to create the universe apart from any advisers. In fact, he has the "creative skill" *[tibunōṯ]* normally given to artisans (Exod 31:3), and the ability to achieve "order" *[mišpāṭ]* according to his heavenly pattern (cf. 1 Kgs 6:38; Ezek 42:11).[34] Isaiah therefore presents the incompara-

[32] R. N. Whybray, *Isaiah 40–66* (Greenwood: Attic, 1975; NCBC; Grand Rapids: Eerdmans, 1981) 53–54.

[33] R. N. Whybray, *The Heavenly Counsellor in Isaiah 40:13–14* (Cambridge: University Press, 1971) 18.

[34] Waltke, "The Creation Account in Genesis 1:1–3," *BSac* 133 (529, 1976) 31–32.

bility of Yahweh as creator, who himself planned the creation of the universe and then implemented his plan by his *rûaḥ*. Creation was planned by the *rûaḥ yhwh,* who then moved to bring the heavens, earth, sea, and mountains into existence.[35]

Creation by Word and Spirit: Psalm 33:6

Psalm 33 is a song of praise and thanksgiving, in which the community of faith acknowledges the work of Yahweh as creator, sustainer, and Lord of history. The psalm is a reflection on the creation narrative of Genesis 1, which further presents the nature of God's creative acts. The principal theme is Yahweh's lordship over nature and over human history. It is the power of Yahweh's word in creation to which the community now appeals for help in its present state of need.

Verse 6 states specifically that "By the word of the Lord were the heavens made, their starry host by the *rûaḥ* of his mouth." Here the psalmist recalls the creation account and emphasizes the connection between the spoken word and the presence of the *rûaḥ,* which brings the word to fulfillment. Verses 6–9 present the work of Yahweh through his creative word.

The concept of creation by the word of God is not unique to Israel. The Egyptian myth of "The Creation by Atum" gives some indication of a spoken word being fulfilled, but "The Theology of Memphis" is quite explicit in reference to the word of Ptah and creation.[36] J. A. Wilson, in reference to the Memphis theology, states, "Here the god Ptah conceives the elements of the universe with his mind [heart] and brings them into being by his commanding speech [tongue]. Thus, at the beginning of Egyptian history, there was an approach to the Logos Doctrine."[37] Upon completion of Ptah's task it is said, "And so Ptah was satisfied, after he had made everything, as well as all the divine order."[38] This concept also occurs in Mesopotamia and reflects a common ancient Near Eastern tradition.

---

[35] Cf. J. D. W. Watts, *Isaiah 34–66,* (WBC; Waco: Word, 1987) 90–91; C. Westermann, *Isaiah 40–66: A Commentary* (OTL; trans. D. M. G. Stalker; Philadelphia: Westminster, 1969) 50.

[36] J. A. Wilson, *ANET,* 3–6. cf. K. Koch, "Wort und Einheit des Schöpfergottes in Memphis und Jerusalem," *ZTK* 62 (1965) 251–93.

[37] *ANET,* 4, note lines 48–60.

[38] *ANET,* 5.

It is doubtful, however, that the OT accounts are dependent on the Egyptian parallels. G. F. Hasel concludes that the creation narrative "knows only of creation by an effortless, omnipotent, and unchallengeable divine word which renders the so-called similarity between the Egyptian mantic-magic world and the Hebrew effortless word of Genesis 1 as 'wholly superficial.' "[39]

In the OT, a number of references speak of Yahweh's intervention and creation by the word. Isaiah says, "so is my word that goes out from my mouth: It will not return to me empty, but will accomplish what I desire and achieve the purpose for which I sent it" (Isa 55:11; cf. 40:26; 44:24–28; 48:13; 50:2; Ezek 37:4; Pss 33:6, 9; 104:7; 147:4, 15–18; 148:3–5). In many of these references, the word and subsequent fulfillment of the word by God's power are indicated. In Psalm 33:6 the connection between the speaking of God and the activity of God is unmistakable.[40] Stated poetically, the breath of God when speaking is meant and its effectual results are evident in what is created. As the breath of God's mouth goes out *[rûaḥ]*, the stars and created elements are brought into existence. The creative word of the Lord brings into reality the heavens and the earth.[41] There is an inner correspondence between the Spirit of God as the breath of life going forth from God and the word of God as the breath of his mouth (Isa 11:4). The use of the term *rûaḥ* in the creation event as understood by the psalmist, but here stated poetically, indicates that the spoken word of God is brought into existence by the *rûaḥ,* which is the active, creative, and vital presence of God.

The Role of Wisdom Personified in Creation: Proverbs 1:23

In the book of Proverbs, Wisdom takes on a unique status as a person. Wisdom is personified as a preexistent companion of God at creation (Prov 8:22–31) and as an itinerant female teacher

[39] Hasel, "Polemic Nature," 90.

[40] Steck, *Schöpfungsbericht,* 46, 236, n. 971; cf. W. H. Schmidt, *"dāḇar," TDOT,* 3.121. cf. Isa 55:10f.

[41] H. J. Kraus, *Psalmen: 1–63, Biblischer Kommentar,* 1 Teilband (Neukirchener Verlag des Erziehungsvereins GmbH, 1979) 262. cf. H. J. Kraus, *Theologie der Psalmen* (Neukirchener Verlag des Erziehungsvereins GmbH, 1979) 72ff.

(1:20–33; 8:1ff.; 9:1ff.).[42] Wisdom actively pursues eager listeners in the marketplaces of life in order to impart knowledge and understanding to those who desire assistance (1:20–33). The benefits that Wisdom offers her listeners include business acumen and riches (3:16), honor (3:16f., 35), and long life (3:22; 13:14). Therefore, seeking Wisdom is a profitable endeavor (2:4; 3:14; 8:11, 19; Job 28:15–20). Failure to embrace Wisdom as a companion (Prov 4:6–8; 7:4; 8:17) turns blessing into calamity.[43]

In these passages, Wisdom is not only like a gift given to the seeker, which makes the individual capable of fulfilling God's purposes in the world, but she is a person who pours forth her wisdom. "If you had responded to my rebuke, I would have poured out my heart *[rûaḥ]* to you and made my thoughts *[dᵉḇārîm]* known to you" (1:23). W. McKane's translation is more literal, "If you return when I reprove you, I shall pour out my spirit for you, I shall divulge my words to you" (cf. Isa 44:3). His assertion in this context has credence, "The intention here may be to represent Wisdom as a charismatic, spirit-filled person, who pours out on those who are receptive and submissive the spirit of wisdom."[44]

Proverbs 1–9 presents Wisdom's role in creation. The emphasis of Wisdom's role in creation is on the vast intelligence by which she exercised an architectonic function in ordering the world.[45] The purpose and order discernible in the cosmos are now regarded as effects of wisdom.[46] Wisdom and the Spirit of God are often linked in the OT; indeed, it is the Spirit who gives wisdom (cf. Gen 41:38–39; Exod 31:3–4; Deut 34:9; Isa 11:2; Job 32:7–10). Wisdom is a divine attribute because it comes from Yahweh or heaven (Prov 2:6; 8:22–31). The rendering of Proverbs 8:22 and its role in the passage are problematic in that wisdom appears to be created. The NIV reads, "The Lord brought me forth as the first of his works," but the possible options are also noted: "The LORD possessed me at the beginning of his work"; or, "The LORD brought me forth at the beginning of

---

[42] G. T. Sheppard, "Wisdom," *ISBE*, 4.1076.

[43] H.-P. Müller, *"ḥoḵmāh," TDOT*, 4.379–80.

[44] W. McKane, *Proverbs: A New Approach* (OTL; Philadelphia: Westminster, 1970) 274; Note the translation on p. 212.

[45] G. von Rad, *Old Testament Theology* (trans. D. M. G. Stalker; New York: Harper & Row, 1965) 2.448f.; See also his *Wisdom in Israel* (trans. J. D. Martin; Nashville: Abingdon, 1972) 144ff.

[46] Eichrodt, *Theology*, 2.81.

his work." In the fuller context, Wisdom preexisted and was a "craftsman" at Yahweh's side in bringing about the mighty works of creation. Therefore, Wisdom worked together with Yahweh in bringing into reality the heavens and the earth that declare the glory of God (Prov 3:19–20; Isa 40:12–17, 28–31).

In this role, and from an OT viewpoint, Wisdom has more affinities to the work of the *rûaḥ* in creation than it does to the preincarnate, only begotten Son of the Father (as suggested by J. B. Payne based on a number of NT passages: Luke 11:49; Matt 23:34; Col 2:3; 1 Cor 1:24, 30; John 1:1–18).[47] In the OT, wisdom is usually seen in practical action and is given by the Spirit of God (Exod 31:3; Gen 41:38f.). The intertestamental period also shows Wisdom's role in creation (Wis 7:22; 8:1, 6; Sir 24:3–5), and specifically refers to Wisdom as the Spirit in the context of preserving creation, "Because the Spirit of the Lord has filled the world, and that which holds all things together knows what is said" (Wis 1:7). Building on this correspondence, the book of James in the phrase "every good and perfect gift is from above" may refer to the Holy Spirit (Jas 1:17) and thus reflect the OT gift of wisdom through the Spirit. The one lacking in wisdom is instructed to ask God, who gives wisdom impartially (Jas 1:5–8, 16–18; 3:13–18; cf. Matt 7:7–11; Luke 11:13).[48] In this sense one can say that "James has a wisdom pneumatology, for wisdom in James functions as the Spirit does in Paul; wisdom helps one stand, delivers one from 'the flesh,' . . . and produces the fruit of the Christian life."[49]

Victory Over Chaos: Job 26:13

In response to the assertion of Bildad, that God is awesome and the establisher of order, Job illustrates the power of

---

[47] J. B. Payne, *The Theology of the Older Testament* (Grand Rapids: Zondervan, 1962) 171.

[48] J. A. Kirk claims, "The Holy Spirit is perhaps conceived of as the supreme good gift, for God will give everything to those who ask Him right up to the giving of the Holy Spirit, provided that faith is present." "The Meaning of Wisdom in James," *NTS* (1969) 25. See also W. R. Thompson, "The Epistle of James—A Document on Heavenly Wisdom," *WTH* 13 (1978) 7–12.

[49] P. Davids, *Commentary on James* (NIGTC; Grand Rapids: Eerdmans, 1982) 56.

Yahweh in and over creation. The translation of Job 26:12–13 according to N. C. Habel is, "By his power he stilled the sea; By his understanding he smote Rahab. His breath *[rûaḥ]* stretched out the heavens and his hand pierced the Evil Serpent."[50] By using the language of myth, Job refers to God's power over creation whereby creation occurs after the subjugation of the primordial chaos.

The theme of a chaotic sea out of which comes a monster who is consequently conquered and then formed into parts of the cosmos is common in the ancient Near East. Therefore, it is not surprising that Israel employs the language of myth in poetic passages in order to convey Yahweh's superiority over whatever claims other nations make. In Israel's literature, mythic claims are transformed to show Yahweh's victory over the chaos monster.

Some of these monsters are called Rahab (Isa 51:9; Pss 87:4; 89:11; Job 9:13; 26:12), Leviathan (Isa 27:1; Pss 74:14; 104:26; Job 40:25), Behemoth (Isa 30:6; Job 40:15), Yam (Isa 51:9f; Ps 74:13f.; Job 3:8; 7:12; 26:12), the dragon (Isa 51:9; 27:1; Jer 51:34; Ezek 29:3; Job 7:12), and the serpent (Isa 27:1; Amos 9:3; Job 26:13).[51] In many of these passages, the writers seek to affirm God's control over creation and the forces of chaos. In Job's situation, therefore, the passage emphasizes that God, who in the past conquered the evil forces of chaos and brought forth order by the *rûaḥ,* would also now bring victory to Job's circumstances and transform chaos into order.

In summary of our discussion of the activity of the *rûaḥ* in creation of the universe, we have considered numerous texts in the OT concerning the nature and theology of creation in the Hebrew understanding. Many of the OT concepts are unique to Israel. A vital element of Israel's understanding of creation that is often overlooked is the nature of the Spirit's work. The texts here discussed show the active involvement of the Spirit's presence in creation. Through the *rûaḥ,* God brought the invisible spoken

---

[50] N. C. Habel, *The Book of Job: A Commentary* (OTL; Philadelphia: Westminster, 1985) 364.

[51] *ANET,* 67, lines 85–101, 131–32; cf. H. Gunkel, "The Influence of the Babylonian Mythology Upon the Biblical Creation Story," *Creation in the Old Testament* (ed. B. W. Anderson; Philadelphia: Fortress, 1984) 33–44. B. W. Anderson, *Creation Versus Chaos* (Philadelphia: Fortress, 1987) 15ff.; F. R. McCurley, *Ancient Myths and Biblical Faith: Scriptural Transformations* (Philadelphia: Fortress, 1983) 11ff.

word into physical reality. This is the significant background to the prophetic experience of Spirit reception, inspiration, and utterance of the spoken word, which was then expected to be fulfilled and realized in the experience of the nation. The word and the *rûaḥ* are thus vital correlatives in the work of creation.

The Presence of God in the Sanctuary

The presence of God is manifested in numerous and often anthropomorphic ways in the OT. The manifestations of God may be indicated as the divine face, arm, hand, or eyes, or by the cloud and other theophanic displays. M. G. Kline concludes: "By these terms the Glory is identified as the personal presence of God and as the power of God stretched forth to act in the exercise of his sovereignty."[52] In many of the contexts where God's presence is manifested, the Spirit of God is signified (Exod 40:34ff.; cf. Num 11:16–17, 25; 1 Kgs 8:10–11; Ezek 43:4–5; Hag 2:5–9). In fact, the glory-cloud may be depicted as a "Spirit-temple" out of which the Spirit moves to effect the will of God.[53] The creation narrative of Genesis 1–3 presents Eden as a sacred temple, a palace or world mountain, where God crowns the garden with his presence. "The garden planted there was holy ground with guardianship of its sanctity committed in turn to men and to cherubim (Gen 2:15; 3:24). It was the temple-garden of God (Isa 51:3; Ezek 28:13, 16; 31:9), the place chosen by the Glory-Spirit who hovered over creation from the beginning to be the focal site of his throne-presence among men."[54]

Heaven and earth are established as a royal residence or temple for the Creator. "The cosmology of the OT is fond of describing creation as a tabernacle which God has pitched (cf. Ps 104; Job 9:8; Isa 40:22) or a house which God has established (with pillars, windows, and doors; Job 26:11; Gen 7:11; Ps 78:23)."[55] Eden is thus a microcosmic version of a sanctuary, a holy place where God dwells by the Spirit (Gen 1:2). Just as the Spirit brings the word of God into reality, so Spirit-endowed artisans bring the

[52] Kline, *Images of the Spirit,* 18–19.
[53] Ibid., 21.
[54] Ibid., 35–36.
[55] W. A. Gage, *The Gospel of Genesis: Studies in Protology and Eschatology* (Winona Lake, Ind.: Carpenter, 1984) 54.

revealed plan for the tabernacle into reality (Exod 31:1–11). Throughout the OT, the Spirit is present in some form during all sacred construction projects, be it the creation of Eden, the Mosaic tabernacle, the Solomonic or exilic temple. In the tabernacle and temple construction, Edenic motifs such as carvings of flowers, palm trees, and cherubim appear frequently (1 Kgs 6:18, 29, 32, 35; 7:18ff.; Ezek 41:18ff.). Rivers that fructify the earth, as well as the tree of life, are found in the original garden and also in the eschatological sanctuary (Ezek 47; Rev 21–22; cf. Gen 2:10–14).[56]

The concept of a temple is not unique to the nation of Israel but is a common feature in the world of the ancient Near East. The ancients understood a temple to be the architectural embodiment of the cosmic mountain, which was the point of contact between heaven and earth.[57] This sacred place does not necessitate an actual building but represents the divine dwelling place where the worshiper communes with the deity (cf. Exod 24:11). The temple issues waters of life which flow from a spring within the building and represent the primeval waters of creation which give life and bring fertility. In their architectural orientation temples often express the idea of a graduated ascent toward heaven that directs the people heavenward in their focus.[58] The plan and measurement of the temple are believed to be a revelation from the deity to the king who is responsible for carrying out the directives.[59] In the OT, the instructions for the tabernacle are revealed in a similar manner (Exod 25–31; 1 Chron 28:6–19; cf. Heb 8:1–5) and are carried out by Spirit-endowed individuals (Exod 31:1–11).

Closely associated with the temple building is the presence of God, who indwells the temple as his throne. Revelation takes place within the sanctuary, which is the symbol of blessing and God's dwelling among the people. In the tabernacle or in the tent of meeting, God meets with Moses and manifests the divine glory (Exod 19:16–23; Num 11). The tabernacle is the central focal point for the community (Deut 12:1–14), and as such is the

---

[56] Kline, *Images of the Spirit,* 41. Further on this, see J. D. Levenson, *Theology of the Program of Restoration of Ezekiel 40–48* (HSM 10; Atlanta: Scholars, 1976) 25–36.

[57] McCurley, *Ancient Myths,* 125–64.

[58] R. E. Clements, *God and Temple* (Oxford: Blackwell, 1965) 1–16.

[59] W. J. Dumbrell, *The End of the Beginning* (Australia: Lancer Books, 1985) 38ff.

central unifying institution in ancient Near Eastern society. The temple expresses the political rule of God over the people. As sacred and holy space, temple precincts are off limits for the general public (cf. Exod 19:12–13, 21–24; 1 Sam 6:19-20) and call for respect and reverence. After God "plants" Eden and "puts" Adam and Eve in his sanctuary, they defile it just as Israel would do in the sanctuary of Canaan, where God "plants" them (Exod 15:17). The result of irreverence for the presence of God and persistent sin is the ultimate covenant curse: expulsion from Eden and Canaan (Deut 28), and later in history, out of the temple itself (John 2:13–16).

The transfer from the tabernacle to the temple did not change the fundamental understanding of temple theology. Associated with the temple building, which David prepares for and which is completed by Solomon, is the concept of rest from enemies (2 Sam 7:1; cf. Ps 132) and the subsequent establishment of the dwelling place of God (cf. Gen 2:2). Underlying the initiative for temple building is the necessary commissioning by God. The human builders understand that although God will dwell in the temple, he can not be restricted to one place (1 Kgs 8:1ff.). God's acceptance of the temple as a place of prayer and a place for seeking divine guidance is indicated by the glory of his presence filling his temple (1 Kgs 8:11; cf. Exod 19:9–25; 40:34–38). Whereas the glory of God is declared through nature and fills the whole earth (Pss 19:1; 29:1–3, 9; 57:5; 108:5; 113:4), God's special presence is manifested in the temple, where the divine presence dwells among the people.

After the destruction of the Solomonic temple in 587 BC, the returning exiles dedicate the exilic temple in 515 BC, which lasts five hundred years until destroyed by Herod the Great.[60] Through Spirit-inspired oracles Haggai serves to encourage the exilic community in their work. In Haggai 2:5b he comforts the exiles: "My Spirit remains among you. Do not fear." Not only does he emphasize that Yahweh's strengthening presence is among them to fulfill his purpose, but he goes on to indicate that the temple will again be filled with God's glory. This term does not suggest glory as in the splendor of a building.[61] It signifies

[60] H. W. Wolff, *Haggai: A Commentary* (trans. M. Kohl; Minneapolis: Augsburg, 1988) 75.

[61] Despite Wolff's suggestion to the contary, ibid., 77.

the "filling" of the temple with the presence of God through the Spirit. From the temple, which is Yahweh's house (1:2, 4; 2:3, 7), God's presence would now issue forth divine blessing and shalom (2:15b, 19b).

The OT prophets cry out at the abuse of the temple and its corruption (Jer 7; 26:1–19). The wrong understanding of the temple precincts amounts to the rejection of Yahweh's rule and therefore, the symbol of the divine presence is removed from among them. The destruction of the temple is viewed as the result of social, moral, and religious decadence and disobedience to Yahweh's commandments. Misplaced trust in the temple leads to its removal and the departure of God's glory (Ezek 10:3–19). This leads to the blueprint for a new temple that will function as Yahweh's throne in a holy city. Ezekiel 43:1–12 narrates the return of God's presence to the new temple. The prophet is transported by the Spirit to the inner court, where the glory of God fills the temple (43:5). After the destruction of the temple, Jerusalem-Zion becomes the place where God will dwell with the people. The prophets present Zion as an Edenic paradise. There, the sacred stream flows from Zion as a symbol of the divine guardianship over the mountain and God's faithful people (Isa 8:6–7). It functions as an instrument of regeneration to bring healing to God's ailing people (Isa 33:20–24).[62] In Ezekiel 47:1–10, 12 the prophet expands the benefits of the stream in the context of Israel's life after redemption. J. D. Levenson summarizes:

> Nature has been healed, giving forth its best at every moment. The economic conditions which call forth human abuses have been eliminated. The serenity of Zion has, through the ever-growing stream, spread throughout the Land. Zion has become the source of redemption; the Temple is the mechanism for the disbursal of abundant grace for the whole population. When the presence of God has returned to the navel of the world, the Land is transfigured through the life-giving stream thus renewed.[63]

Therefore, the restoration of the Edenic mountain in Scripture is to be identified with the eschatological exaltation of Zion as the cosmic mountain of the North (cf. Isa 51:3; Jer 17:13; Ezek 28:13–14; 40:2; 47:12; Pss 36:8–9; 46; 125:1–2). However, the hopes

---

[62] Levenson, *Theology,* 12.
[63] Ibid, 13.

and desires for Zion and the temple in the exilic community are largely thwarted and again relegated to a future fulfillment (cf. Hag 1:15–2:9; Joel 3:17–18; Zech 1:7–17; 14:8; Ezra 4:1–4).

In Qumran, the temple imagery was applied to the community, which was viewed as a temple in which God dwelt (4QFlor 1, 1–13). This text was an exposition of the promise of Nathan concerning the "house of David" that the Qumran community believed to be fulfilled in them (cf. Amos 9:11f.). As the temple of God, they were an exclusive group of chosen people called to holiness.[64] In the community, God as builder worked through the agency of the priest, the righteous teacher (cf. Matt 16:18). The community as a "temple" believed themselves to be the inheritors of the Zion tradition which promised security against enemies. They believed they were the place from where God's truth proceeded. The temple was the place of atonement and judgment.

The closest correspondences with the Qumran concept appear in 2 Corinthians 6:14–7:1. The Qumran community believed they were indwelt by the Spirit of God according to Ezekiel 37:27 and Leviticus, "I will put my dwelling place among you, and I will not abhor you. I will walk among you and be your God, and you will be my people" (26:11–12). This belief led to the tenet of separation and fellowship with God.

With the advent of Jesus, the development of temple theology is taken a step further. Jesus' understanding of the temple as a house of prayer leads to the cleansing of the temple (Mark 11:12–20; Matt 21:12–16; John 2:13–16). The cleansing episode in Mark is framed by the temple entry and the cursing of the fig tree, which symbolizes the cultus. Its withering portrays God's judgment on the temple, which has failed to be the place of worship for all the nations (Mark 11:17; cf. Isa 56:7). In light of this, Jesus is pictured as the new temple (Mark 1:10f.; 9:7) on whom the Spirit and the glory of God rest. His body is the temple made without hands in whom the glory of God "tabernacled" (John 1:14). His body would be raised to create the new temple that would be a place of worship for both Jew and Gentile (John 2:19; 14:58; Mark 12:9ff.; cf. Eph 2:20–22; 1 Pet

[64] L. Gaston, *No Stone On Another* (Leiden: Brill, 1970) 164ff.; B. Gärtner, *The Temple and the Community in Qumran and the New Testament* (Cambridge: University Press, 1966) 30ff.; R. J. McKelvey, *The New Temple: The Church in the New Testament* (Oxford: University Press, 1969) 46–53.

2:4–10). This reality is seen in the worship of believers as they gathered together for prayer and communion (Acts 2:46; 3:1; 4:11).

It is Paul who takes the temple imagery and applies it directly to believing communities (1 Cor 3:16ff.; 2 Cor 6:16–17). In the context of 2 Corinthians 6:16–17, the stress on separation is clear. Believers are set apart for specific purposes, and Paul indicates the antithesis strongly: "What agreement has the temple of God with idols? For we are the temple of the living God." The emphasis is on the unique nature of the Corinthian community, who are the temple of God and therefore subject to ethical obligations. Thus, the OT Scriptures about God indwelling the temple are fulfilled in the NT community of believers. As R. J. McKelvey puts it, "God no longer dwells with his people in a sanctuary which they make for him; he dwells in them and they are his temple."[65]

In 1 Corinthians 6:19–20, Paul takes the imagery of the temple and applies it in context to the individual's body, which is reserved for God. The Spirit of God dwells in the individual and therefore sanctifies the body, which must not be defiled with prostitutes.[66] In the context of the popular belief that what is done in the body cannot impede the life of the Spirit, Paul makes it clear that, "Because the body is God's, one must not use it in illicit intercourse; instead, one must make it a chaste temple whereby to honor God."[67] Both the community and individuals have moral and spiritual obligations to fulfill. Ephesians 2:19–22 refers to the church universal as God's temple where believers of every race may gather together as a holy sanctuary indwelt by the Spirit. This text and the rich imagery it employs present the fullest development of Paul's conception of the church as God's temple. Thus, a vivid picture is set before the church, not only of its moral obligations as God's dwelling place but of its great privilege to commune with God in unity.[68]

[65] McKelvey, *New Temple,* 95.

[66] G. D. Fee, *The First Epistle to the Corinthians* (NICNT; Grand Rapids: Eerdmans, 1987) 263–65.

[67] C. K. Barrett, *A Commentary on the Epistle to the Corinthians* (2d ed.; London: Adam & Charles Black, 1968) 151.

[68] See McKelvey, *New Temple,* for an in-depth discussion on Ephesians 2:20–22, 1 Peter 2:4–12, and other relevant texts.

The Nature of the Spirit's Role in the Creation of Humankind

References to God's creation of humankind by his *rûaḥ* are relatively infrequent in the OT. However, this remains an important element in establishing the theological understanding of Israel concerning the creation of humankind. The psalmist claims, "Know that the Lord himself is God; It is he who has made us, and not we ourselves" (Ps 100:3). Concerning the nation, Moses summarizes the general OT theological understanding by asking, "Is he not your Father, your Creator, who made you and formed you?" (Deut 32:6). The theological truth of humankind's creation at the hands of God is often asserted concerning the individual (Pss 71:6; 89:48; 94:9; 139:13, 15; 149:2) but is also extended to the creation of communities and groups. Thus, not only are Jacob and Israel created and redeemed by God, but God promises to pour out the *rûaḥ* on their offspring, enabling them through his blessing to fulfill their commission by God (Isa 43:1; 44:2–21; 54:5; Hos 8:14; Deut 32:6, 15, 18; cf. Isa 1:2; 64:7). The individual lament psalms address the creator in hopes of salvation (Job 10:3, 10–12; 14:15; 35:10; Pss 22:10f.; 119:73; 138:8). God also created his servant for his purposes, one who would be anointed for his service (Isa 49:5; cf. 42:6; 49:8; Jer 1:5).[69]

Some specific concepts concerning the creation of humankind are provided in texts asserting the vital role of the *rûaḥ* in granting life to humankind. The OT also abounds with substantives such as *lēḇ*, *nep̄eš*, and *bāśār*, which are often in parallel with *rûaḥ*. The consideration of these parallel terms becomes vital for determining the OT understanding of human beings. This section primarily considers passages that indicate the role of the *rûaḥ* in the creation of humankind, but also considers important parallel terms and the relationship of Genesis 1:26–27 to Genesis 1:2.

Humankind in the Image of God: Genesis 1:26–27

Within the creation narrative, and in the context of filling the earth, God determines to create humankind. The clause "Let

[69] R. Albertz, *Weltschöpfung und Menschenschöpfung: Untersucht bei Deuterojesaja, Hiob und in den Psalmen* (Stuttgart: Calwer, 1974) 26–53.

us make man in our image, in our likeness" has received much attention as to its significance for anthropology. The survey by C. Westermann on the exegetical views that Genesis 1:26–27 have inspired indicates the voluminous literature written on the subject. Interpretations fall into several groups of categories that feature (1) a distinction made between the natural and supernatural likeness to God; (2) the likeness of God consisting of spiritual qualities or capacities; (3) the image and likeness of God as seen in the external form; (4) the image as the person as a whole; (5) the person as God's counterpart; (6) the person as God's representative on earth; plus other views that are more speculative and obscure.[70] In summarizing these interpretations, Westermann claims that in many cases, false hermeneutical presuppositions led to an approach of the text that was not intended. He claims that the stress lies not on the question of the nature of humankind but on the action of God in the creation of humankind. He encourages an interpretation that deals with the passage as a whole, but he himself sees the text as an independent phrase that was later inserted into the narrative as a whole. We cannot resolve these issues here, but intend to note the relevant material in relation to the involvement of the *rûaḥ* in Genesis 1:26–27.

Concerning the plural references in this text and others (cf. Gen 3:22; 11:7), explanations include the "plural of majesty," the "plural of deliberation," and "the divine assembly" motif. The first two are objectionable grammatically and contextually, whereas the last is generally considered theologically objectionable because it assumes that angelic beings were involved in the act of creation.[71] But M. G. Kline's thesis of the theophanic glory-cloud may explain the angelic presence in a more acceptable manner. Based on an overview of texts in the OT and NT, Kline refers to God's presence at creation and other redemptive events as the "theophanic glory-cloud." While this concept is developed more fully in other texts, we cannot dismiss its relevance in Genesis 1:2 and 1:26–27. His thesis that "the theophanic

[70] Westermann, *Genesis: 1-11*, 148-55.

[71] For details on these views, refer to P. D. Miller, Jr., *Genesis 1–11: Studies in Structure and Theme* (JSOT 8; Sheffield: University of Sheffield Press, 1978) 9–26. F. W. Gesenius, E. Kautzsch, and A. E. Cowley, *Gesenius' Hebrew Grammar* (1910) 124, n. 2, 398. D. J. A. Clines, "The Image of God in Man," *Tyndale Bulletin* 19 (1968) 53–103.

Glory was present at the creation and was the specific divine model or referent in view in the creating of man in the image of God" does have credence within the OT teaching of creation.[72] In the context of Genesis 1, the creation of man is the focus of the narrative. Humankind is the pinnacle of creation, and the *rûaḥ ᵓᵉlōhîm,* which effected the daily creative acts, is now involved in the action of creating humankind.

The theophanic cloud represents the presence of God in heaven that is normally invisible to humankind. When accessible, God is viewed to be the king of glory in the midst of heavenly beings (1 Kgs 22; Isa 6; Job 1-2). The throne is surrounded by angelic beings, but is transported by cherubim and directed by the *rûaḥ* (Ezek 1). This heavenly council superintends the acts of creation, and God by his *rûaḥ* carries out his creative activities while the heavenly council observes and acknowledges his great power. Job indicates that the activity of the angels in response to creation was worship: "the morning stars sang together and all the angels shouted for joy" (Job 38:7). They too were created beings (Ps 148:2, 5), and the presence of cherubim in the garden is also evident in Genesis 3:24. Thus, the cosmos has the character of a royal temple within which resides the glory and presence of God and the angelic entourage (Isa 66:1). In the microcosm, the temple and humankind are also overshadowed by the presence of God. "God created man in the likeness of the Glory to be a spirit-temple of God in the spirit."[73] Whereas this concept becomes clearer in the OT and specifically in the NT (1 Cor 3:16), it is the relevant background to the specific references that indicate the role of the *rûaḥ* in the creation of humankind (see below).

The key aspects that the image of God signifies in the OT and in the ancient Near East are summarized most ably by D. J. A. Clines. These include the concept of the statue in the round. Whereas the god was represented in the ancient Near East by a statue, in the OT human beings represent a psychosomatic unity in their totality. Israel's God could never be represented by a statue, but humankind could represent God on earth. Thus, human beings are a faithful and adequate representation of God but not an exact copy. Furthermore, human beings in the image of God possess the life of the one they

[72] Kline, *Images of the Spirit,* 21ff.
[73] Ibid., 21.

represent, and epitomize the presence of the one represented. As God's representatives, they function as God does by ruling over the earth with the word (Gen 2:19). In their work, human beings follow the six-day cycle that God illustrated in the six days of creative work followed by rest (Gen 1:28). The image concept also entails kingship, which in the ancient Near East was usually reserved for the king.[74] However, the functions of humankind on earth are often noted in royal terms in the OT, and the royal imagery is democratized to include all of humankind. Thus, the psalmist declares: "What is man that you are mindful of him, the son of man that you care for him? You made him a little lower than the heavenly beings and crowned him with glory and honor. You made him ruler over the works of your hands; you put everything under his feet" (Ps 8:4–6).

The Creation of Humankind: Psalm 104:30

Commentators point out the numerous similarities between Psalm 104 and the "Hymn of Aton."[75] Both these hymns are concerned with creation and the origins of the cosmos. In the Aton hymn from Amarna, the following lines are particularly similar to Psalm 104:27–30. In the hymn it is claimed: "Thou settest every man in his place, Thou suppliest their necessities; Everyone has his food, and his time of life is reckoned . . . The world came into being by thy hand, According as thou has made them. When thou hast risen they live, When thou settest they die. Thou art lifetime thy own self, For one lives (only) through thee."[76] The content of Psalm 104 is mainly a celebration of God's creative work in Genesis 1 which inspires the psalmist to praise the creator. In this context of worship, verses 29b–30 refer mainly to the creation of humankind and beast, but also indicate the continuous work of God in preserving and renewing the earth. In reference to God's creatures, the psalmist states, "You take away their *rûaḥ*, they

---

[74] Clines, "Image of God," 53–103.

[75] Cf. *ANET,* 369–70. The similarities are now accepted to be a result of common themes and traditions in the ancient Near East rather than literary dependence. Cf. P. C. Craigie, "The Comparison of Hebrew Poetry: Psalm 104 in the Light of Egyptian and Ugaritic Poetry," *Semitics* 4 (1974) 10–21.

[76] *ANET,* 370–71.

die and revert to the dust; you send out your *rûaḥ,* creatures are made, and you renew the surface of the ground." Whereas similar claims are made in some Egyptian literature, this passage features Yahweh's Spirit as the giver of physical life to humankind (cf. Gen 2:7; 6:17). As noted in chapter 1, the breath of life concept is not referred to as "spirit" in the ancient Near East. In a hymn to Amon-Re, the claim is made, "It is you who have placed the breath of life in every nose, so that what your two arms have created may remain in life."[77]

Psalm 104 is not just a reflection on the initial creation of humankind and beast but refers to the on going involvement of Yahweh in creation. Every generation is to recognize and affirm that it is the product of Yahweh's creative activity through the process of reproduction. Yahweh replenishes both humankind and the animal kingdom.[78] Human beings are viewed to be utterly dependent on Yahweh's continued creative activity. W. Eichrodt summarizes: "Hence every living thing in the world is dependent on God's constantly letting his breath of life go forth to renew the created order; and when its vital spirit from God is withdrawn every creature must sink down in death. Thus, *rûaḥ* is at all times plainly superior to Man, a divine power within his mortal body subject to the rule of God alone."[79] When the *rûaḥ* is given to humankind, life is the inevitable result. When it is taken away, the living being is transferred into the realm of the dead (cf. Gen 3:19; Job 34:4, 14ff; Ps 146:4).

The Animating Power of Life: Job 32:8; 33:4; 34:14

A number of texts in Job present the understanding of Job and Elihu concerning the nature of humankind's existence. The *rûaḥ* of God is clearly the animating life force that initiates respiration and life. Job says, "As long as I have life within me, the breath *[rûaḥ]* of God in my nostrils, my lips will not speak wickedness" (Job 27:3). In this passage, and in a number of others (32:8; 33:4; 34:14), the *rûaḥ* and the *n^{e}šāmāh* are parallel constructs that underline the fact that life comes from God. Elihu

[77] O. Keel, *The Symbolism of the Biblical World: Ancient Near Eastern Iconography and the Book of Psalms* (trans. T. J. Hallet; New York: Crossroad, 1985) 210.

[78] L. C. Allen, *Psalms 101–150,* (WBC; Waco: Word, 1983) 34.

[79] Eichrodt, *Theology,* 2.47–48.

claims, "The spirit *[rûaḥ]* of El made me; the breath *[n^e^šāmāh]* of Shaddai gives me life" (33:4).[80] This text accents humankind's formation by the *rûaḥ*, as well as the subsequent life force that is bestowed on the physical body through the life breath.

Life and Wisdom for Skillful Living

In his speech, Elihu justifies his right to speak because of the *rûaḥ* within him that is shared by all humanity. The spirit in this context seems to have a dual role. On the one hand, the *rûaḥ* gives life to humankind, and on the other, the *rûaḥ* is almost personified with Lady Wisdom through whom mankind may find wisdom for skillful living (cf. Prov 1:23; 8:22–31).[81] This example is an indicator of the frequent connection in the wisdom literature between creation and wisdom. This is further clarified by Job 32:7–8, where the *rûaḥ* and *n^e^šāmāh* of Shaddai are given to man as the source of insight and understanding which is available to all mankind. "I thought, 'Age should speak; advanced years should teach wisdom.' But it is the spirit *[rûaḥ]* in a man, the breath of the Almighty, that gives him understanding."[82] Therefore, in addition to the theological conception of humankind's creation through the *rûaḥ*, the *rûaḥ* is also understood to be the source of inner wisdom that Elihu possesses by virtue of his creation as a human at the hands of Shaddai.

Although Habel claims that the life-giving spirit (Job 27:3) and the wisdom-imparting spirit are identical (cf. Gen 41:38; Dan 5:12; Exod 31:3) and not to be considered the charismatic gift, Elihu does claim to have wisdom above that of the elders.[83] Therefore, Elihu understands that he has a special endowment of wisdom that the elders do not have by virtue of their creation by Yahweh.[84] A distinction is made between the commonsense wisdom available to all humankind and the special endowment of wisdom for leadership and administration given only to some,

---

[80] Habel, *Job,* 455. The LXX translates the verse, "The divine spirit is that which formed me, and the breath of the Almighty that which teaches me."

[81] Habel, *Job,* 464.

[82] Cf. J. E. Hartley, *The Book of Job* (NICOT; Grand Rapids: Eerdmans, 1988) 434.

[83] Habel, *Job,* 451.

[84] M. H. Pope, *Job* (AB; 3d ed.; Garden City: Doubleday, 1973) 247.

at particular times and for specific tasks, such as in the experience of Joshua (Deut 34:9; cf. Isa 11:2f).

That God is the giver of life also indicates that he has the power to withdraw life. In this connection, Job claims, "If he plans in his heart to gather his spirit *[rûaḥ]* and breath *[n^e^šāmāh]* to himself, all flesh expires at once and humankind returns to the dust" (Job 34:14).[85] God has the ability and the right not only to give and to preserve life but also to remove the breath and *rûaḥ* of life which would result in the annihilation of humankind (cf. Ps 104:29; Gen 6:5–7, 13).

The opposite of the preservation of humankind, which happens when God gives life by the *rûaḥ,* is death, which occurs when God returns human beings to dust or clay (*ʾadāmāh*) by withdrawing the *rûaḥ*. Just as the *rûaḥ* of God is necessary to breathe life into the macrocosm for creation to take place, so the *rûaḥ* is required in the microcosm of a human being for life to exist.

The Creation of Humankind and the Divine Breath: Genesis 2:7

This verse uses *n^e^šāmāh*, a synonym term for *rûaḥ,* to indicate the animating principle of life. In the Writings, *rûaḥ* and *n^e^šāmāh* are often parallel terms referring to God's breath, which gives life to all creatures. At times *n^e^šāmāh* may refer to human breath (1 Kgs 17:17; Isa 42:5; Dan 10:7). Breath is God's gift that initiates life and respiration (Job 34:14; 36:4; Isa 2:22). Isaiah 57:16 includes both terms: "I will not accuse forever, nor will I always be angry, for then the spirit *[rûaḥ]* of man would grow faint before me—the breath *[n^e^šāmāh]* of man that I have created" (cf. Deut 20:16; Josh 10:40; 11:11, 14; 1 Kgs 15:29; Ps 150:6). If a distinction is to be made between the terms, *rûaḥ* would be considered as featuring the dynamic vitality of life, while *n^e^šāmāh* distinguishes between life and death. In other passages, *n^e^šāmāh* may indicate the capacity for feeling and knowing, as in Job 32:8: "But it is the spirit in a man, the breath of the Almighty, that gives him understanding."[86]

---

[85] Habel, *Job,* 473.

[86] See Bratcher, "Biblical Words Describing Man: Breath, Life, Spirit," 202. See also D. C. Arichea, Jr., "Translating Breath and Spirit," *BT* 34 (April, 1983) 209ff.

The Genesis creation account records that humankind was created on the sixth day. Verse 1:27 emphasizes God's work in the creation of humankind through the threefold repetition of the term *bārā*ʾ. The use of this word makes clear that God is solely responsible for and capable of creating humankind. The term always points to God's acts of creation and in Genesis 1:1 and 2:3–4 refers to creation as a whole. Theologically, *bārā*ʾ expresses "the incomparability of the creative work of God in contrast to man's things."[87] Whereas Genesis 1 gives a summary account of the creation of humankind, Genesis 2:7 indicates that God "formed" *[yāṣār]* the human and then "breathed" into the nostrils "the breath of life" *[nišmāṯ ḥayyîm]*. It is this action that not only begins physical life, but constitutes man "a living being" *[nep̱eš ḥayyāh]*. The term *nep̱eš* is usually used to designate a person as a complete individual, that is, it refers to a whole person. Physical life is stressed by the word *ḥāyāh,* which again differentiates the living from the dead. Texts that contrast death to life often note that idols who do not have the *rûaḥ* (Jer 10:14; 51:17) are devoid of life.[88] Without the *rûaḥ,* humankind returns to dust (cf. Ps 104:29; Gen 3:19; Job 10:9; 34:14f).

It is not only humankind who receives the breath of life from God but "every living creature" (Gen 6:17; 7:15, 22). But the distinction between humans and beasts is asserted in that humans have the divine breath directly breathed into them. Adam then shows his superiority over the animals by naming them. Although animals are said to have the *nišmāt ḥayyîm* or the *rûaḥ ḥayyîm* in them, the main difference between a human being and God is spiritual in nature (cf. Isa 42:5; Job 26:4; 27:3).[89] Whereas humankind and beast share in the breath of life, they are different in function and nature (cf. Exod 11:7; 19:13; Lev 20:15). The gift of the woman who is presented to Adam and who stands at his side (Gen 2:21) is equal to Adam and unique from the animals who are "put under his feet" and subjugated to his rule (Ps 8:6ff.; Gen 2:18f; 1:26–28).

---

[87] K. H. Bernhardt, "*bārā*ʾ," *TDOT,* 2:246-47.

[88] For a clearer understanding of the anthropological distinctions between these terms, see Wolff, *Anthropology;* Johnson, *Vitality,* 22, 27–29; Eichrodt, *Theology,* 2.136f.; H. Lamberty-Zielinski, "*nišāmāh,*" *TWAT,* 5.670–73.

[89] Eichrodt, *Theology,* 2.121. Johnson, *Vitality,* 27–29.

Blessing and Spirit

The OT concept of blessing is particularly suggestive in its relationship to the Spirit. Just as all creation is brought into reality by God through the Spirit, so it is the Spirit of God that gives animating life to humankind and makes that life capable of reproduction and creativity (cf. Gen 5:1ff.; 4:19–26). At times the Spirit gives a special ability or charisma for creative and sacred duties (Exod 31:1ff.). In the OT it is often the blessing of God that brings about the positive effects of fertility, long life, prosperity, and security. From the beginning, the ability of humankind to fulfill the commands of God depends on God's blessing. Therefore, the fundamental necessity for a person's success in fulfilling God's mandate is the blessing conferred on an individual. The commands: "Be fruitful and increase in number; fill the earth and subdue it. Rule over the fish of the sea and the birds of the air and over every living creature that moves on the ground" (Gen 1:28, 22; 5:2; 9:1), are impossible to discharge were it not for God's blessing. God enables humankind to fulfill the divinely imposed obligations through his conferred blessing.

Isaiah 44:3 shows the harmonious relationship between the promised blessing and its subsequent fulfillment through the work of the Spirit: "For I will pour water on the thirsty land, and streams on the dry ground; I will pour my Spirit on your offspring and my blessing on your descendants." Through this beneficent act of Yahweh, the divine promises and blessings will be realized. God is the source of both the blessing and the Spirit. Thus, the gift of fertility is given by God, who opens the barren womb (Gen 17:16, 20; 22:17; 25:11; 28:3). God's blessing brings vitality, health, prosperity, and abundance to the people of God (Deut 1:11; 7:13–15; 28:1–14). The blessing is tangible and visible and indicates God's favor, which witnesses may observe (Isa 51:2; 61:9).

Although the spoken blessing and its fulfillment were tied to magical connotations or the repetition of formula sayings in the ancient Near East, the OT evidence is distinctive. The experience of the blessing involves a relational dimension. J. Scharbert says: "In the OT the blessing is almost always attributed to God or closely connected with him. The godly man knew that the only kind of benedictory wishes he could utter were those which God alone could bring to reality. Since a blessing can be brought to reality by God alone, and since it denotes an attachment with or a strengthening of solidarity, it is necessary that the person uttering the blessing be in fellowship with God, seek it, or be worthy of it."[90] Therefore, the blessings of God were not activated through just any spoken formula such as the priestly blessing: "The Lord bless you and keep you; the Lord make his face shine upon you and be gracious to you; the Lord turn his face toward you and give you peace" (Num 6:24–26). While this blessing called for God's beneficence to be turned towards his people, the blessing was only as effective as the obedience of the people. Their experience of power that brings happiness, prosperity, success, respect, fertility, security, peace, and contentment was only a reality when they walked in obedience to God's commands.[91] Disobedience and rebellion brought the opposite affects of blessing on the people and actually "grieved the Holy Spirit" (Isa 63:10). The curse brought the reversal of covenant blessings on them (Deut 28).

The relationship between Spirit and blessing is also evident in the second part of humankind's OT commission to "subdue" and to "rule." Just as humankind depends on God for the blessing to enable fertility, success, and prosperity, so they depend on God to enable their work of subduing and ruling. This is vividly portrayed in the creation account where God forms Adam, breathes into him the breath of life, and puts him in the garden to "take care of it" (Gen 2:7–15).

In the OT, the role of ruling and subduing is a royal function. God chooses representatives to rule over his people. He works through individuals like Noah and Abraham whom he blesses and enables for their roles in the history of salvation. Moreover, God selects leaders and endows them with the Spirit of God to fulfill the divine purposes in history. In fact, most of the references concerning the Spirit of God in the OT are in relation to leadership for the purposes of ruling in the kingdom of God. This theme will be discussed more thoroughly in chapter 4 where we discover that the successful rule and blessing of God is experienced only where charismatic leaders are endowed with the Spirit for their royal functions.[92] Ultimately, it is through the

---

[90] J. Scharbert, *"brk," TDOT,* 2.303.

[91] Ibid., 304.

[92] See W. J. Dumbrell, "Spirit and Kingdom of God in the Old Testament," *RTR* 33 (1974) 1ff.

messianic rule of God's chosen, anointed king that God's initial purposes for humankind are realized.

In the NT, the Spirit of God comes on the chosen one of God who goes about his work of subduing and ruling (Matt 3:16–17; Mark 1:10–12; Luke 3:21–22; 4:14ff.). He is not only anointed for his work by the Spirit but is miraculously conceived by the Holy Spirit (Matt 1:18–23). His work includes teaching, preaching, exorcism, deliverance, and healing. When the time for transferring his work comes he gathers the disciples and says, "Peace be with you! As the Father has sent me, I am sending you" (John 20:21). In an act reminiscent of the creation formation of Adam, he then breathes on the disciples, saying, "Receive the Holy Spirit." Their work is then clearly set forth: "If you forgive anyone his sins, they are forgiven; if you do not forgive them, they are not forgiven" (20:21–23). Jesus clarifies the nature of God's commission in this text and in that of Matthew 28:16–20. However, he underscores the necessity of the disciples to wait for the reception of the Spirit that will enable their work in the kingdom of God. They are to receive the "heavenly blessing" before venturing forth in the work of the kingdom (Luke 24:49; Acts 1:4–5). In Peter's Pentecost sermon he emphasizes the fulfillment of the OT promise of the poured-out Spirit (Acts 2:29–47) with the subsequent blessings enjoyed in the new community of God's people.

Water as a Symbol of the Spirit of God

The symbolism of water in reference to the Spirit of God in the OT is not as obvious as some writers claim. But some passages certainly suggest that the symbolism of water and the work of the Spirit are connected. The key facets where this is evident are in passages where water is the source of life, where water is used in reference to cleansing and purification rites, and where water indicates renewal and restoration. Water lends itself to figurative descriptions of the Spirit's work in giving and sustaining life, renewal, and purification.

Water as Chaos and Other Metaphors

The context for the use of metaphors must be carefully considered. Water is often symbolic of the chaotic situation on earth, not only in primeval times where it indicates the uninhabitable situation on earth, but also in times when life was threatened by chaotic floods. In the ancient Near East, floodwaters symbolized the evil, chaotic forces that threatened life and fertility on earth. Only as God intervenes by separating the water and creating the sky and land does life on earth become possible (Gen 1:6, 9).

Proverbs 5:15–18 uses water metaphorically for the satisfaction found in marital sex. The son is encouraged to "drink water from your own cistern, running water from your own well." He is warned not to indulge in illicit sex by satiating his thirst for love outside the marriage bond. The water metaphor also pertains to the experience of salvation: "Surely God is my salvation; I will trust and not be afraid. 'The LORD, the LORD is my strength and my song; he has become my salvation.' With joy you will draw water from the wells of salvation" (Isa 12:2). As a result of God's blessing, humankind may also be likened to a fertile garden. "You will be like a well-watered garden, like a spring whose waters never fail" (Isa 58:11). Moreover, the pouring out of water may symbolize contrition (Exod 4:9; 1 Sam 7:6), illustrate the pouring out of wrath (Dan 9:11), and refer to a drink offering (Gen 35:4; Jer 32:29).

Water and Life

The main symbolic connection between water and Spirit is in its life-giving dimension. Jeremiah 2:13 refers metaphorically to God as a "fountain of living water," indicating the divine ability to give and maintain life. "They have forsaken me, the spring of living water." Life without water is impossible just as spiritual life is impossible without God and the *rûaḥ*. The psalmist shows his spiritual thirst for God in the metaphor: "O God, you are my God, earnestly I seek you; my soul thirsts for you, my body longs for you, in a dry and weary land where there is no water" (Ps 63:1). The psalmist understands that just as God provided water from the rock during the wilderness wanderings when water was scarce, so God will provide for spiritual well-being (Exod 17:1–7; Num 20:8–13; Deut 8:11ff.; Ps 78:16–20; 114:8; Neh 9:20). It is in its life-sustaining capacity that water is used to symbolize the life-giving aspect of the Spirit of God. Thus, rain, dew, rivers, and streams are often used metaphorically to suggest renewal and restoration—the satiating of physical and spiritual thirst.

In Genesis, vegetation is nurtured by the streams coming up from the earth to water the ground. The trees and vegetation in the garden are fructified by the river flowing from Eden. The four rivers that branched from it are the Pishon, Gihon, Tigris, and Euphrates. Water in subterranean streams and rivers was necessary to sustain the life of humankind, as well as both flora and fauna. Water fructified the land and through its continual flow sustained and preserved life in Eden.

The theme of water flowing from the sacred place illustrates the OT concept of God and his throne as the source of life (cf. Jer 17:13; Ezek 47:1; Ps 36:8–9). In the OT, the "mountain of God" concept presents the theological dimension of the sacred place as a cosmic mountain which is the Garden of Eden, Jerusalem or Zion, and the temple. The element of water is featured from the beginning of the OT where Eden is the world mountain. The great river flowing through Eden sufficiently provides the life-sustaining element. In Ezekiel, the life-sustaining stream begins as a trickle from beneath the temple and then swells to a great river that brings life and abundance to all creatures. In this eschatological vision, God's blessings that are issued through the fructifying powers of water are granted not only to Israel but to the whole world. The imagery in which this restoration and blessing are conveyed is the river flowing from the Lord's dwelling. This is also envisioned in other passages. "A fountain will flow out of the Lord's house and will water the valley of the acacias" (Joel 3:18). "On that day living water will flow out from Jerusalem" (Zech 14:8; cf. Rev 22:1ff.).

In the OT, water is one of the crucial blessings provided by God to sustain life. God's blessing is also necessary in order for humankind to fulfill God's instructions to "be fruitful and multiply." God confers power to reproduce, multiply, and fill the earth through his blessing (Gen 1:22, 28; 9:1, 2). The necessity of water for fertility and fruitfulness is indicated in many passages that feature God's blessing through rain and dew. God's dwelling place is figuratively compared to a "cloud of dew" (Isa 18:4). In Isaac's blessing of Jacob, Isaac requests that the "heaven's dew" be granted to Jacob. In other words, Isaac asks that the dew which makes fertile and prosperous be Jacob's portion (Gen 27:28). God is the source of both physical and spiritual blessings (Deut 33:28; Ps 133:3; cf. Isa 45:8; Zech 10:1; Job 36:26f.; 37:6). God opens the heavens, the storehouse of bounty, in order to send rain on the obedient people of God (Deut 28:12; Jer 10:13; Ps 135:7). The curse, however, reverses this provision when through divine judgment God withholds the rains (1 Kgs 17:1; cf. 1 Sam 5:6). Just as God's blessing is necessary for humankind to fulfill God's instructions to fill the earth, so later, particularly in regard to leadership, is God's Spirit a necessity to bring about his dominion in the earth through anointed, charismatic leaders. Through the Spirit, God brings blessing and restoration to the people of God: "For I will pour water on the thirsty land, and streams on the dry ground; I will pour out my Spirit on your offspring and my blessing on your descendants" (Isa 44:3).

Water for Cleansing, Renewal, and Restoration

The cleansing properties of water for purification rites are obvious. "Running" or "living" water symbolically portrays the cleansing functions of ritual ablutions. For example: "I will sprinkle clean water on you, and you will be clean; I will cleanse you from all your impurities and from all your idols. I will give you a new heart and put a new spirit in you; I will remove from you your heart of stone and give you a heart of flesh. And I will put my Spirit in you and move you to follow my decrees and be careful to keep my laws" (Ezek 36:25–27). A running stream or a fountain of running water is prescribed in the purification rites (Lev 15:13; 2 Kgs 5:10–13; cf. 2 Sam 11:2–4). Priests must consecrate themselves by washing in water (Num 19:1–10; cf. Lev 14:5f., 50–52). In the context of Ezekiel 36:25–27, Yahweh addresses Israel, who had defiled themselves by improper conduct and actions out of step with the covenant. In order to vindicate God's name among the nations, Yahweh promises to purify Israel from defilement and indicates the restoration process that will be initiated. This process appeals to the cleansing metaphor of water in parallel with the work of the Spirit in the nation's return to God.

In Isaiah 32:14, spiritual transformation and renewal are indicated through the symbolic outpouring of the Spirit, who acts on humankind to bring about restoration just as water would renew the desert and make it fertile ground. The Lord also promises Israel a spiritual renewal: "For I will pour water on the thirsty land, and streams on the dry ground; I will pour out my Spirit on your offspring and my blessing on your descendants" (Isa 44:3). Water, Spirit, and blessing are integral concepts in these contexts. Indeed, the Spirit and living water are often eschatological images indicating renewal. At the feast of

Tabernacles, which was the third of the annual feasts celebrating a bountiful harvest, it was common not only to give thanks for God's abundant blessings, but to offer prayer for rain for the next harvest (cf. Exod 23:16; 34:22; Lev 23:33–36, 39–43; Num 29:12–32; Deut 16:13–16; Ezek 45:25; Zech 14:16ff.). The ingathering of the harvest preceded the start of the rains and the coming of the heavier dew.[93] Thus, the celebrations included thanksgiving for the bountiful harvest and anticipation for the rains that would fructify the earth and thereby bring forth agricultural blessings. In the exilic texts noted, the pouring out of the Spirit was longed for as the certain sign of God's dwelling among the people (Joel 2:28–29). Just as the rains were longed for to give a bountiful physical harvest, so in the messianic age the rains of the Spirit were desired to bring cleansing, renewal, spiritual blessing, and restoration.

---

[93] H. J. Kraus, *Worship in Israel: A Cultic History of the Old Testament* (trans. G. Buswell; Richmond: John Knox, 1966) 62ff.

3

The Spirit and God's People

I will give you a new heart and put a new spirit in you; I will remove from you your heart of stone and give you a heart of flesh. And I will put my Spirit in you and move you to follow my decrees and be careful to keep my laws. You will live in the land I gave your forefathers; you will be my people, and I will be your God. (Ezekiel 36:27–28)

Throughout the history of Israel, the Spirit was actively involved in specific phases of the nation's experience. For instance, the establishment of Israel as a nation by Yahweh is brought about by the intervention of the *rûaḥ* in the exodus event. In a subsequent generation, David attributes his victories as king of the nation to the intervention of Yahweh by the *rûaḥ*. The prophets also recognize the involvement of the *rûaḥ* in the establishment, preservation, judgment, and restoration of the people of God. The purpose of this chapter is to investigate the role that the *rûaḥ* plays in each of these activities. A number of images and symbols of the Spirit are also considered in their relevant contexts.

The Establishment of God's People: Introduction

The OT is for the most part the record of God's dealings with Israel. God established Israel as a nation by delivering them from the bondage of the Egyptians. At times, the forming of the nation is described as a creation. "But now, this is what the Lord says—he who created you, O Jacob, he who formed you, O Israel: 'Fear not, for I have redeemed you; I have summoned you by name; you are mine' " (Isa 43:1). In every subsequent generation, the Israelites recalled the exodus as the foundational event that constituted them as a nation. The importance of the exodus event is emphasized in the book of Exodus by its repetition. First it is recorded in narrative form (Exod 14), and then it is presented poetically (Exod 15). The "Song of the Sea" is one of the main sources for the central deliverance event of the nation, as well as one of the most archaic accounts in the OT.[1]

The deliverance of Israel through the Sea of Reeds is emphasized not only in the book of Exodus but throughout the Hebrew canon. The Israelites considered the exodus event as the supernatural intervention of God on their behalf (cf. Pss 78:13; 136:13ff.; 114:1f.; Neh 9:11). The prophets found in the exodus accounts the images and terms that in turn would describe their freedom from captivity to come. A variety of descriptions of God's action in the exodus event are also employed in the OT. Isaiah uses the exodus typology in approximately ten passages in chapters 40–55. In 51:9–11, the prophet encourages Israel to reflect on God's action in the exodus event and features "the arm of the Lord" as the powerful force behind their redemption: "Awake, awake! Clothe yourself with strength, O arm of the Lord; as in days gone by, as in generations of old. Was it not you who cut Rahab to pieces, who pierced that monster through? Was it not you who dried up the sea, the waters of the great deep, who made a road in the depths of the sea, so that the redeemed might cross over?" The exodus theme also permeates hymns, narratives, and even legal documents throughout Israel's history.[2] The exodus became the paradigm of salvation for Israel and a symbol of judgment for the nation's enemies. For this reason, the presence of the *rûaḥ* in the exodus event is vital for

[1] F. M. Cross, "The Song of the Sea and Canaanite Myth," *Canaanite Myth and Hebrew Epic* (Cambridge: Harvard University Press, 1973) 123; cf. J. Bright, *A History of Israel* (3d ed.; Philadelphia: Westminster, 1982) 122.

[2] B. W. Anderson, "Exodus Typology in Second Isaiah," *Israel's Prophetic Heritage* (ed. B. W. Anderson and W. Harrelson; New York: Harper & Brothers, 1962) 181–82. Cf. P. D. Hanson, *The People Called: The Growth of Community in the Bible* (San Francisco: Harper & Row, 1986) 11. Significant exodus texts in the prophets are: Isa 10:24, 26; 11:15–16; Jer 2:6– 7; 7:22, 25; 11:4; 23:7–8; 16:14–15; 31:32; 32:20–22; 24:13–14; 63:12ff.; Ezek 20:5f.; Hos 2:14–15; 11:1; 12:9, 13; 13:4–5; Amos 2:9–10; 3:1–2; 9:7; Mic 6:4.

explaining how Yahweh expressed the divine power on behalf of God's people.

The Context of the Exodus Event: Exodus 13:17–14:8

In the narrative account of the exodus event the writer presents the plans of Yahweh and Pharaoh that set the scene of the predominately religious struggle between Yahweh and the gods of Egypt. In this context the people of God find themselves confronted by the troops of Egypt and cry out to Moses and Yahweh for deliverance. In the narrative, Moses stretches out his hand in obedience to Yahweh's direction, and the Sea of Reeds is split in half. This is accomplished by a strong easterly "wind" *[rûaḥ]* through which Yahweh drives back the sea and brings about deliverance for the nation. In this account, and in the majority of OT summaries that reflect on the exodus, the splitting of the sea becomes an important feature of the deliverance.

The poetic account of the exodus event has a few different details from that of Exodus 14 concerning the manner of Yahweh's intervention. Some of the differences are due in part to the genres of the two accounts, but other variations have to do with the theological understanding of Yahweh's intervention on Israel's behalf. This is seen particularly in the passages that use *rûaḥ* to describe Yahweh's mediation in the account. The first part of the hymn of Exodus 15:1–12, which describes the victory of Yahweh over the Egyptians, does not mention the splitting of the sea. Rather, the poetic account presents a storm-tossed sea that is directed against the Egyptians by the instigation of Yahweh and his *rûaḥ*.[3] The sea in the poetic version is the passive instrument God uses to defeat Israel's enemies. In short, the *rûaḥ* in the narrative is Yahweh's wind, but in the poetic account the *rûaḥ* of Yahweh is "breathed out." Thus, the poetic account describes the active presence of the *rûaḥ* in the exodus event, through whose action the nation is established as God's people.

Yahweh's Messenger: The Divine Breath

In Exodus 15, the verses indicating Yahweh's divine intervention state that the victory is achieved when the *rûaḥ* of

[3] Cross, *Canaanite Myth*, 131.

Yahweh is "breathed out." F. M. Cross and B. S. Childs translate the key phrase in Exodus 15:8 as "at the blast of your nostrils *[ʾap̱]*" and in verse 10, "You blew with your breath."[4] The word "*ʾap̱*" is often used metaphorically to refer to anger, either human or divine. It also refers to the nostrils and indicates the organ of breathing or heavy breathing.[5] In the LXX, Exodus 15:8 is translated "by the breath of your anger *[thymos],*" and in 15:10, "you sent forth your wind." This first rendering suggests angry snorting or intensified breathing. Although snorting or anger is implied by the word *ʾap̱* in some contexts (cf. Ps 18:8; Job 4:9), there is no suggestion of anger directed at the water in Exodus 15:8. It is true that God unleashes his anger against the Egyptians (15:7), but he is not angry with the waters, a theme sometimes evident in ancient Near Eastern mythic patterns.

In verse 8, the *rûaḥ* of Yahweh's nostrils *[ûḇrûaḥ ʾappeyḵā]* causes the waters to "pile up," "surge," and "congeal." The context does not refer to a *chaoskampf* with the sea.[6] In fact, the waters in obedience to Yahweh stand up like an army for God.[7] The activity of the *rûaḥ* is similar to the action of Yahweh that describes intervention by his "right hand" (15:7, 12, 17; cf. Isa

---

[4] Ibid., 131ff.; B. S. Childs, *The Book of Exodus* (OTL; Philadelphia: Westminster, 1974) 221ff.

[5] Cf. *BDB*, 60.; E. Johnson, "*ʾānaph, ʾāph,*" *TDOT,* 1.351–54.

[6] The poetic account of the exodus event incorporates mythological language and patterns that are also evident in Canaanite literature. Thus, Cross argues that Israel adopted the episode of the sea as symbolic of their redemption and creation as a community and merged it with myths of creation. A summary of the mythic pattern preserved in the Song of the Sea is: (1) the combat of the Divine Warrior and his victory at the Sea; (2) the building of a sanctuary on the "mount of possession" won in battle; and (3) the god's manifestation of "eternal" kingship. Cf. Cross, *Canaanite Myth,* 138, 142. On the mythic cycle of Baal and ʿAnat, and the pattern described here, see pages 112–120 and *ANET,* 129ff. Caution must be exercised concerning the *chaoskampf* motif in Exodus 15, however. Whereas some OT passages allude to Egypt as Rahab or the dragon based on the Song of the Sea (Isa 51:10; Ps 77:17–21), the motifs of a conflict in Exodus convey the actual, historical deliverance event of Israel from Egypt which constituted her as a nation as described in the historical narrative of Exodus 14. This event is the act of God which gave birth to the nation of Israel through the divine intervention at the Sea of Reeds by his *rûaḥ*. Cf. Day, *God's Conflict,* 86.

[7] Neve, *Spirit of God,* 8.

51:9–11). With his right hand, Yahweh releases his power to defeat the enemy. Yahweh stretches out his hand and the earth swallows the Egyptians (Exod 15:12), the effect of which was similar to the sea covering them (15:10). Thus, "by the *rûaḥ* of your nostrils" is a further description of how Yahweh defeated the enemy by releasing his Spirit.

The intervention of Yahweh by his Spirit is highlighted by the description in verse 10, "but you blew with your breath *[rûaḥ]*." Here the overwhelming power of Yahweh is asserted. The enemy is conquered with a "breath" through which Yahweh's *rûaḥ* is released to deliver Israel. The *rûaḥ* causes the waters to become turbulent, which in turn effects the overthrow of the enemy. In verses 8 and 10 *rûaḥ* should not be translated by the term wind. Although the wind is often used by God, it is only "breathed out" or "blown out" by God in a metaphoric sense.[8] The result of Yahweh's intervention by the *rûaḥ* brings about the defeat of the Egyptians. The exodus journey marks the beginning of Yahweh's leadership and guidance for Israel. Yahweh leads the people of God to Mount Sinai where they formally enter a covenant bond (Exod 15:13, 17; 19:1ff.). Yahweh redeems them in order to "plant" them on the "holy mountain" and to establish them as the people of God. Thus, the Song of the Sea focuses on the victory that is procured by the direct intervention of Yahweh and the *rûaḥ*.

The significance God's action of deliverance by the Spirit is reiterated by Isaiah. When reflecting on the great exodus event and on the identity of the one who brought them through the sea, the prophet says: "Where is he who set his Holy Spirit *[rûaḥ]* among them, who sent his glorious arm of power to be at Moses' right hand, who divided the waters before them, to gain for himself everlasting renown, who led them through the depths?" (Isa 63:11b–12). God exercised great power through the Spirit by leading the people through the divided sea. This phenomenon

[8] Knight comes to the same view as we do in this text, but he follows the rendering "Thou didst blow with thy wind" and suggests that the effect of the blowing wind is the effect of the will of God as God blows upon the sea. He comments, "In the same way that the Word does not return unto God void, neither does the Spirit of God blow without effectively bearing the will of God." G. A. F. Knight, *A Christian Theology of the Old Testament* (London: SCM, 1959) 84–85. His conclusion is warranted if he follows the analogy of God breathing out his *rûaḥ* and thus accomplishing his will.

was recorded for the sake of each generation to indicate the power of Yahweh. It is the foundational event for the nation. Just as creation is brought into reality by the Spirit for all humanity, so in the exodus event the Spirit brings Israel through the sea and establishes the people of God in Canaan. Through the *rûaḥ*, Israel is born, delivered, established, nurtured, and sustained (cf. Isa 42:5).[9]

The Pillar of Cloud and of Fire

The function of the "pillar of cloud and pillar of fire" *[ᶜammûḏ ᶜānān, ᶜammûḏ ᵓē]* in Exodus is similar to the work of the *rûaḥ* in some texts. The cloud column is active in the deliverance of Israel at the Sea of Reeds (Exod 13:21–27). The pillar guides at night as well as during the day (13:21; 24:15–18; Num 9:15) and is present during times of provision for the people of God. When God judges the Egyptians, the pillar of cloud hides and protects Israel from their enemies (Exod 14:19) and then throws the army into a panic (14:24). Miriam also faces punishment for opposing God's prophet when Yahweh speaks from the cloud (Num 12:5, 10). The cloud is present and active when Moses receives revelation from Yahweh at the tent of meeting (Exod 33:7–11). These correspondences indicate a strong relationship between the work of the *rûaḥ* and the pillar of cloud and fire.

Various views concerning the nature of the pillar of cloud and fire have been set forth. Some offer naturalistic explanations such as the smudge pot or firebrand at the head of the army. Others believe that the Sinai theophany with its meteorological or volcanic imagery from Exodus 19 is here extended to the pillar of cloud and fire motif.[10] T. W. Mann seeks to identify the pillar from the Ugaritic term for "messenger" and finds the OT link in the mythological storm motif (Pss 18; 68; Hab 3). Thus, "The pillar of cloud served as a graphic, literary, theological symbol within the Yahwistic narrative of the crossing of the sea."[11]

---

[9] Knight, *Christian Theology*, 85.

[10] These were set forth by U. Cassuto and M. Noth respectively. Cf. T. W. Mann, "The Pillar of Cloud in the Reed Sea Narrative," *JBL* 90 (1971) 15–30.

[11] Mann, "Pillar of Cloud," 30.

B. S. Childs' view regarding the supernatural events of the exodus is informative here. He indicates that due to critical examination, scholars often seek to explain the supernatural occurrences by natural events that they claim the author extends into the supernatural in order to articulate the theological meaning. Childs indicates that this approach is not compatible with the intention of the biblical author. "Likewise, the assigning of historical validity to the natural events and theological meaning to the supernatural is also a move which is entirely incompatible with the inner dynamic of the biblical witness."[12] In relation to the pillar of cloud and fire, there is no warrant to seek naturalistic explanations when the text clearly describes the movement, function, and presence of the cloud through which Yahweh speaks and guides his people.[13]

The main role of the pillar is guidance and protection. This is the dominant theme in Exodus 13:17–14:31. "By day the Lord went ahead of them in a pillar of cloud to guide them on their way and by night in a pillar of fire to give them light, so that they could travel by day or night. Neither the pillar of cloud by day nor the pillar of fire by night left its place in front of the people" (13:21–22). Here the people of God embark on their pilgrimage to the promised land. It is not surprising, in the light of the threatening conditions, that God gave a visible beacon for the people to see while on their journey (cf. Exod 40:38). In most of God's early appearances to individuals and to Israel the divine presence is manifested in a variety of visible ways. In 14:20, the same pillar of cloud moves behind the camp of Israel, before the crossing of the Reed Sea, in order to protect and conceal them from the Egyptian army. From the cloud, Yahweh "looks down" on the enemy and throws them into a panic, adding to their confusion (14:24). In this activity, Yahweh is indeed a warrior on behalf of the people of God (15:1–4).

The same theme of guidance is emphasized in the book of Numbers. Here God's people are pilgrimaging to the promised land. In the opening chapters, they are ready for battle, unified,

[12] Childs, *Exodus,* 228.

[13] See R. K. Harrison, *Numbers* (WEC; Chicago: Moody, 1990) 158–65. Another approach is to suggest that the palace pillars of 1 Kings 7:15 were fiery cressets and that these may have been read back into Exodus narratives to explain God's guidance. See G. H. Davies, "Pillar," *IDB,* 3.817.

disciplined, and obedient. The presence of God is in their midst, symbolized by the cloud.[14] The cloud not only leads the people during the day and night but it also regulates their times of travel and times of rest (Num 9:15–23). "Whenever the cloud lifted from above the tent, the Israelites set out; wherever the cloud settled, the Israelites encamped" (9:17; cf. Exod 40:34–38; Neh 9:12–19; Ps 99:7).

In addition to the guidance and leadership theme, the cloud also functions in a revelatory mode. This is the manner in which Yahweh speaks to his people through his prophet (Exod 19:9, 16). On Sinai, Yahweh also reveals himself in smoke and fire (19:21–24; Deut 5:4–5). Even after the people request Moses to mediate God's word to them, Yahweh still reveals the divine word and will to Moses through the cloud (Exod 20:18–21; cf. Deut 31:15). Exodus 33:7–11 indicates how Yahweh reveals his word to Moses "face to face." The pillar of cloud descends on the "tent of meeting" when Moses enters it. Although the nature of this tent and the revelatory experience surrounding it are in a sense mystical, the evidence shows that this was Yahweh's chosen way to communicate with Moses and to instill reverence and respect for the Mosaic office in the people.[15] In the incident where Aaron and Miriam oppose Moses, the pillar of cloud descends on the tent. From the cloud Yahweh rebukes Miriam and smites her with leprosy for her participation and irreverence for the Mosaic office (Num 12:5, 10).

Another important text indicating that the *rûaḥ* and the pillar of cloud function together is Numbers 11:25. Here Yahweh shares the Spirit that is on Moses with the seventy elders. "Then the Lord came down in the cloud and spoke with him, and he took of the Spirit that was on him and put the Spirit on the seventy elders. When the Spirit rested on them, they prophesied, but they did not do so again." Through the cloud that enshrouds and through the *rûaḥ,* Yahweh brings about the divine will by enabling the chosen leaders. In this text, God visibly manifests the divine presence to the people and moves upon the elders, who show their reception of the Spirit by prophesying.

---

[14] W. J. Dumbrell, *The Faith of Israel* (Grand Rapids: Baker, 1988) 48–49.

[15] A number of critical problems are evident in the texts which refer to the tent of meeting. See Childs, *Exodus,* 582ff.; and S. Westerholm, "Tabernacle," *ISBE,* 4.703.

This event bestows authority on the elders in the eyes of the people and endows the elders with the Spirit in order for them to fulfill their ministry.

Many texts from the period of Israel's wilderness wanderings merge the cloud and the pillar motifs, at times making it difficult to differentiate the symbols. However, the main concern of these texts is to feature the cloud and the pillar of cloud as the location of Yahweh's presence to lead, speak, or act. The pillar or the cloud plays a role in each special revelation of Yahweh.[16] In addition to these symbols, the angel of the Lord is also at work in connection with the pillar of cloud. In Exodus 14:19, the angel of the Lord moves with the pillar to protect Israel. "Then the angel of God, who had been traveling in front of Israel's army, withdrew and went behind them. The pillar of cloud also moved from in front and stood behind them, coming between the armies of Egypt and Israel." In other texts, the angel of the presence was sent in response to Israel's cry for deliverance (Num 20:16; cf. Exod 23:20–23; Isa 63:9). Although the angel of the Lord is active before the exodus (Gen 16:7, 9–11; 22:11, 15; 31:11; Exod 3:2), the angel is the distinct helper of Israel during the wilderness pilgrimage and acts as the emissary of Yahweh.[17] The main differentiation evident in the various texts describing the presence and activity of God is between the cloud and the angel of the Lord. Kline comments: "Although the Angel is identified with God, he may also be distinguished as one who is sent by God on a mission or who himself refers to the Lord in the third person. In this fact that the Angel is distinguishable from God, there is a basis for his being a prophet-figure, even though also a divine figure."[18]

Therefore, the pillar of cloud and fire functions with the angel of the Lord and with Yahweh to bring about the divine will for the people of God. Much like the activity of the *rûaḥ,* the pillar serves to guide, protect, reveal, and even judge people to fulfill the work of Yahweh. The cloud hides the "face of God" but visibly indicates the presence of God among his people. It is noteworthy that the pillar of cloud and fire begins leading Israel before the exodus event, through the

---

[16] A. Oepke, "*nephelē,*" *TDNT,* 4.905.
[17] Eichrodt, *Theology,* 2.24ff.
[18] Kline, *Images of the Spirit,* 71.

wilderness trial, and up to the point of resting on the tabernacle. At the tabernacle the goal of God's redemptive work, the worship of God, is achieved. The presence of God now rests on his earthly dwelling. The symbols of Yahweh's presence are transferred to the tabernacle (cf. Num 9:22).[19] Through the cloud, the glory and presence of Yahweh are imparted. When the tabernacle is completed "the cloud covered the Tent of Meeting, and the glory of the Lord filled the tabernacle" (Exod 40:34ff.). Here at the end of the book of Exodus, the narrative features the presence of God in the midst of the people at worship.

The Preservation of God's People: Introduction

The providential hand of God is evident throughout the pilgrimages of the covenant people. Whether in the experiences of Abraham and the promised seed, or in God's providential care for Israel through the life and work of Joseph in Egypt, it is evident that history is directed by Israel's God. During the wilderness wanderings, God provides protection, food, and water to sustain Israel (Exod 16:4; Num 11:7; Ps 78:24–25). Throughout the conquest period it was God who directed the military operations in Canaan and gave the land as an inheritance to Israel (Josh 5:13–5; Ps 44:1–8). This providential activity is also evident during the monarchy period (Pss 23; 78:70–71). One common denominator in these times of preservation is the presence of the *rûaḥ* in the lives of God's chosen leaders to sustain and preserve the elect people of God. The specific work of sustaining the people by the Spirit is evident in the lives of Joseph, Moses, Joshua, Gideon, David, and Elijah (cf. ch. 4 below). It is observed that these leader's efforts are successful due to the Spirit's presence with them. In addition to these references, however, are texts that specifically indicate Yahweh's providential care by his *rûaḥ*.

[19] See V. H. Matthews, "Theophanies Cultic and Cosmic," *Israel's Apostasy and Restoration: Essays in Honor of R. K. Harrison* (ed. A Gileadi; Grand Rapids: Baker, 1988) 312. Also, T. W. Mann, *Divine Presence and Guidance in Israelite Traditions: The Typology of Exaltation* (Baltimore: John Hopkins University Press, 1977) 165–66.

The Preservation of God's People: 2 Samuel 22:16 and Psalm 18:16

The role of the king during the monarchy is to preserve justice, to provide leadership, and to protect the established people of God. It is through the king that Yahweh seeks to shepherd and preserve the nation. Psalm 18 and 2 Samuel 22 are a royal psalm in which King David acknowledges the acts of Yahweh on his behalf to protect him and deliver him from his enemies.[20] The psalm is a fitting testimony to the successful life granted to the king by Yahweh. The books of Samuel vividly record the dangers David experiences from a crazed Saul (1 Sam 19ff.). David's struggles with the house of Saul (2 Sam 2ff.) and his enemies the Philistines (5:17–25) subjected him to many military dangers. There was also the threat of wild animals (1 Sam 17:34–37). All of these dangers were overcome with the help of Yahweh. "The Lord gave David victory wherever he went" (2 Sam 8:14b; cf. 2 Sam 7). The successful reign of the king is attributed to the endowment of the *rûaḥ* on David. This endowment is both prospective, "So Samuel took the horn of oil and anointed him in the presence of his brothers, and from that day on the Spirit of the Lord came upon David in power" (1 Sam 16:13), and retrospective (2 Sam 22:8ff.). Moreover, the intervention of Yahweh through which David is assisted is also described with reference to the *rûaḥ*. The psalm in the book of Samuel functions much like the Song of the Sea (Exodus 15) which gives praise to Yahweh for the deliverance of Israel from their enemies. This is David's victory song for Yahweh after experiencing the victories granted to him.

As a royal psalm its unifying theme is the relationship between God and the king. Common themes that bind royal psalms together include "divine adoption, the throne's stability,

[20] Davidic authorship is probable due to a number of factors including, a) the orthographic evidence which indicates an early date; b) the linguistic archaisms occur only in the oldest Hebrew and Canaanite literature; c) the language and style of the theophany derives from ancient Canaanite sources; d) the literary associations with other theophanic texts point to an early date for its composition; e) the inclusion of the poem with "The Last Words of David," shows that an old tradition associated the psalm with the early monarchy. Cf. Cross and Freedman, "A Royal Song of Thanksgiving: 2 Samuel and Psalm 18," 20.

the prophecy of Nathan, prayers for the king and oracles promising the king happiness and prosperity."[21] One of the king's roles as vice-regent was to represent the people before God and God before the people, a representation often referred to as "corporate personality."[22] In the deliverance of the king, therefore, the people of God are also preserved and sustained.

The Context of the Psalm

The intervention of Yahweh described by the *rûaḥ* comes in a context where the king reflects on his past experiences. When he cried out to Yahweh from the depths of his various dilemmas, the Lord was attentive to his cry. Yahweh's response is described as a theophany, which results in the deliverance of his helpless servant (cf. Ps 18:7–15; Deut 33:2f.; Ps 97:2f.). J. K. Kuntz summarizes the unique manifestation of Yahweh in theophany as: "A temporal, partial, and intentionally allusive self-disclosure initiated by the sovereign deity at a particular place, the reality of which evokes the convulsion of nature and the fear and dread of man, and whose unfolding emphasizes visual and audible aspects generally according to a recognized literary form."[23]

Psalm 18 describes Yahweh's intervention in theophanic and cataclysmic terms, in answer to the cry of the petitioner. The account of the theophany employs the language and imagery of the *chaoskampf* to emphasize Yahweh's cosmic authority and power. From the beginning of the theophany the passage highlights the awesome power and effect of Yahweh's presence. In verses 7 and 15, the presence of Yahweh is depicted as moving the very depths of creation in response to the servant's petition. God's anger is clearly manifested against the enemies of the servant. The first two lines of verse 8 are in synonymous parallelism and feature the vented anger *[ʾap̱]* of Yahweh.[24]

---

[21] L. Sabourin, *The Psalms: Their Origin and Meaning* (New York: Alba House, 1974) 335. Other royal psalms include Psalms 2, 18, 20, 21, 45, 72, 101, 110, 132, and 144:1–11.

[22] S. Mowinckel, *The Psalms in Israel's Worship* (2 vols.; trans. D. R. Ap-Thomas; Nashville: Abingdon, 1962) 1.60.

[23] J. K. Kuntz, *The Self-Revelation of God* (Philadelphia: Westminster, 1967) 45.

[24] J. Bergman, "*ʾānaph, ʾaph,*" *TDOT,* 1.348.

As in Exodus 15, Yahweh is pictured as a warrior but now appears as a rider on the cherubim. This is an apparent polemic against Baal, who is referred to as "the Rider on the Clouds."[25] This imagery portrays Yahweh's intervention as coming "on the wings of the wind." In other OT and ancient Near Eastern literature, wings often represent the protection of the deity, who like a bird covers its young with its wings (Pss 17:8; 57:1; 61:4; 63:7; 91:3).

The efficacy of Yahweh's intervention is now described in terms reminding us of the great exodus event and creation. As in the beginning, God speaks. His voice goes forth in a thunderous clamor. The voice of Yahweh often accompanies the manifestation of God's power both in the ordinary storms of nature (Job 37:4f.; Pss 29:3ff.; 104:7) and in the extraordinary theophanic storm phenomena (Pss 46:7; 68:34; Isa 30:30).[26] The cosmic reverberations of the theophany come to an end in Psalm 18:16. Yahweh's intervention is depicted in terms that reflect his victory over chaos and the pharaoh in Exodus 15. It is at the rebuke of Yahweh and the "*rûaḥ* of his nostrils" that "the valleys of the sea are exposed and the foundations of the earth laid bare." The term "rebuke" denotes the threatening manifestation of God's anger that drives away "everything that is symbolized by chaos in nature and revolt in history."[27] Thus, the intervention of Yahweh is connected to the word that effectively brings deliverance to the king. The *rûaḥ,* which is parallel with "rebuke," indicates Yahweh's presence to effect and activate the word for the salvation of the servant on behalf of God's people. Israel's neighbors claimed that it was Baal who had such powers: "Baal opens rifts in the clouds. Baal gives forth his holy voice, Baal discharges the utterance of his lips. His holy voice convulses the earth . . . the mountains quake, A-tremble are . . . east and west, earth's high places reel. Baal's enemies take to the woods."[28] In Psalm 18, the king affirms that it is Yahweh who overcomes all the tyrannical forces that threaten to overwhelm the king, and by the *rûaḥ* he brings the word of rebuke into effect, the results of which cause the foundations of the earth to convulse.[29]

---

[25] *ANET,* 132; cf. Ps 68.
[26] M. G. Kline, "Primal Parousia," *WTJ* 72 (1972) 245.
[27] A. Caquot, *"gār," TDOT,* 3.51.
[28] *ANET,* 135.
[29] P. C. Craigie, *Psalms 1–50* (WBC; Waco: Word, 1983) 174.

In this summary of David's successful reign as king of Israel, he attributes his victories and successes to the intervention of Yahweh on his behalf. Not only was he elected to be king and anointed for his task, but the *rûaḥ* of Yahweh came on him to enable him to fulfill his duties (1 Sam 16:13). At the end of his reign, David acknowledges that his triumphs are victories wrought by Yahweh. To summarize and highlight this, the psalmist describes Yahweh's work of preserving him and the nation in terms of theophanic display in which the *rûaḥ* takes an active part in defeating the king's enemies.

Preservation Through Guidance

The *rûaḥ* was also involved in the guidance of the nation through its chosen leaders who were dependent on Yahweh for direction and instruction (cf. Ps 78:70–71). Yahweh's prerogative to lead Israel according to his plan is evident throughout the historical literature. His ability to deliver the nation and lead them into Canaan was proof of his commitment to Israel (Pss 105; 106; 135; 136). This is illustrated in the holy war led by Yahweh for the conquest of Canaan. Entrance into the land of Canaan as an inheritance was a reminder that all victories were to be fought and directed by Yahweh. It was to Yahweh that the people were to look for help, deliverance, and victory. Throughout the monarchy, however, Israel was tempted to trust in their military might for protection rather than rely on Yahweh.

Trusting in Yahweh: Isaiah 31:1

Isaiah 31:1 is a proclamation of woe declared by Yahweh. "Woe to those who go down to Egypt for help, who rely on horses, who trust in the multitude of their chariots and in the great strength of their horsemen, but do not look to the Holy One of Israel or seek help from the LORD." This censure is followed by the reminder that the Egyptians are just men and their horses are just flesh, not *rûaḥ* (30:3). The oracle is spoken by Isaiah during the time of revolt led by Hezekiah against Sennacherib (703–701 BC).[30] Rather than turning to Yahweh for security, the leaders turned to Egypt for protection. In this pe-

[30] O. Kaiser, *Isaiah 13–39: A Commentary* (OTL; trans. R. A. Wilson; Philadelphia: Westminster, 1974) 283–85. See J. K. Hoffmeier, "Egypt as an Arm of Flesh: A Prophetic Response," *Israel's Apostasy and Restoration,* 88f.

riod, Egypt was also weak and in need of assistance. The prophetic rebuke specifically addresses the leaders who devised their plans apart from the direction and oracle of Yahweh (cf. 2 Kgs 21:22ff.; Jer 37:17ff.; 38:14ff.). Instead of consulting "my *rûaḥ*," the leaders contrived an alliance with Egypt and ratified it according to their plans and wisdom. The term *šāʾal* in the OT is often a technical term used for inquiring of the deity for guidance, often through an oracle (cf. Josh 9:14; 1 Sam 23:2; 30:8).[31] Prophets who were inspired by the *rûaḥ* were, therefore, to be consulted for direction and guidance through the Spirit. Unfortunately, Israel often inquired of pagan deities instead (cf. Ezek 21:21).

Spirit or Flesh? Isaiah 31:3

Another passage from the same context of 703–701 BC sets forth the antithesis between trust in God and trust in humanity. "But the Egyptians are men and not God; their horses are flesh [*bāśār*] and not spirit [*rûaḥ*]" (Isa 31:3). The differences in the nature of God and flesh, and the strength of God and flesh, are here distinguished (cf. Hos 11:9; Ezek 28:2, 9). God is never referred to as *bāśār* in the OT; rather, this term is reserved for humankind and beasts.[32] The word is contrasted with *rûaḥ* to indicate the necessity for humankind's complete dependence on God and the Spirit.[33] Instead of looking for allies and military assistance, God directs Israel to seek direction from the *rûaḥ*, which in this context is the source of power and guidance.[34] The important lesson for Israel to learn in this situation is to reject the temptation to seek assistance from frail friends. The text highlights their failure to seek Yahweh's help and guidance by the *rûaḥ*. Psalm 20 illustrates the positive steps of faith which the faithful are to take: "Now I know that the Lord saves his anointed; he answers him from his holy heaven with the saving power of his right hand. Some trust in chariots and some in horses, but we trust in the name of the Lord our God" (20:6–7).

[31] Kaiser, *Isaiah 13–39*, 285; G. G. Cohen, "*šāʾal*," *TWOT*, 2.891.

[32] Wolff, *Anthropology*, 24–31.

[33] N. P. Bratsiotis, "*bāśār*," *TDOT*, 2.330.

[34] H. C. Leupold, *Exposition of Isaiah* (Grand Rapids: Baker, 1968), 488. Cf. A. R. Johnson, *The One and the Many in the Israelite Conception of God* (Cardiff: University of Wales Press, 1961) 14ff.

Thus, the Spirit-anointed king will be rescued and directed by the powerful "right hand of God" in contrast to those who put their trust elsewhere.

Comfort in God's Presence: Psalms 51:11 [13 MT], 139:7, and 143:10

God's preservation and comforting presence for Israel was not just reserved for the nation but was also available to the individual (Exod 33). Just as God led the people as a nation (Ps 44:1–8), so he also cared for the individual (Ps 23:3–4). The individual was free to look to Yahweh for guidance in private matters. Often in the individual laments, the petitioner cries out to God for protection or deliverance, which he trusts will be granted. Although the reality of Yahweh as preserver and sustainer of people is set forth in many passages of the OT, the role of the *rûaḥ* in this activity seems to be a late development (note Gen 28:15; 49:24; Exod 14:29–30; Deut 1:30–31; Pss 31:20; 32:6). In Psalm 51, the petitioner acknowledges the presence of Yahweh on his behalf and trusts the deity to forgive, protect, guide, deliver, and especially remain with him.

In this psalm, the term *rûaḥ* occurs four times. In three of the occurrences, the psalmist refers clearly to his own *rûaḥ*. He desires a renewed "steadfast spirit" (51:10 [12 MT]), a "willing spirit" (51:12 [14 MT]), and a "broken spirit" (51:17 [19 MT]). In verse 11, however, he pleads, "Do not cast me from your presence or take your Holy Spirit *[rûaḥ qoḏᵉḵā]* from me [13 MT]." Here the psalmist acknowledges his need for Yahweh's presence in his life. He expresses the necessary changes required in his own spirit but pleads with God not to leave him bereft of his presence in a similar fashion to Moses' request, "If your Presence does not go with us, do not send us up from here. . . . What else will distinguish me and your people from all the other people on the face of the earth?" (Exod 33:15–16). In David's case, he is reminded of King Saul's experience. He fears the loss of the Spirit and the ensuing results that accompanied the Spirit's departure from Saul (1 Sam 16:14ff.).

Psalm 139:7 underlines the reality of God's omnipresence as the petitioner queries, "Where can I go from your Spirit *[rûaḥ]*? Where can I flee from your presence?" The psalmist understands that the vital power of Yahweh's presence by the *rûaḥ* and God's "face" will preserve him in the time of need. The psalmist asserts the impossibility of being removed from God's presence in cosmological and geographical terms (139:8–10). Even if the psalmist seeks to escape, Yahweh will still be there to guide him (139:10). Thus, the psalmist cries out to Yahweh, trusting that Yahweh will intervene in his situation and bring deliverance and guidance by the *rûaḥ*. Moreover, in Psalm 143:10, the psalmist speaks of the *rûaḥ* as present not only to guide but also to give counsel and instruction (cf. Neh 9:20). "Teach me to do your will, for you are my God; may your good Spirit *[rûaḥ]* lead me on level ground. For your name's sake, O LORD, preserve my life." In each of these examples, the petitioners acknowledge their need for God but they also indicate that through God's presence and Spirit their needs will be met.

The Judgment of Humankind: Genesis 6:3

Shortly after the creation and fall of humankind, the intensification of sin became a sad factor in the relationship of God with humanity. The structure of Genesis 3–11 is presented according to the sin, speech, mitigation, and punishment themes.[35] In the enigmatic passage Genesis 6:1–8, the depravity of the "sons of God" is featured. Of the various interpretations of the identity of the "sons of God," including that of the Sethites, angels, and dynastic rulers, the context and theology of the passage argues for the last. Tyrannical and polygamous rulers threatened the extinction of the godly seed by prevailing over it.[36] In despair over the actions of these individuals, Yahweh utters the resolution: "My Spirit *[rûaḥ]* will not contend with man forever, for he is mortal; his days will be a hundred and twenty years" (Gen 6:3). The nature of the work of the *rûaḥ* in this passage is disputed. Is the *rûaḥ* simply involved as the animating principle of life or is there a spiritual element implicated in the context? Has God given them up to the consequences of their own behavior? Has God severed all ties of fellowship with humanity?

[35] D. J. A. Clines, *The Theme of the Pentateuch* (Sheffield: JSOT, 1986) 63.

[36] See D. J. A. Clines, "The Significance of the 'Sons of God' Episode (Genesis 6:1–4) in the Context of the 'Primeval History' (Genesis 1–11)," *JSOT* 13 (1979) 33–46. See also Hamilton, *The Book of Genesis: Chapters 1–17*, 261–9.

Numerous difficulties surrounding this text are evident, but a consensus concerning the work of the *rûaḥ* is forming. Some of the difficulties concern the reading of the term *yāḏôn* as "contend, strive, or judge." Because this is a *hapax legomenon,* the philological meaning of the term is disputed. Thus, many commentators follow the context of the passage and the LXX *katameinē* to read *yāḏôn* in the sense of "to remain, stay, abide." Therefore, through God's judgment, he will now limit the life span of humanity. Although individuals lived long, extended lives (Gen 5:2f.; 11:10–26), now God's *rûaḥ,* which denotes the life-giving power and animating principle of life on which every creature depends, will be diminished in its length of abiding with humankind.[37] God imposes limits on human life in order to keep human beings from an eternal existence in the state of sin (cf. Gen 3:22).[38] Indeed, one generation, apart from Noah and family, will be wiped from the face of the earth (Gen 6:7). Therefore, the *rûaḥ* of God that imparts life and vitality in humankind can be withdrawn at the will of God, resulting in the loss of life (cf. Job 34:14–15; cf. Gen 2:7).

The Judgment of God's People

The establishment of Israel as God's people through the exodus event and the covenant with Yahweh was threatened by apostasy. As a covenant partner, Israel received the many blessings of the covenant grant, but the gifts also required the nation to live up to certain obligations. Whereas Yahweh was committed to fulfill many promises on behalf of the people, obedience and right ethical behavior on the part of the covenant partner were expected.[39] The history of Israel from the wilderness wanderings throughout the period of the monarchy reveals the persistent idolatry and sin of the nation. The prophetic response addresses the failures of the leaders, who at times were corrupt,

---

[37] G. J. Wenham, *Genesis 1–15* (WBC; Waco: Word, 1987) 141f. J. H. Sailhamer, "Genesis," *Expositors Bible Commentary* (Grand Rapids: Zondervan, 1990) 2.76–78.

[38] Westermann, *Genesis 1–11,* 374.

[39] B. K. Waltke, "The Phenomenon of Conditionality within Conditional Covenants," *Israel's Apostasy and Restoration: Essays in Honor of R. K. Harrison* (ed. A. Gileadi; Grand Rapids: Baker, 1988) 123–39; K. Baltzer, *The Covenant Formulary* (Philadelphia: Fortress, 1971) 11–12.

greedy, and unfaithful in their appointed duties (Amos 3:15; 5:10–13). The cultus was perverted (4:4–5), social injustice was rampant, and idolatry common (Hos 4:4–6, 12–13; 7:6–7). The foreign policies of Israel greatly compromised their heritage of faith in Yahweh as warrior (cf. Jer 2:9–13, 23–25; 3:1–5; Hos 7:1–7; 8:4). The people of God acknowledged their circumstances as deserving divine judgment, but Judah did not learn from Israel's disaster (2 Kgs 17; 24:20–25:21; Jer 3:6ff.; Ezek 23; Lam 1:12–14; 2:1f.; 3:40–42).[40] The Deuteronomic history also summarizes Israel's rebellion against Yahweh (Deut 6:10–12; 8:18; 9:4–6; Josh 22–23; Judg 2–3; 1 Sam 12; 2 Kgs 17).

At the threat of the impending curses promised for disobedience, the prophets cried out against the unfaithfulness of God's people. A great variety of sins led Israel to the prospect of enduring the ultimate covenant curse—Israel would be torn from their land (Deut 28:64). Failure to live in the land by faith and responsible behavior led to the threat of invasion by foreign nations, whom Yahweh used to punish his people (Isa 10:5–7; 30:27ff.; 37:22ff.; Jer 25:8–15; 27:5ff.). Nations who used excessive harshness in disciplining God's people were in turn punished by God (Jer 10:24–25; 27:11–13; 35:8–10). The deportations of Israel by the Assyrians began in 733 BC (2 Kgs 15:29) and continued until after the capture of Samaria (2 Kgs 17:6). Judah's deportations began around 597 BC by the Babylonians and continued to about 582–581 BC (Jer 52:28).[41]

A fundamental expression of Yahweh's wrath against Israel and her enemies occurs in Isaiah's prophecy. Numerous terms are used in the OT to portray the anger and wrath of God.[42] As already mentioned, the term *rûaḥ* means "breath" or "anger" in some texts (Judg 8:3; Isa 25:4; 30:28; Prov 16:32; 29:11). This anthropomorphic meaning probably derives from the increased respiration due to excitement associated with sudden emotion. Because of God's zealous love for people, divine jealousy and anger are expressed in a similar manner as when infidelity is discovered in the marriage bond.

---

[40] Cf. P. R. Ackroyd, *Exile and Restoration* (OTL; Philadelphia: Westminster, 1968) 43f., 77.

[41] *ANET,* 284–85; Bright, *A History of Israel,* 273ff.

[42] Cf. Johnson, "*ʾānaph,*" 351ff.

Punishment and Cleansing: Isaiah 4:4

The structure of the oracles of Isaiah fluctuates between promise and threat.[43] The first chapter of Isaiah presents the programmatic events of judgment to come. Jerusalem is portrayed as an apostate city whose sins have come to full measure and now deserve punishment. Isaiah 1 is an indictment proclaiming covenant breach, a perverted cult, and the failure of Israel to be the people of God. Therefore, their punishment was justified.

The sins of Israel call for a process of cleansing that involves a "*rûaḥ* of judgment *[mišpāṭ],*" and a "*rûaḥ* of fire *[bᶜr]*" (cf. Isa 28:6). "The Lord will wash away the filth of the women of Zion; he will cleanse the bloodstains from Jerusalem by a *rûaḥ* of judgment and a *rûaḥ* of fire" (4:4). This oracle follows a prophecy of judgment that describes Yahweh's action of cleansing for those who are punished. The word *mišpāṭ* is a legal term used of right judgment, justice, or of a decision rendered. In Isaiah 4:4 it refers to the thought of punishment due to the intervention of God.[44] Yahweh will set things in order by punishing the wrongdoer. A cultic purifying is here implied that brings the individual into a right relationship with Yahweh (cf. Isa 1:16; Prov 30:12; Exod 29:4; 40:12).[45]

The word *bᶜr* usually appears in contexts where the wrath of God is manifested, as well as in theophanic passages (cf. Isa 30:33; 42:25). The wrath of God is like a fire that is used to punish the wicked but may also be used to purify or refine the community.[46] Numerous anthropomorphic images refer to God's tongue or breath as instruments of fire. "See, the Name of the Lord comes from afar, with burning anger and dense clouds of smoke; his lips are full of wrath, and his tongue is a consuming fire" (30:27). The breath *[rûaḥ]* of the Lord is likened to a stream of sulfur (30:33), and the wrath of God may be poured out in fiery anger (Ezek 21:31; 22:31). In these passages, the opposite effect of God's beneficence, which is often "poured out" on his people through the Spirit, is experienced. In this sense, God is

---

[43] P. R. Ackroyd, "Isaiah 1–12: Presentation of a Prophet," VTSup 29 (Leiden: Brill, 1978) 16ff.

[44] B. Johnson, "*mišpāṭ*," *TWAT,* 5.102.

[45] O. Kaiser, *Isaiah 1–12,* 87–88.

[46] H. Ringgren, "*bᶜr*," *TDOT,* 2.202–4.

like a consuming fire that burns, refines, and on occasion destroys (cf. Num 16:35; Deut 4:24; Ps 78:21).

In Isaiah 11:15, the prophet looks forward to the branch from Jesse who will exercise judgment by the Spirit. The remnant will be restored and the enemies of Israel punished by "a scorching wind" *[rûaḥ]* (cf. Isa 27:8; 30:28; 40:7; Hos 13:15), which may refer to the hot east sirocco or metaphorically to a foreign power. In these passages the presence of God is manifested in a theophany that not only destroys the enemies of Israel but purifies the nation through a mitigated punishment. In Isaiah 4:4, the sins of Israel will be put aside by Yahweh's purifying work through his *rûaḥ*. The results expressed in 4:5-6 indicate the expected consequences: "A life in a fertile land, life without guilt in sure protection, afforded and prepared for by God himself, in the community of the city of God."[47]

In short, when Yahweh's anger is aroused, the judgment of Yahweh on the people of God results in punishment. This may include the removal of God's people from the divine presence (2 Kgs 17:17b—18), but it also results in a process of refinement and purification through the *rûaḥ*. Yahweh subsequently restores the people of God into the divine presence.

Grieving the Spirit

Isaiah 63:7–19 is a reflection on the deeds that Yahweh accomplished on behalf of Israel. It takes the form of a community lament, however, because God's gracious acts for the chosen people were met with rebellion and obstinacy rather than praise and adoration. The consequence of their sin was due to their poor response to the work of Yahweh through the *rûaḥ*. Isaiah records the lament: "Yet they rebelled and grieved his Holy Spirit *[rûaḥ qoḏ^{e}šô]*. So he turned and became their enemy and he himself fought against them" (Isa 63:10). The result of their transgression was that they "grieved his Holy Spirit." The piel form of *ʿāṣaḇ* indicates the sorrowful response of the *rûaḥ* due to the consequence of Israel's failure to acknowledge the one who "brought them through the sea" and who it was that set "the Holy Spirit" among them to guide and deliver them: "Then his people recalled the days of old, the days of Moses and his people—where

[47] Kaiser, *Isaiah 1–12*, 88.

is he who brought them through the sea, with the shepherd of his flock? Where is he who set his Holy Spirit among them, who sent his glorious arm of power to be at Moses' right hand, who divided the waters before them, to gain for himself everlasting renown, who led them through the depths?" (Isa 63:11–13a).

In Isaiah 63, the exodus event and the miracles wrought by Yahweh are attributed to the presence of the *rûaḥ qoḏešô,* who exercises power to perform miracles on behalf of God's people. This passage marks an important step toward the use of 'Spirit' "in relation to God in which each and all of his acts can be attributed to his Spirit or to God's Holy Spirit."[48] The community of faith recognizes the exodus and the resulting "rest" as the provision of Yahweh by his *rûaḥ* (v. 14), and they now lament their improper response which caused their punishment. With a return to covenant loyalty, the community could petition Yahweh to intervene once again. Thus, the repentant community recognizes that their judgment was the result of grieving the *rûaḥ*. Moreover, they also realize that restoration will be affected by the renewed work of the Spirit on their behalf.

The Spirit as Person

Discussions concerning the deity and personality of the Spirit in theology books mainly revolve around NT texts and philosophical dialogue. Although the deity of the Spirit of God in the OT is usually not denied, the personality of the Spirit is generally doubted.[49] The Spirit of God in both the OT and the NT seems to prefer a veiled role. This makes it more difficult to show the Spirit's work as a person rather than just a way of indicating God's work, will, power, and activity. In addition, J. B. Payne's contention that the OT emphasizes the unity of God and avoids

[48] Westermann, *Isaiah 40–66,* 389.

[49] The discussion concerning the person of God and the personality of the Spirit is mainly evident in older biblical theology books. The interests of systematic theological dialogue are usually apparent there. See Payne, *The Theology of the Older Testament,* 166–76; G. F. Oehler, *Theology of the Old Testament* (trans. G. E. Day; Grand Rapids: Zondervan, n.d.) 141–42; A. B. Davidson, *The Theology of the Old Testament* (Edinburgh: T. & T. Clark, 1904) 126–29. See also M. J. Erickson, *Christian Theology* (Grand Rapids: Baker, 1983) 845–63.

the revelation of trinitarianism to guard against polytheism may be valid.[50] But the main difficulty in presenting the personhood of the Spirit in the OT is due to the OT focus on the deeds of the Spirit in relation to humankind. Thus, nonpersonal words and phrases are used to describe the Spirit as divine energy, as a wind and fire, as light and space.[51]

References to the *rûaḥ* in relation to God in the Hebrew conception are understood as the extension of God's personality through which the divine plans are effected. Thus, Hebrew thought usually associated the *rûaḥ* with power, ability, creativity, and saw it as an extension of the presence of God. The *rûaḥ* was understood descriptively to indicate God's activity and presence in some way. It may be going too far to state that the OT presents an ontological understanding of the *rûaḥ* as a person throughout the Hebrew canon. Although A. B. Davidson claims that the language used of the Spirit expresses the conception of the Spirit as a distinct person, he states that the idea of personality is not one we should expect to find in the OT.[52] The term *rûaḥ* in its various translations is conceived of as an impersonal force. However, P. K. Jewett's summary is helpful here:

> The Hebrews, it would seem, spoke of God in this way because they conceived of him in his essential being as the invisible Power (Energy) behind all that is, the creative Breath by which the living creature, indeed the whole universe, is animated. Yet in the context of the Old Testament as a whole it is evident that this animating Power, this creative Breath, is not understood as an impersonal force but rather as a living Subject. The personal Energy which God is in himself, the Breath by which he calls worlds into being (Ps 33:6) is, in the first instance, the Energy by which God wills to be who he is. He is who he is by his own act; that is, his being is *personal* being, being that can be understood only as a self-determined "self," an "I."[53]

---

[50] Payne, *Theology*, 167. Payne goes on to discuss the four OT figures that witness to the truth of the trinity, namely the Angel of the Testament, the Wisdom of God, The Spirit of God, and the divine Messiah., 167ff. He concludes that there are genuine suggestions of the persons that make up the Godhead in the OT.

[51] Moltmann, *Spirit of Life*, 10.

[52] Davidson, *Theology*, 127f.

[53] P. K. Jewett, "God Is Personal Being," *Church, Word, and Spirit: Historical and Theological Essays in Honor of Geoffrey W. Bromiley* (ed. J. E. Bradley and R. A. Muller; Grand Rapids: Eerdmans, 1987) 274.

From the many possessive suffixes and construct states with *rûaḥ* and the divine name, it is evident that the Hebrews did perceive the *rûaḥ* to be an independent personality in some instances (cf. 1 Kgs 22:21–22; Isa 63:11; Ps 51:11). Both personal activities and some dispositions are ascribed to the *rûaḥ* (Gen 6:3; 2 Sam 23:2; Isa 4:4; 63:10; Neh 9:20). It has been argued that three divine persons are referred to in Isaiah 48:16, where the prophet records, "And now the Lord God has sent Me, and His Spirit" (NASB). However, it seems more likely that this refers to a royal leader (or prophet) who claims to be commissioned and sent by Yahweh and the Spirit. Others claim that in Isaiah 61:1 the divinity is working together in a threefold manner: "The Spirit of the Sovereign Lord is on me, because the Lord has anointed me to preach good news to the poor." In this passage the Lord anoints the Messiah with the Spirit. It is implied that the *rûaḥ* was not only a divine messenger who had the power to effect the divine will but was also believed to be a person.

Perhaps J. Moltmann's attempt to develop a "trinitarian pneumatology" out of the experience and theology of the Holy Spirit provides the most fruitful recent discussion on the personhood issue. His methodology involves a deductive investigation into the metaphors that express the operation of the Spirit. He claims that "in the operation of the Spirit we experience the operation of God himself, and all the metaphors used for the Holy Spirit are metaphors for God in his coming to us, and in his presence with us."[54] Thus, this form of revelation helps us to understand God in general, and how God relates to humankind in particular. Moltmann's study into the metaphors for the experience of the Spirit in the OT leads him to this definition: "The personhood of God the Holy Spirit is the loving, self-communicating, out-fanning and out-pouring presence of the eternal divine life of the triune God."[55] To say more than this does lead into a speculative intrusion into the OT references. The NT develops the ontological conception of the Spirit as a person in much greater detail as one would expect in the progressive revelation of Scripture.[56] The NT revelation of the Spirit as the

[54] Moltmann, *Spirit of Life,* 286.

[55] Ibid., 289. See ch. XII for his discussion of personal, formative, movement, and mystical metaphors, 268ff.

[56] Oehler, *Theology,* 142, cautions, "Though we must not read the New Testament doctrine of the Trinity into the Old Testament, it is yet

Third Person of the Trinity is necessary to appreciate fully the pneumatology of the OT. At the same time, the NT conception of the Spirit as a person is based on and is developed from the OT Scriptures.

The Restoration of God's People

The threat of judgment that the prophets so eloquently expressed "by the word of the Lord" came to pass on Israel, Judah, and their enemies alike. This was not the last word, however, for intermingled with the word of judgment came the hope of restoration. During the period of exile, the prophets grew in their understanding of the *rûaḥ* and applied the necessity of the involvement of the *rûaḥ* to the new life and transformation that would come about within the people and within nature. In passages dealing with the influence of the *rûaḥ yhwh* in the exile, it is evident that the people realized Yahweh's continued presence with them. This reality revitalized and renewed their hopes as a nation for restoration to their land.[57] The prophets not only gave adequate reasons for the exile of God's people but they spoke of a new beginning and a return to their land. In order to experience the restoration and renewal prophesied, however, the people were called on to respond in repentance, faith, and covenant loyalty.

Hope for Transformation: Isaiah 32:15

The hope for restoration and all that it implied is particularly evident in Isaiah. Chapters 40–55 contain the most vivid images of the restoration longed for. There will be fertility and an abundance of water in the land (Isa 40:1ff.; 41:17–20; 49:19ff.). The people of God will be reestablished in a covenant relationship with Yahweh (55:3–5; 45:9f.). Cities will be rebuilt, repopulated, and God's blessings will abound (44:24–28).[58] The content of Isaiah 32 refers to a future time when renewal within the

undeniable that we find the way to the economic Trinity of the New Testament already prepared in the doctrine of the Malakh and of the Spirit."

[57] Cf. R. J. Sklba, " 'Until the Spirit from on High Is Poured out on Us' (Isa 32:15): Reflections on the Role of the Spirit in the Exile," *CBQ* 46 (1984) 1–3.

[58] Ackroyd, *Exile,* 135.

nation will take place.[59] It addresses some of the major problems that the nation faced, particularly problems within society. The need for renewal is evident in every part of society, where injustice, unrighteousness, and rebellion are tolerated.

But how will change and transformation be effected? Isaiah points to the coming *rûaḥ* as the necessary element for change. Renewal will not come "till the *rûaḥ* is poured upon us from on high." The phrase "from on high" refers to the heavenly abode of Yahweh from where the Spirit of God descends (cf. Isa 57:15; Jer 25:30; Ps 144:7). Verbs that refer to the *rûaḥ* as being "poured out" are frequent in prophetic literature (Isa 32:15; 44:3; Ezek 39:29; Joel 2:28–29 [3:1–2 MT]).[60] They portray metaphorically the blessings brought by the Spirit just as the rain brings about the fructification and fertility of the earth. The association of the *rûaḥ* with the pouring out of oil in the ritual of anointing, that developed during the time of Moses, continued during the period of the monarchy (Exod 28:41; 1 Sam 10:1).

The result of the Spirit's coming will be the initiation of a radical transformation among the people. Following the denunciation of the complacent women and their judgment (Isa 32:9–14), the prophet depicts the transformation of the barren soil as indicative of the transformation of the human heart brought about by the Spirit.[61] Justice and righteousness will reign. Security and peace will finally prevail. The coming of the Spirit, which will change the character and nature of the people, indicates a new attitude to the lordship and rule of God. It is evident from the prophecy that Isaiah refers to a future period, perhaps the messianic age when justice and righteousness will characterize the day. Thus, the prophet grants a vision of hope

---

[59] The authorship and dating of Isaiah 1–66 has been debated at length in OT introductions. However, the passages which we examine here concerning the *rûaḥ* are best understood when the canonical shaping of Isaiah and its theological context are considered. The present canonical shape emphasizes that the message of Isaiah is one of promise not only for Israel but for God's people in every age. Chapters 40–66 bear witness to the fulfillment of the prophetic word in chs. 1–39 and further apply the word to the community. Cf. B. S. Childs, *Introduction to the Old Testament as Scripture* (Philadelphia: Fortress, 1979) 326–33; Ackroyd, *Exile,* 230.

[60] Albertz and Westermann, "*rûaḥ, Geist,*" 2.751.

[61] H. M. Wolff, "The Transcendent Nature of Covenant Curse Reversals," *Israel's Apostasy and Restoration* (ed. A. Gileadi; Grand Rapids: Baker, 1988) 323.

for the possible transformation and renewal that God will bring about by the *rûaḥ* in the lives of his people and in nature.

The Judgment of Edom: Isaiah 34:16

In another text from the 8th century BC, Isaiah uses Edom as an example of God's judgment. Edom was often denounced for its wickedness, and punishment is promised accordingly (cf. Jer 49:7ff.; Ezek 25:12ff.; 35:1ff.; Amos 1:11f.). Judgment will be harsh and Edom will be completely desolated. The beasts of the field will inhabit Edom's land. Within this context, verses 16–17 underline the veracity of the prophetic word: "For it is his mouth that has given the order, and his Spirit *[rûaḥ]* will gather them together." The frequent connection between the spoken word and the *rûaḥ* that will carry it out is clear in this passage. God will set things in order through the work of his *rûaḥ*. Just as God will gather the people together for blessing, so also will the animals be gathered together as a sign of judgment over Edom.

Spiritual Blessings: Isaiah 44:3

After an oracle reviewing Israel's unfaithfulness, the prophet turns to a salvation oracle indicating God's further care for the chosen people. They are encouraged and granted assurance by Yahweh's word: "For I will pour water on the thirsty land, and streams on the dry ground; I will pour my Spirit *[rûaḥ]* on your offspring, and my blessing on your descendants" (Isa 44:3). The passage affirms that the promises of God will be made effective by the coming of the *rûaḥ*. The blessed state will be brought into reality by the Spirit. The context refers to the forming of the nation by Yahweh and points to the new life that will come to the descendants of Jacob. The *rûaḥ* will effect a positive response to the God of Jacob's forefathers. A new religious commitment will be motivated by the *rûaḥ*. In this context, the *rûaḥ* expresses the divine power that creates life in humanity and nature. It is here parallel to the blessing of God that is the vitality bestowing fertility. Not only does God breathe life into the people's physical offspring, God also provides the *rûaḥ*, that enables them to live skillfully and successfully in the divine presence.[62]

[62] Cf. C. W. Mitchell, *The Meaning of BRK 'To Bless' in the Old Testament* (Atlanta, Georgia: Scholars, 1987) 57.

Spirit and Word: Isaiah 59:21

In the context of Isaiah 59, verse 21 seems to be an addition to the preceding community lament, which is a reflection by the community on their past sins of apostasy, deceit, and injustice. Now that their time of punishment is over, however, their hopes for a complete restoration and fulfillment of the glorious images that the prophet proclaimed do not seem evident. In this passage, the prophet assures and encourages the disheartened community: " 'As for me, this is my covenant with them,' says the Lord. 'My Spirit *[rûaḥ]*, who is on you, and my words that I have put in your mouth will not depart from your mouth, or from the mouths of your children, or from the mouths of their descendants from this time on and forever.' " This prophecy points to the expectation of the realization of the prophetic word for all Israel. The word and the *rûaḥ* operate together and assert the reality that the covenant promises will be fulfilled from generation to generation in the experience of God's people (cf. Isa 42:6; 49:8; 54:10; 55:3; 61:8). The word is an assurance that the *rûaḥ* will not depart from the people. The theology of the Spirit as presented here during the exile is an important vehicle for affirming monotheism. "By divine Spirit, Yahweh could be mysteriously present in many lands, transcending limitations of space and time."[63]

A New Spirit: Ezekiel 36:27

Ezekiel prophesied during the period between 593 and 571 BC. The prophet spoke to numerous exiles and used a variety of methods to convey his message. After a period of time when many prophets avoided the term *rûaḥ,* Ezekiel began to emphasize the work and nature of the Spirit. It was evident from the circumstances of the people that God had scattered Israel and punished them for their obstinate disobedience and rebellion (Ezek 20). But, Yahweh promised to vindicate his name that was profaned among the nations because of the situation of the exiles (36:20–23). The vindication of Yahweh's name and the cleansing of the people could be effected only by divine intervention and

[63] Sklba, "Until the Spirit," 13.

a new creative act that would restore the people to a covenant relationship with God.[64]

The essence of the "new thing" that God would do was tied to the persistent sin of Israel and the defilement of the land. The problem was Israel's evident inability to fulfill the command of obedience and faithfulness to the covenant bond (Exod 19:1ff.; cf. Jer 13:23; Ezek 2:3–8; 15–16). Israel had failed to uphold their side of the covenant and for the most part did not submit to Yahweh's lordship. Now they had come to the end of themselves and it was clear that divine help was imperative. Therefore, the great announcement brought hope to the exiles: "I will give you a new heart and put a new spirit *[rûaḥ]* in you; I will remove from you your heart of stone and give you a heart of flesh. And I will put my Spirit *[rûaḥ]* in you and move you to follow my decrees and be careful to keep my laws" (Ezek 36:26–27; cf. 11:19; 18:31; 37:14).

The terms employed in these passages are reminiscent of Jeremiah 31:31–34, which signifies the internalization of religion by way of the "new thing" that Yahweh was ready to do.[65] This passage is found in the "Book of Comfort" (Jer 30–33), which outlines the restoration of Israel and Judah. Jeremiah 31:31–34 particularly presents hope for restoration to the exiles (586 BC). Although the new covenant indicates new features such as the universal knowledge of God (Jer 31:34), universal peace, security, prosperity, and possession of the Spirit (Isa 4:2; Jer 32:41; Ezek 34:25–27; 37:26; Hos 2:18; Joel 2:32ff.), it was not new in the sense of "better." It was new in the sense that Yahweh was prepared to put the law in the hearts of the people, enabling them to live in accordance with the covenant obligations through the power of the *rûaḥ*.[66] The goal of Yahweh's actions was to bring about a new attitude toward him, where the reality of "I will be their God, and they will be my people" would be experienced as it was originally intended (Ezek 36:28; Jer 7:11; 11:4; 24:7; 30:22; 31:1, 34).

---

[64] Cf. W. Zimmerli, "*rûaḥ* in the Book of Ezekiel," *Ezekiel 2: A Commentary on the Book of the Prophet Ezekiel Chapters 25–48* (Hermeneia; trans. J. D. Martin; Philadelphia: Fortress, 1983) 566–68.

[65] R. North, "*ḥādā*," *TDOT*, 4.236–39.

[66] Cf. W. C. Kaiser, Jr., *Toward an Old Testament Theology* (Grand Rapids: Zondervan, 1978) 234; Waltke, "The Phenomenon of Conditionality," *Israel's Apostasy and Restoration*, 136–37.

The intervention of Yahweh in the circumstances of God's people involved gathering the people to their own land (Ezek 36:24), purifying and cleansing them from defilement (36:35), and replacing the "heart of stone" with a "new heart" and a "new spirit." The intent of this is clearest in verse 27 which indicates that Yahweh's Spirit would be given in order to motivate the recipients to follow his decrees and keep his laws. Yahweh would actively participate in man's obedience and as a result vindicate his name (36:36).[67] Moreover, intermediaries such as priests and prophets would no longer have a monopoly on the personal knowledge and Spirit of God. The promise is democratized to include all of God's people.

Ezekiel and the Living Bones: Ezekiel 37

The vision of the valley of bones is structured in two sections, with verses 1–10 presenting the vision and verses 11–14 the interpretation. The question put to the prophet is whether the bones can come to life. His answer indicates the thrust of the whole passage—only God knows whether the nation of Israel can be restored to their former glory. The nature of the restoration depends on the coming of the Spirit.

The term *rûaḥ* in Ezekiel 37:5, 6, 8, and 10 is closely related to the "breath of life" given to all human beings apart from which existence is impossible (cf. Gen 2:7; Eccl 12:7). In this context, *rûaḥ* is the animating principle of life that makes a person a living being. Here it refers to the nation as a whole. In verse 9, however, *rûaḥ* is a pervading wind moving over the world that comes into the dead bodies from the four corners of the world. These are descriptive passages that are then summarized in verse 14. Yahweh declares, "I will put my Spirit *[rûaḥ]* in

[67] Eichrodt suggests that *rûaḥ* in Ezekiel 36:26 means the organ of spiritual life in the sense of disposition and ethical determination. The act of God is thus a bestowal of a new will and a new attitude of spirit to the things of God. In this sense, Eichrodt refers to a person's spirit which is affected by God's action. *Ezekiel: A Commentary* (OTL; trans. C. Quin; Philadelphia: Westminster, 1970) 499–500. In 36:37, however, Eichrodt sees a further development of meaning from the theology of Isaiah where the Spirit as the power of God's being brings about religious submission and obedience. The Spirit now permeates individuals, transforms them, and gives them power to shape their lives in accordance with God's commands.

you and you will live, and I will settle you in your own land." Thus, the people of God are encouraged by the promise of new life through the *rûaḥ*. The purpose of this event is to make clear to Israel that God is the one (37:13–14) who brings to fulfillment the divine promises and thereby vindicates his name. The emphasis of the passage is on the supernatural life-giving power of Yahweh, who alone can renew and restore the nation back to life in their land.

Abiding Presence: Ezekiel 39:29

A reaffirmation of Yahweh's purpose to gather the exiles to their land in Ezekiel 39:29 comes after the prophecy against Gog and Magog (Ezek 38–39). In the prophecy the nation is faced with the possibility of further threat from other nations even after God's "resurrection" of the nation is asserted in chapter 37. Regardless of possible future hostile aggressors, Yahweh will reveal himself by gathering the exiles and by "pouring out" his *rûaḥ* on the house of Israel. "I will no longer hide my face from them, for I will pour out my Spirit *[rûaḥ]* on the house of Israel, declares the Sovereign Lord" (39:29). Therefore, despite any future threats against the nation, Yahweh pledges to bless and abide with Israel.

New Life: Joel 2:28–29 [3:1–2 MT]

The two main parts of the book of Joel consist of a judgment oracle (1:1–2:12), and an oracle of salvation (2:18–3:21). At the heart of the book is the passage concerning God's eschatological activity, "And afterward I will pour out my Spirit *[rûaḥ]* on all people" (2:28). The fulfillment of this prophetic word will occur "afterward." This phrase is a transition from the oracles of judgment to a message of hope and promise for a more distant time.[68] It is then that Yahweh will "pour out" *[šāp̄ak]* the *rûaḥ* on "all flesh" *[kol-bāśār]*. The verb *šāp̄ak* is often used in reference to the pouring out of liquids (Gen 9:6) but also to the "pouring out of the soul" in prayer (Ps 62:9; 1 Sam 1:15). In Joel 2:28–29, however, God performs the action of "pouring" (cf. Ezek 39:29;

---

[68] H. W. Wolff, *Joel and Amos* (Hermeneia; trans. W. Janzen et al.; Philadelphia: Fortress, 1977) 65. Cf. W. A. VanGemeren, "The Spirit of Restoration," *WTJ* 50 (1988) 84–87.

Zech 12:10). A symbolic element is indicated here as is the case in the ritual of anointing performed by priests and prophets. The *rûaḥ* in this context is given by God, not in the sense of animating life, nor for a special gift, but to convey his immediate presence to the recipients. The other consequences are perhaps secondary to this reality of an intimate relationship with God, which was often limited to those in leadership roles. The presence of God implies that a new and vibrant relationship with God will be possible through the event of receiving the "poured-out" *rûaḥ*. A refreshing, revitalizing work is implied, as Wolff explains: "The pouring out of God's spirit upon flesh means the establishment of new, vigorous life through God's unreserved giving of himself."[69] This announcement is as revolutionary as the "new heart" and "new spirit" prophesied by Jeremiah (31:33–34) and Ezekiel (36:26–27).

Yahweh's action in pouring out the Spirit has extensive effects. "I will pour out my Spirit on all people. Your sons and daughters will prophesy, your old men will dream dreams, your young men will see visions. Even on my servants, both men and women, I will pour out my Spirit in those days" (Joel 2:28f.). The thrust of the passage indicates that the coming transformation brought about by the *rûaḥ* will radically change social conditions in the community. All people will be privileged possessors of the Spirit, not just the prophets. In fact, both sons and daughters will function as prophets. All people will have access to the words of Yahweh and to communion with him. Social status will no longer be a criterion for Spirit reception. The programmatic desire of Moses is here affirmed and moved a step closer to fulfillment: "I wish that all the LORD's people were prophets and that the LORD would put his Spirit on them!" (Num 11:29; cf. Exod 19:3–6). Therefore, the charismatic endowment of the gift is extended to the whole community.[70] The reference to "all

[69] Wolff, *Joel and Amos*, 66.

[70] L.C. Allen, *The Books of Joel, Obadiah, Jonah, and Micah* (NICOT; Grand Rapids: Eerdmans, 1976) 98–99. The nature of the manifestations which accompany the coming of the Spirit will be addressed in chapter 5. For now we note that the recipients of the *rûaḥ* will prophesy, dream, and see visions. The word "prophesy" in this context is the niphal perfect form of *nibba* which is often associated with intelligible speech and somewhat different from the hithpael form associated with ecstatic behavior (cf. Num 11:25–27; 1 Sam 10:5–6, 10–12). Cf. J. Jeremias, "*nābîᵓ*," *THAT*, 2.11. However, it is the same *rûaḥ* which motivates the recipients to prophesy intelligibly

people" is qualified in Numbers 11:29 to refer to God's people. Thus, Wolff claims that "all flesh" means everybody in Israel only, while the other nations should expect judgment (4:1ff.).[71] This seems to be the understanding of Peter in Acts 2, until his rooftop vision and experience with the Gentiles in Acts 10. In the NT the gift of the Spirit is democratized to both Jew and Gentile alike. There the condition for Spirit reception is Peter's conclusion to his Pentecost sermon: "Repent and be baptized, every one of you, in the name of Jesus Christ for the forgiveness of your sins. And you will receive the gift of the Holy Spirit. The promise is for you and your children and for all who are far off—for all whom the LORD our God will call" (Acts 2:38–39). Peter's views were revolutionized to a greater extent through his visionary experience (Acts 10:9ff.) and visit to Cornelius' house (cf. Acts 10:23–11:18).

Yahweh's Presence: Haggai 2:5

The oracles of Haggai in 520 BC mainly address Zerubbabel the governor and Joshua the high priest of Judah. After the edict of Cyrus (ca. 538 BC), a number of exiles returned to Judah under the leadership of Sheshbazzar (Ezra 1:11f.), Ezra (ca. 458 BC), and Nehemiah (ca. 445 BC). Although these oracles are primarily addressed to the leaders of Judah, they are also for the whole community which was distressed by the opposition to their temple building and discouraged by the poor harvest (Hag 1:3–12; cf. Ezra 5:14–16).

To encourage the returnees, Haggai's message affirms the presence of Yahweh with them (1:13; 2:5). Yahweh also takes an active part in motivating the leaders and people alike. Yahweh "stirred up" the *rûaḥ* of Zerubbabel, Joshua, and the whole remnant. The verb "stir," which affects the *rûaḥ,* is often used when Yahweh motivates people to action. In other passages, Yahweh may "incite" individuals to battle (Jer 51:11; 1 Chron 5:26; 2 Chron 21:16), he may "move" Cyrus to perform his will (2 Chron 36:22–23), or he may "stir up" the remnant to return to

---

or ecstatically. The emphasis in Joel seems to underline the quality of relationship which was enjoyed by the prophets alone. Now "all flesh" could know and enjoy the gift of prophecy, visions, and dreams—all for the purpose of knowing God.

[71] Wolff, *Joel and Amos,* 67.

Jerusalem (Ezra 1:5). The human *rûaḥ* is the place where Yahweh works to motivate and inspire God's people to complete the house of the Lord.[72]

In Haggai 2:5, however, it is specifically Yahweh's *rûaḥ* that is with the remnant to encourage and assure them. They are reminded that as Yahweh was with the people throughout the exodus events, so now he abides *[ᶜōmeḏeṯ]* with them (cf. Exod 29:45). Just as the presence of God led and remained with Israel in the "pillar of cloud and fire" during the exodus period, so now he was with them during their difficult times (Exod 33:8; cf. Isa 63:7–14). The participle *ᶜōmeḏeṯ* makes clear that Yahweh was not only with them in the past but continued to be with them to the present. The emphasis in Haggai on the presence of God is connected to the temple, which was the symbol of God dwelling among the people. It is the place from where the divine blessing and shalom issue. The remnant is assured of Yahweh's continued presence by the *rûaḥ* among them that encourages them to complete the work of temple building.[73]

By the Spirit: Zechariah 4:6

Zechariah was a contemporary of Haggai who brought a similar message to the remnant of Israel. His prophecy shows concern for the temple-building, the community, and the new age.[74] Featured in Zechariah's prophecy is the temple-building project and the role of leadership in the construction work. Zechariah 4 is a vision emphasizing the centrality of God in the community and God's direction for the temple through the leadership of Zerubbabel and Joshua. In the vision the prophet is shown a gold lampstand with a bowl, seven lights, and two olive trees (4:2–3).

The answer to the question "What are these?" (4:5) is not given until a word for Zerubbabel is proclaimed (4:14). The interjection of this word serves to highlight the authority and source of power for the "two anointed ones" who are the representatives of the Lord. The oracle is connected by the repetition

---

[72] D. L. Petersen, *Haggai and Zechariah 1–8: A Commentary* (OTL; Philadelphia: Westminster, 1984) 58–59.

[73] Ackroyd, *Exile,* 154ff. cf. P. A. Verhoef, *The Books of Haggai and Malachi* (NICOT; Grand Rapids: Eerdmans, 1987) 100–101.

[74] Ackroyd, *Exile,* 170–217.

of the name Zerubbabel and the link between the symbolism of oil, *rûaḥ*, and the anointed ones.[75] The interpretation of the two anointed ones, who are initially the two olive trees standing beside the lampstand, invites a symbolic interpretation that becomes more frequent among the exiles. One symbol used to illustrate the refreshing nature of the *rûaḥ* being poured out is the water of dew or rain. Another symbol was the aromatic oil that would invigorate and possibly heal. Usually the anointing oil conferred on the recipient the authority to fulfill a specific assignment in addition to consecrating them for such a task.[76]

The word to the governor is, "Not by might *[ḥayil]* nor by power *[kōaḥ]*, but by my Spirit *[rûaḥ]* says the Lord Almighty" (4:6). The main emphasis in this statement relates to the source of strength needed for the completion of the temple construction. Negatively, it will not be accomplished by military or human strength alone.[77] Positively, the presence of God, who grants the necessary resources to enable the remnant in their building of the temple, will "by his Spirit" intervene. Therefore, just as the Spirit of God was present to bring the acts of creation into reality, and just as the Spirit enabled the craftsmen in their construction of the tabernacle (Exod 35:30–36:1), so also now in the second temple construction does God pledge his presence to fulfill the construction of the temple. The promise of restoration will be accomplished and brought to reality by the presence of the Spirit of God.

The Spirit Gives Rest: Zechariah 6:8

In the eight visions of Zechariah, the prophet sees a number of horses and chariots dispersed in various directions. They come out from the presence of the Lord and evidently are his messengers. Chariots in the ancient Near East served as transportation for kings and were also symbolic for the military presence of a deity (Isa 66:15; Jer 4:13).[78] The prophet's attention

---

[75] Neve, *Spirit of God,* 103. Cf. Petersen, *Haggai and Zechariah 1–8,* 171–73, for the view that 4:6b–10 is an interpolation.

[76] Sklba, "Until the Spirit," 11–12.

[77] The phrase "not by might" recalls Israel's "watchword in holy war." See G. von Rad, *Old Testament Theology* (trans. D. G. M. Stalker; New York: Harper & Row, 1965) 2.285.

[78] Petersen, *Haggai and Zechariah 1–8,* 265.

is directed northward and he is told, "Look, those going toward the north country have given my Spirit *[rûaḥ]* rest in the land of the north" (6:8).

This text poses a number of difficulties, but the implication is that in the land of the north, where the people of God are in exile, the purpose of God in judgment is realized. In this sense, "my Spirit" has the connotation of anger being set aside. The *rûaḥ* is assuaged, the time of judgment is over, and the time for restoration has come.[79] With Yahweh's work done, the transition in the passage turns to the work of the exiles. Zechariah 6:9–15 emphasizes that the necessary elements required for temple construction will be made available now that the *rûaḥ* is at rest. The rest brought about by the *rûaḥ* is not limited to the exilic period (cf. Isa 63:14; Ezek 37:1). The term *nûaḥ* [rest] brings to mind the promised rest into which Yahweh led Israel (Deut 12:10; Josh 21:44–45). The renewal and the rest brought about by the *rûaḥ* are connected. Not only does Yahweh lead his people into a physical land of bounty which is their rest, but he gives them spiritual rest through his *rûaḥ* (cf. Ps 95; Heb 4).[80] Now all the resources for the task at hand are available. Donations to fund the building are collected, the key figures in directing the project are authorized, and more exiles will return to help with the restoration and building of the temple. Also implied in this reference is the work of the *rûaḥ* in bringing the spoken prophetic word into reality. Zechariah associates the fulfillment of the word with the operation of the Spirit in the community (Zech 1:6; 4:6; 7:12).[81]

In Zechariah 12:10 the Lord says, "I will pour out on the house of David and the inhabitants of Jerusalem a spirit *[rûaḥ]* of grace and supplication." The verb "pour" is used again as in other texts (Isa 32:15; 44:3; Ezek 39:29; Joel 2:28-29), but the context implies that God brings about a disposition of "grace and supplication." The work of the *rûaḥ* is to bring about a response of grace and supplication. The nation will mourn for the one "they have pierced" (Zech 12:10b).

---

[79] Cf. Petersen, *Haggai and Zechariah 1–8,* 272ff.

[80] Cf. H. D. Preuss, *"nûaḥ,"* *TWAT,* 4.300.

[81] Eichrodt, *Theology,* 2.64–65. Eichrodt notes, "It was the spirit which gave rise to the word of God uttered in times past and now of normative significance in the present, and which is at the same time the power of giving life to the community."

In summary of the results and experiences which the coming of the Spirit brings about in Israel's restoration, J. Moltmann presents the following ramifications:

> The experience of God which is expected from the coming of the Spirit is 1. *universal*—no longer particular, but related to 'all flesh' in the whole breadth of creation; 2. *total*—no longer partial, effective in the human 'heart,' in the depths of human existence; 3. *enduring*—no longer historically temporary, but conceived as the 'resting' or 'dwelling place' of the Spirit; 4. *direct*—no longer mediated through revelation and tradition, but grounded on the contemplation of God and his glory.[82]

Therefore, the intention of God for the covenant people is finally realized. God established the nation and cared for Israel, but their rejection of God's attention on their behalf resulted in judgment. Yet, through the Spirit of God, a new arrangement and experience was initiated to bring the intentions of God into reality: "I will be their God, and they will be my people."

[82]Moltmann, *Spirit of Life*, 57.

4

The Spirit of God in Israel's Leadership

So Samuel took the horn of oil and anointed him in the presence of his brothers, and from that day on the Spirit of the Lord came upon David in power. (1 Samuel 16:13)

The Spirit of the Sovereign Lord is on me, because the Lord has anointed me to preach good news to the poor. (Isaiah 61:1a)

Israel had the unique privilege, among its ancient Near Eastern neighbors, of being led by Yahweh. From the time of the exodus, the history of Israel presents the care and guidance with which Yahweh leads the people of God. Yahweh chooses individuals to whom authority is delegated for the purpose of leading Israel according to the divine design. In every stage of their history, Yahweh gives Israel leaders who are enabled for their various roles by the *rûaḥ*. In doing so, God through the Spirit sought to preside theocratically over his people.[1] This chapter is an investigation into the role that the *rûaḥ* played in Israel's leadership in order to discover the nature of charismatic administration. The major sections of the chapter discuss the key passages referring to the role of the Spirit in the

---

[1] W. J. Dumbrell in noting this emphasis concluded that, "the presence of the Spirit in the Old Testament is normally confined to the leadership of Israel and has in view the preservation of the concept of the theocracy; or otherwise stated, the theological function of the Spirit appears to be to implement and sustain the Old Testament notion of the Kingdom of God." "Spirit and Kingdom of God in the Old Testament," 1.

leadership of Joseph, Bezalel and Oholiab, Moses, Joshua, the seventy elders, the judges, the kings, the prophets, and the priests.

The Spirit and Joseph: Genesis 41:38

The role of the Spirit is often conspicuous in connection with major leadership figures who were responsible for administrative, military, or judicial functions in the nation. However, the *rûaḥ* is also given to one of the patriarchs at a crucial period in the history of God's people. Even before the time of a severe famine in Canaan, God began ordering the life and circumstances of Joseph to prepare him for the role of preserving the chosen people. Genesis 50:20–21 summarizes the patriarch's experience in Joseph's reply to his brothers: "You intended to harm me, but God intended it for good to accomplish what is now being done, the saving of many lives. So then, don't be afraid. I will provide for you and your children." God's providential activity is observed throughout the Joseph narratives and includes the work of the Spirit to bring Joseph to the place of influence in the pharaoh's court.

The narratives concerning the life and events of Joseph begin with and include a number of dream scenarios followed by their interpretations. From the beginning of the narratives, Joseph's experience of exaltation is foreshadowed in the dreams of the sheaves and the stars (Gen 37:1–11). But, the unfavorable response of the brothers to Joseph's dreams brings about the humiliation of Joseph to the place where he is a domestic housekeeper in the residence of the commander of pharaoh's guard. In this setting, and subsequently as an attendant in the prison, Joseph proves his administrative abilities and stewardship. He also proves his ability to interpret the dreams of the pharaoh's imprisoned officers. Consequently he is called to the pharaoh's court to interpret his traumatic dreams.

The first occurrence of the phrase *rûaḥ ʾelōhîm* in association with a particular leadership skill occurs in Genesis 41:38. The pharaoh recognizes a special endowment of wisdom in Joseph because of his ability to interpret dreams. The pharaoh asks his officials: "Can we find anyone like this man, one in whom is the spirit of God?" E. A. Speiser's translation captures the essence of the question: "Could we find another like him, one so endowed with the divine *rûaḥ*?"[2] Although this utterance, which attributes Joseph's unique ability to the *rûaḥ* *ʾelōhîm,* comes from a pagan king and reflects an ancient Near Eastern conception, the text records Joseph's initial response to the problem. When called upon to interpret the pharaoh's dream, Joseph replies, "I cannot do it but God will give Pharaoh the answer he desires" (Gen 41:16). Therefore, Joseph recognizes that his ability to interpret the dreams of the cupbearer and the baker (Gen 40) is not an inherent skill but a revelation of God.

In the Joseph narratives his dreams are not just ordinary ones but revelatory dreams. God is presented as giving both the dream and the interpretation. Both the Egyptian and Mesopotamian royal courts employed wise men, seers, and diviners to translate what was considered a divinely inspired dream. In Genesis 41 the pharaoh's court was unable to understand the dream. However, in Joseph's case, more than any other influence, it was the presence of the *rûaḥ ʾelōhîm* that gave Joseph not only the skill to interpret dreams but also his great wisdom and administrative ability. The recognition of his skills earned him the high position of vizier in Egypt and providentially placed him in a position to help God's people.[3] As a reward for assisting the Pharaoh in this Joseph is given the royal seal and authority of the king. Through God's enabling insight and wisdom, Joseph is promoted to the place where he uses his influence to settle the people of God in the ideal land of Goshen and to provide for their physical needs.

The Spirit and Bezalel and Oholiab

The role of the Spirit in the creation of the universe reflects the OT notion of divine involvement in the construction of the sacred place. Just as the macrocosm was creatively constructed by the divine word and brought into reality by the Spirit of God,

---

[2] Speiser, *Genesis,* 310.

[3] See T. N. D. Mettinger, *King and Messiah: The Civil and Sacral Legitimation of the Israelite Kings* (Lund: Gleerup, 1986) 250; Neve, *Spirit of God,* 119; K. A. Kitchen, "Joseph," *ISBE,* 2.1127–29.

so the tabernacle required divine revelation and skill in its construction (Exod 25–31). The tabernacle was to be the portable expression of divine kingship in the midst of Israel. The tabernacle required careful workmanship and attention in its construction. Skill and wisdom were necessary in the making of the garments and furniture. The natural skills of artisans and craftsmen were apparently insufficient for this sacred task.

God selected Bezalel to oversee the construction project and enabled him for the task. Exodus records God's action, "I have filled him with the Spirit of God, with skill, ability, and knowledge in all kinds of crafts." Bezalel was also responsible for making the anointing oil, which often symbolizes the Spirit of God in some texts (Exod 37:29). In addition to artistic skill, the *rûaḥ ᵓelōhîm* is given to both Bezalel and Oholiab in order to equip them to teach others how to perform all the necessary tasks involved in completing the sacred tabernacle (Exod 31:3; 35:30ff.). Thus, the Spirit of God provides the artistic abilities and the skills of instruction to God's selected artisans for this important project. In these examples, the role of the *rûaḥ* illustrates the diversity of gifts associated with the Spirit of God.

The Spirit and Moses

In the OT, Moses is clearly the paradigmatic representative of Israel's leaders. Not only does Moses present the nation's religious beliefs, but he is used by God to lead Israel out of Egypt in order to bring them to Sinai. There, they enter into a covenant with Yahweh and become the people of God. Moses is the chosen mediator of God who reveals to Israel the nature and attributes of Yahweh, as well as the requirements of the covenant bond. From the beginning, Moses is personally confronted by the presence of God and the angelic messenger (Exod 3). Through theophanies and the Spirit, God speaks directly with his servant and reveals his will to Israel (Exod 19:16–20; 33:7–10; Num 12). Moses is the chosen mediator for presenting God's law to the people (Exod 24:4, 12).

The responsibility of leading a large group of people poses many hardships and frustrations for Moses, but he is equipped and sustained in his task by Yahweh's presence. The biblical evidence that Moses gives leadership by the *rûaḥ yhwh* is implicit for the most part in the Pentateuch, but made explicit in Numbers 11 and in Isaiah 63. For instance, the transfer of the *rûaḥ* from Moses to the seventy elders assumes that authority throughout Moses' leadership era comes by the *rûaḥ* (Num 11:16ff.). In the passage of the transfer of the Spirit directed by Yahweh, it is said: "I will take of the Spirit that is on you and put the Spirit on them" (Num 11:17c). That Moses serves by the Spirit is clearly demonstrated. The presence of Yahweh with Moses is so "potent" that it can be shared among the seventy without diminishing its effectiveness in Moses' responsibilities or authority. This narrative indicates Moses' role as God's exemplary prophet (Deut 18:15–18), mediator, and intercessor for the nation (Exod 33:12–16; Num 11:1f.; 12:13; 14:16b–19).

Moreover, Isaiah 63:7–14 presents Israel's understanding that God led the nation by the *rûaḥ* through the leadership of Moses. "Where is he who set his Holy Spirit among them, who sent his glorious arm of power to be at Moses' right hand, who divided the waters before them?" (Isa 63:11c–12a). The rebellion of the nation is directed not only against Moses, but particularly against the rule of God. They "rebelled" against him and thereby "grieved" his Holy Spirit (cf. Ps 78:4). Isaiah 63:7ff. makes explicit the presence of the Spirit during Moses' leadership experiences through which the many miracles of God are accomplished (Exod 6–11; cf. 1 Sam 12:6–8; Ps 105:26–37). It is the *rûaḥ* that enables Moses to lead the people of God through the wilderness and in the performance of his duties.

In short, the many roles Moses played as leader of Israel, judge, lawgiver, prophet, intercessor, miracle worker, and provider were successful because of the presence of God that remained with him and the *rûaḥ* on him that brought God's plans and miracles into reality.[4]

The Spirit and Joshua

When the burden of leading Israel became overwhelming for Moses, particularly in the judicial duties he performed (Exod 18:13–16), he was instructed to set apart seventy elders for consecration to leadership responsibilities. Among the seventy was

[4] J. K. Hoffmeier, "Moses," *ISBE,* 3.423–24.

Joshua, a servant of Moses (Exod 24:13; 32:17) and a military field commander (Exod 17:9–13). As successor to Moses, however, Joshua was specifically set apart for leadership by Yahweh and commissioned for his military and administrative tasks (Num 27:16–23; cf. Deut 31:1–29). His main responsibilities included the leading of Israel in holy war (Josh 1:2–5; cf. Deut 1:37f.; 3:28; 31:7), as well as the administration and supervision of the land inheritance allotments (Josh 1:6–9; 13:7ff.).

The ability to perform his duties is not attributed directly to a period of apprenticeship with Moses but to the recognition that Joshua was a man in whom was the *rûaḥ* (Num 27:18). Although the endowment of *rûaḥ* is specifically noted as taking place at the same time as the seventy elders received the *rûaḥ*, Joshua's role in leadership was distinct. Joshua was filled *[mālēʾ]* with the *rûaḥ* of wisdom *[ḥoḵmāh]* (Deut 34:9). The presence of the Spirit with Joshua provided him with wisdom and skill to function as leader and administrator during the conquest period.

Moreover, significant typological parallels are featured between the leadership of Moses and Joshua that indicate that miraculous occurrences took place in both their public roles. Isaiah 63 attributes these miracles to the presence of the Holy Spirit and to the powerful arm of God. Yahweh was, therefore, present with Joshua as he was with Moses (Josh 1:5; 3:7). The transfer of power from Moses to Joshua served to give authority to Joshua before the people. Joshua is told: "Today I will begin to exalt you in the eyes of all Israel, so that they may know that I am with you as I was with Moses" (Josh 3:7). One of the similar miracles performed through Joshua was the parting of water (Josh 3:17; cf. Moses in Exod 14:21–23, 29; 15:8). Both leaders interceded for the nation (Josh 7:7; cf. Deut 9:25–29), and both met the Lord on sacred ground (Josh 5:15; cf. Exod 3:5).[5]

Leadership by the Spirit Democratized

An important element in the narrative of Numbers 11 occurs when Eldad and Medad, who are outside the camp when

[5] See B. K. Waltke, "Joshua," *ISBE*, 2.1133f.; J. A. Thompson, *Deuteronomy: An Introduction and Commentary* (Tyndale OT Commentaries; Downers Grove, Ill.: InterVarsity, 1974) 320.

the Spirit is transferred from Moses to the elders, also receive the *rûaḥ* and prophesy (Num 11:25–26). Joshua objects to this activity of prophesying and complains to Moses, perhaps believing that this ecstatic activity is reserved only for Moses and the elders gathered before him. But, Moses assures him that Spirit possession/reception is a necessary endowment for leadership—it is a paradigmatic requirement for all who assume leadership duties. Furthermore, Spirit possession/reception is a programmatic imperative—it is not just reserved for prophets and leaders but is an aspiration for all of God's people.[6] The external activity of prophesying confirms publicly the transfer of leadership authority from Moses to other individuals.

In short, Numbers 11 and Isaiah 63, in addition to other divine presence motifs, make clear that the leadership of Moses is successful due to the divine endowment of the Spirit. In the transfer of the *rûaḥ* from Moses to the seventy elders and Joshua, the imperative of the *rûaḥ* for leadership is set forth. Just as the exodus and wilderness wanderings are characterized by charismatic leadership, so the conquest of Canaan is characterized by the charismatic leadership of Joshua. The term "charismatic" refers to the divine gift of the *rûaḥ* that comes on a chosen individual and grants a person the Spirit that is responsible for the supernatural power and skill required to fulfill administrative duties. The transfer episode is therefore both paradigmatic and programmatic. It is progressively carried further in Joel's statement, "I will pour out my Spirit on all people" (Joel 2:28).

The Spirit and the Seventy Elders

The term *zāqēn* is used most often in the OT in reference to a member of a social group who holds an office or special position within that group.[7] It is probable that the office of elder originated on account of the need for tribal representation at important community meetings. Elders voiced the concerns of their communities and exercised local jurisdiction (cf. Ruth 4:1–12). As was common in the ancient Near East, elders met at the city

[6] See R. Stronstad, *The Charismatic Theology of St. Luke* (Peabody, Mass.: Hendrickson, 1984).

[7] J. Conrad, "*zāqēn*," *TDOT*, 4.123.

gate for decision making and business transactions (Deut 21:1–9, 18–21; 25:5–10). They played an important role in every period of Israel's history (Exod 24:1–9; Num 11:16, 24f.; 2 Kgs 10:1, 5; Ezek 8:1; 14:1).[8]

The narrative of Numbers 11 presents the growing problems that Moses had with administering Israel (cf. Exod 18). In answer to Moses' frustrations and plea, Yahweh directs him to gather together seventy of Israel's elders who were known as leaders and officials among the people. They were to present themselves at the Tent of Meeting for a public gathering, and there Yahweh would take of the *rûaḥ* that was on Moses and share the *rûaḥ* with the elders (Num 11:17). Accordingly, as they gathered for the ceremony of investiture, Yahweh came down in a cloud, spoke with Moses, and then took of the *rûaḥ* on him and shared the *rûaḥ* with the elders (11:25). Subsequently, the elders prophesied.

This narrative is usually interpreted either to support the authorization of the elders for leadership or taken to legitimize ecstatic prophecy in prophetic circles. The passage, however, makes clear that the activity of prophesying was limited to this one occurrence (11:16, 24). Prophesying was an external sign to signify the internal reality of Spirit reception for leadership purposes and for public observation to indicate God's endowment. The ecstatic behavior initiated them for their administrative roles with Moses.[9] By this public manifestation of the *rûaḥ,* the elders' authority was ratified before the people just as Moses' leadership was ratified by God through signs and wonders, and the reality of intimate, face-to-face communication (Exod 3:14; 33:12–23; Num 12). Whereas the act of prophesying served to publicly endorse the elders as newly appointed leaders, the *rûaḥ* served to enable them with the necessary resources for their task.[10]

---

[8] See R. de Vaux. *Ancient Israel* (trans. J. McHugh; New York: McGraw Hill, 1965) 1.69–70.

[9] See Z. Weisman, "The Personal Spirit as Imparting Authority," *ZAW* 93 (1981) 229.

[10] See P. J. Budd, *Numbers* (WBC; Waco: Word, 1984) 128. Commentators who try to make an aetiology of this passage in order to promote the office of prophet or ecstatic bands (Num 11:17ff.) do so unnecessarily. Budd claims, "In both components—the empowering of the elders and the activity of Eldad and Medad—there is evidently a concern that possession of the spirit should play its part in the professional institutions,

The Spirit and the Charismatic Leadership of the Judges

The main purpose of this section is to highlight the role of leadership during the period of the judges, and to feature the significance of the *rûaḥ* in the experience of the "charismatic judges." The conquest of Canaan was a united effort led by Joshua. The record of the conquest continues to be presented in the book of Judges. In Judges, however, individual clans try to claim the "unconquered" land allotments given to them by Joshua. With the death of their leader, Israel was without a centralized government. Joshua did not transfer his authority nor did he appoint a successor.

Two types of persons are referred to as judges during this period. The "major judges" are Othniel (Judg 3:7–11), Ehud (3:12–30), Deborah and Barak (4:1–24), Gideon (6:1–8:28), Jephthah (10:6–12:7), and Samson (13:1–16:31). The "minor judges," who also "judged Israel," are Tola, Jair, Ibzan, Elon, Abdon (10:1–5; 12:8–15), and Shamgar (3:31). Although the nature of their leadership was sporadic and localized, the activities of the judges were definitely for the benefit of "all Israel," not just for a particular clan. This is made clear from the predominant use of the name "Israel" throughout the narratives. The term Israel appears more times in the book of Judges than in any other OT book.[11] Even though the activities of the judges focus only on a few tribes at a time, the overall concern remains Israel's fidelity to Yahweh as a nation.

Characteristic of the era in which Israel had no centralized government was the reluctance of individuals to get involved in the life of the nation in order to alleviate the suffering induced by their oppressors. The charismatic judges were not the only leaders during the period of the judges. Elders continued to exercise judicial and political responsibilities as long as normal

---

represented by the elders and in the charisma of men freely raised up by God to declare his word" (pp. 126–27). In our view, Numbers 11:16 and 11:24 do not support this assumption.

[11] See B. Lindars, "The Israelite Tribes in Judges," *Studies in the Historical Books of the Old Testament* (ed. J. A. Emerton VTSup 30; Leiden: Brill, 1979) 95ff.; D. I. Block, "The Period of the Judges: Religious Disintegration under Tribal Rule," *Israel's Apostasy and Restoration* (ed. A. Gileadi; Grand Rapids: Baker, 1988) 41–45.

conditions existed. Unfortunately, they were either unable or unwilling to take initiatives to resolve conflicts within the nation. When the oppressors afflicted the people to the point of a state of emergency, they turned to "savior" figures (Judg 6:12; 11:8–11).[12] The charismatic judge was then able to rally the support of the people, who recognized that the judge was endowed with the *rûaḥ*.

The term "charisma" is a theological notion that "conveys the idea of God's spiritual gifts, bestowed upon people who function as His emissaries and carry out His mission upon the earth."[13] It is the coming of the *rûaḥ* that is responsible for the supernatural power exhibited by the judges, and not a natural, physical endowment of special skills that are normally developed and recognized by the individual and his people.[14] In short, "The deliverer-judge, distinguished by extraordinary qualities and gifts, appeared in his own estimation and in that of his devotees as a divine agent delivering his people from national crisis, an act which imbued him with supreme authority within his society."[15] Therefore, when the *rûaḥ* came on these individuals, who were referred to by a variety of titles such as judge (2:16–19), ruler or official (8:14; 9:30; 10:18), leader (11:6), or head (11:6), they were transformed into mainly military figures.[16] Their role as judicial administrators in the forensic meaning of the term was limited.[17] Through the *rûaḥ*, they were enabled to throw off the yoke of their oppressors in a variety of ways.

The problem of apostasy and spiritual lapse is a recurring theme in the book of Judges. This dilemma is emphasized by the theological pattern that occurs throughout the book, either with

[12] Z. Weisman, "Charismatic Leaders in the Era of the Judges," *ZAW* 89 (1977) 404–5.

[13] Weisman, "Charismatic Leaders," 400.

[14] See de Vaux, *Ancient Israel*, 1.93, 151.

[15] A. Malamat, "Charismatic Leadership in the Book of Judges," *Magnalia Dei: The Mighty Acts of God: Essays on the Bible and Archaeology in Memory of G. Ernest Wright* (ed. F. M. Cross et al.; Garden City: Doubleday, 1976) 159.

[16] J. M. Miller and J. H. Hayes, *A History of Ancient Israel and Judah* (Philadelphia: Westminster, 1986) 93f.

[17] Dumbrell, *The Faith of Israel*, 70–71; de Vaux, *Ancient Israel*, 1.150–51. In addition to Samuel's role in war, he was also a circuit judge who administered justice in Israel (1 Sam 7:15f.; 12:3ff.).

all of the following features or with minor variations: (1) Israel does what is evil in Yahweh's sight; (2) Yahweh gives or sells his people into the hand of oppressors; (3) Israel cries out to Yahweh; (4) Yahweh raises up a savior or deliverer; (5) the deliverer defeats the oppressor; and finally (6) the land has rest for an extensive period of time. This pattern is initially and programmatically presented in Judges 2:11–23.[18]

The Spirit and Othniel: Judges 3:7–11

In accordance with the pattern evident in the book of Judges, the episode of Othniel begins with a report of Israel's sin and their consequent eight-year subjugation at the hands of the king of Aram Naharaim. When the people finally cry out to Yahweh, he answers their cry by raising up a "deliverer" *(môšîᶜa)* named Othniel son of Kenaz (3:9; cf. 1:13f.). "The Spirit of the Lord *[rûaḥ yhwh]* came upon him, so that he became Israel's judge and went to war" (3:10a). Here, and in most instances, the feminine form is used: "She came upon him." R. G. Boling states that, "The heavenly functionary *(rûaḥ)* when he does his task on earth loses his masculine identity and becomes an impersonal power or force and can so envelop a man that he becomes capable of extraordinary deeds."[19] The result of this endowment and empowering is a victory over the king of Aram with the subsequent peace in Israel for forty years. In short, Othniel "judges" with the enabling of the *rûaḥ yhwh* and overpowers the enemy.[20] For Othniel, the charisma of the Spirit is mainly realized in a military capacity.

The Spirit and Gideon: Judges 6:1–8:35

Gideon is a typically reluctant candidate for the role of judge. His call is similar to the call of Moses. In reply to the cries of Israel under Egyptian bondage, God confronts Moses with the burning bush and the angel. In Gideon's case, after seven years of harsh oppression by the Midianites, the Israelites cry out to

---

[18] See D. M. Gunn, "Joshua and Judges," *The Literary Guide to the Bible* (ed. R. Alter and F. Kermode; Cambridge: Belnap, 1987) 104–5.

[19] R. G. Boling, *Judges: Introduction, Translation, and Commentary* (AB. Garden City: Doubleday, 1975) 81.

[20] See W. Richter, "Zu den 'Richtern Israels,' " *ZAW* 77 (1965) 61ff.

Yahweh for deliverance. Yahweh sends them a messenger, saying to Gideon: "The Lord is with you, mighty warrior" (Judg 6:12). This greeting is anticipatory of the role Gideon will play, but his self-perception is one of weakness. He considers himself to be insignificant in his family (Judg 6:15). Nevertheless, Gideon is commissioned to save Israel from their oppressors and is promised the presence of Yahweh. In addition to the impoverishment of the nation by the Midianites, Israel also lacks individuals who could stand up against the influences of Baalism and other religious idolatrous practices (1 Sam 6:6, 25–27).

Gideon is "clothed" *[laḇešâ]* with the Spirit of the Lord when threatened by the enemy, and he begins to immediately muster the troops for battle (6:34). The term translated "clothed" is used metaphorically to illustrate the enveloping of Gideon with the Spirit so as to empower him in his task (cf. 1 Chron 12:18; 2 Chron 24:20). The result of his call to arms is staggering in comparison with the characteristic unwillingness of the people to get involved. In order to assure that the victory is credited to Yahweh, the troops are reduced to three hundred men (Judg 7:1–8). With the Spirit of God upon Gideon, "chariots and horses" are insignificant factors. Furthermore, Yahweh exhibits prowess as a warrior through the unconventional warfare that brings victory to Israel (cf. 8:4–17). Thus, the ability to rally individuals is associated with the presence of the *rûaḥ*. Moreover, Gideon is changed from a fearful and reluctant individual (6:36–39) to a wise and courageous warrior (8:1ff.), in contrast to his brother, who is without the *rûaḥ* (8:20). Gideon also strikes a mighty blow against the advance of Baalism and hampers its growth until his death. He is used by God to extend the covenant boundaries to a greater extent than achieved before (7:24–25).

The Spirit and Jephthah: Judges 10:6–18

The episode of Jephthah opens with a report of Israel's sin and their oppression at the hands of the Philistines and the Ammonites for eighteen years. The people express their penitence (10:10, 15) and plead for deliverance. Leaders from Gilead gather together to defend themselves from the Ammonites but discover that they are without a commander. Jephthah the Gileadite is then introduced as "a mighty warrior" (i.e., a professional mercenary). But he is also an illegitimate son and an outcast (11:1ff.). After a band of adventurers gather with Jephthah the elders of

Gilead approach him and offer to make him "head" *[rōʾš]* of the clan if he will lead them in war. Jephthah agrees to the proposition, becomes their "commander" *[qāṣîn]* and leads them in battle. As in the case of Othniel, the *rûaḥ yhwh* comes on Jephthah (11:29) who proceeds to devastate twenty towns (11:32). Although Jephthah exhibited military qualities before his selection as commander, the author no doubt views the victory over the Ammonites as a direct result of Yahweh's divine intervention by the *rûaḥ*. Jephthah receives boldness and power from the Spirit.

The Spirit and Samson: Judges 13–16

The narratives concerning Samson have a number of different features when compared to the other judges. The episodes begin with a report of Israel's subjugation to the Philistines for forty years. As in the case of the barren patriarchal wives, Manoah's wife is barren but is promised a son by the angel of the Lord (13:2ff.). Her son, however, is to be a Nazirite with the programmatic purpose: "he will begin the deliverance of Israel from the hands of the Philistines" (13:5). The threefold Nazirite pledge is to stay away from corpses, to abstain from alcohol, and to refrain from cutting the hair. Samson is to fight the enemies of God through the charismatic empowering of the *rûaḥ*.[21]

After the birth of Samson and the subsequent blessing of Yahweh during his childhood, the *rûaḥ yhwh* began to "stir" *[pāʿam]* or "impel" him to trouble and frustrate Israel's oppressors (13:25). Often these deeds seem petty and childish, but the main purpose of Yahweh is to give the Philistines into Israel's hands. In this way Samson is a thorn in the Philistines' flesh. He instigates battles in which he single-handedly defeats many Philistines. The specific references to the coming of the *rûaḥ* on Samson are followed by a variety of results. In Judges 14:1 Samson goes to Timnah to take for himself a Philistine bride. The editorial note explains that it was Yahweh's purpose through Samson to instigate conflict with the Philistines (14:4). On the way Samson is confronted by a lion, but when the *rûaḥ yhwh* comes on him, he tears the beast apart (14:6). On another occasion Samson receives the *rûaḥ* and then in anger goes to

[21] See J. A. Soggin, *Judges: A Commentary* (OTL; trans. J. Bowden; Philadelphia: Westminster, 1981) 229–30.

Ashkelon and brutally kills thirty men (14:19). In another act of vengeance, Samson attacks the Philistines with a donkey's jawbone and kills a thousand men when the *rûaḥ yhwh* comes on him (15:14ff.).

In all these episodes, the power of Yahweh by his *rûaḥ* is the source of Samson's strength for his exploits. Though Samson often lacks wisdom and discretion, he exhibits the necessary qualifications for the position of deliverer and is used by Yahweh to throw off the yoke of the Philistines. In his last prayer he recalls the power of God and pleads: "O Sovereign Lord, remember me. O God, please strengthen me just once more, and let me with one blow get revenge on the Philistines for my two eyes" (Judg 16:28). Thus, even to his death, the power of Yahweh enables Samson to loosen the grip of the oppressor and kill more when he dies than when he lived (16:30).

Charismatic Leadership in the Judges

The theme of charismatic leadership during the judges period shows Yahweh's active participation in Israel. Yahweh hears Israel's cries of repentance and intervenes to alleviate their suffering. Yahweh delivers the people by raising up an individual endowed with the Spirit. Nevertheless, Yahweh remains the true Judge and leader of the people (11:27). The judges God sends are bestowed with supernatural power, and therefore Yahweh is ultimately entitled to the victory. Because it is God's power, the special characteristics and circumstances of the individual are insignificant. Judges are selected regardless of status (Nazirite or illegitimate outcast), age, or sex.[22] What matters is the transformation of their attitudes, skills, and strength. The *rûaḥ* that comes on them is a dynamic, explosive power that can overtake them and equip them for their specific tasks of salvation.

The key components in the raising up of the deliverer usually include: (1) a crisis period of oppression; (2) the raising up of an individual who is endowed and enabled to motivate people; (3) the gift of *rûaḥ*, which spontaneously empowers the individual at the appropriate time of need; (4) the authority and effectiveness of the individual, not dependent on age, sex,

[22] See Boling, *Judges*, 25ff.; Dumbrell, "Spirit and Kingdom," 4.

ability, status, wisdom, or prowess; and (5) narratives indicating that victories are won by the intervention of Yahweh through the Spirit that enables the judge in his salvation task.[23]

Were all the judges charismatic in the sense of receiving the Spirit for their roles? As is the case with historical and wisdom literature, the principle of selection is applied to episodes included in the book of Judges. The judges who have the *rûaḥ yhwh* come on them are indeed characteristic of the savior figures who perform their feats by the Spirit. Thus, R. de Vaux's claim that the only authority manifest in the period of the judges was charismatic is valid.[24] Israel did not always explicate what was commonly understood. In the case of Deborah, the title of prophet or prophetess is usually given to persons who receive the *rûaḥ* (Judg 4:4). Deborah also exhibits the great ability of rallying people for the task at hand, an ability that is often associated with the *rûaḥ yhwh* (Judg 4:6ff.; 5:12).[25]

The book of Judges emphasizes the ability of Yahweh to preserve the nation of Israel even in the worst conditions. Through the *rûaḥ yhwh,* God maintains the unity of Israel through charismatic deliverers whom he raises up when true repentance is exhibited.[26]

The Spirit and the Leadership of the Kings

The transition from the charismatic judges to that of kingship involves major cultural, economic, and political changes for Israel. The cyclical pattern of apostasy and oppression in Judges continues into the opening chapters of 1 Samuel. But some hope for renewal is indicated by the spiritual piety in the lives of some individuals. In addition to the characters portrayed in the book of Ruth, a number of faithful adherents to Yahweh are presented in 1 Samuel. One of these was Hannah.

---

[23] See Malamat, "Charismatic Leadership," 161–62.

[24] De Vaux, *Ancient Israel,* 1.93. This statement must be taken in the context of the "deliverance" motifs, however, since elders did exercise some authority.

[25] G. F. Moore, *Judges: A Critical and Exegetical Commentary* (ICC; Edinburgh: T. & T. Clark, 1895) 112–13.

[26] See W. J. Dumbrell, "The Purpose of the Book of Judges Reconsidered," *JSOT* 25 (1983) 23–33.

The Song of Hannah plays a special role in establishing the main theological emphasis of 1 and 2 Samuel (1 Sam 2:1–10). The unjust and sacrilegious situation in Israel will be reversed, and in its place Yahweh will give strength to his king and will "exalt the horn of his anointed" (1 Sam 2:10b). The prayer of Hannah is not just a pious request but a foreshadowing of the greater thing Yahweh will do on behalf of his people. The nature of Yahweh and his intentions are here set forth—he who "brings low and also exalts," "who judges the ends of the earth," "who will give strength to his king"—is revealed in the narratives that follow the hymn.[27] In this section I investigate the function of the king who is anointed and endowed with the *rûaḥ* for his role of leadership.

The Rise of Kingship in Israel

The plight of Israel at the hands of the Philistines is presented in the "Ark Narrative," which focuses on the impotence of Israel under the yoke of their oppressors (1 Sam 4–7). Through the leadership of Samuel, however, Yahweh brought about a victory and delivered the nation through holy war (7:10ff.). In this way, Samuel demonstrated the sufficiency of his role as judge and the theological propriety of nonroyal leadership.[28]

A problem arises when Samuel, in his old age, appoints his "wicked sons" as judges to succeed him (1 Sam 8:3). In the light of this action, and perhaps because of a similar disgrace in the family of Eli the priest (1 Sam 2:12ff.), the elders voice their concerns and request a king to rule over them. Samuel's disapproval of their request is similar to the implicit disfavor shown toward kingship in the judges period (Judg 9). Their desire to be like the other nations is ultimately a rejection of Yahweh's kingship (1 Sam 8:7; 10:19; 12:17–19) and a denial of God's divine rule in their midst (Exod 19:3–6). Yahweh takes the initiative, however, and tells Samuel to clarify the nature of kingship and its implications for the people in relation to the covenant. Samuel's presentation is an account of the typical administration of Canaanite city-states complete with their problems and abuses

---

[27] See Childs, *Introduction to the Old Testament as Scripture,* 273.

[28] See P. K. McCarter, *1 Samuel* (AB; Garden City: Doubleday, 1980) 149.

(1 Sam 8:6–17). Although kingship was anticipated in Israel (Deut 17:18–20), it was acceptable only as far as it was compatible with the rule and covenant of Yahweh.[29]

The Spirit and the Leadership of Saul

The Lord responds to the people's request for a king by directing Samuel to "anoint" *[māšaḥ]* a man as "leader" *[nāg̱îḏ]* over Israel who would deliver them from the Philistines. The term "leader" may be interpreted as one who is singled out and designated for office.[30] By virtue of the *nāg̱îḏ* title and the anointing, Saul is strengthened for the function of delivering the people.[31] Yahweh providentially arranges a meeting where Saul and Samuel come together (1 Sam 9). This is followed by the private anointing of Saul by Samuel (10:1). All these events are orchestrated by the Lord, who chooses Saul and directs his anointing by Samuel.

Three signs are to follow the anointing of Saul that serve to confirm his authorization as *nāg̱îḏ* (10:1ff.). The third sign, to verify the prophet's word, is the reception of the *rûaḥ yhwh,* that will "come upon him" *[ṣālaḥ]* (cf. Judg 14:6, 19; 15:14; 1 Sam 10:6, 10; 11:6; 18:10; 16:13), cause him to "prophesy" *[hiṯhnāḇēʾ]* and "change" him (10:6–7). The act of prophesying by Saul and the band of prophets is to be distinguished from that of prophetic inspiration, which conveys a message to the recipient. The ecstatic element indicates an encounter with the *rûaḥ yhwh* that brings about external manifestations in addition to verbal utterances. In this instance, the fulfillment of the three signs would confirm that Yahweh is with Saul. In accordance with the words of Samuel, Saul's heart is transformed and the *rûaḥ ʾelōhîm* comes on him, causing him to prophesy (10:10;

---

[29] A pro-monarchical narrative consisting of 1 Samuel 9:1–10 and 13–14 is often contrasted to an anti-monarchical strand in 1 Samuel 8; 10:17–27; and 12. See B. Halpern, *The Constitution of the Monarchy in Israel* (Chico, Calif.: Scholars, 1981) 149ff. However, it is natural that as important an office as that of king should be carefully considered. Divergent views regarding the monarchy are to be expected in major transition periods.

[30] McCarter, *1 Samuel,* 178. He notes that the significance of the term is its use of Yahweh's prerogative to appoint a "prince" of his choice (186f.). The main difference is the religious-sacral element indicated by "*nâg̱îḏ.*" See G. F. Hasel, "*nāg̱îḏ,*" *TWAT,* 4.204.

[31] Hasel, "*nāg̱îḏ,*" 213.

cf. 19:20, 23). The nature of the "changed heart" may refer to the courage and strength that are part of the charisma needed to perform a deed of valor.[32] Subsequent to the anointing and to the bestowal of the *rûaḥ*, the recipient is enabled to triumph over his enemies. The *rûaḥ* gives Saul the power to carry out his military mandate, which in turn proves that he is filled with divine power.

The manifestation of the *rûaḥ yhwh* at this important transition period to the monarchy is consistent with the OT emphasis that all leadership must be Spirit-endowed. The charisma is fundamental to prove the authority and ability of an individual for the role of "judge" or "king." With the power of Yahweh on him, Saul proves his prowess in his confrontation with the Ammonites (11:1ff.). When he hears of the Ammonite threat, the *rûaḥ ʾelōhîm* comes on him and fills him with anger. Saul is able to muster a staggering number of people (11:8), in a similar manner as in the Gideon episode. Here, the "terror" *[paḥad]* of Yahweh falls on them and motivates them to fight for the nation (11:7). With the Spirit of God, they are able to defeat the Ammonites. In short, Saul's leadership is affirmed by the presence of *rûaḥ* that brings victory to God's chosen one and legitimizes Saul's authority as king (cf. 11:12–15).

The Evil Spirit and the Rejection of Saul

A new section is marked by the introductory formula in 1 Samuel 13:1. The focal point of the narrative is the rejection of Saul as king. Saul seems to have overstepped his authority as king and is accused of not keeping the command of Yahweh (13:13). In all the texts dealing with Saul's fall, he is blamed for violating the covenant. First Samuel 15:25a–30 and 13:10–14 tie his rejection to the laws of holy war, with the latter reference asserting that Saul's line would have been established had he observed his obligations. Saul is accused of disobedience in general (1 Chron 10:13) and of summoning up Samuel's specter in particular (1 Sam 28:3–25; cf. Deut 18:9–11). It is the king's special position and responsibility that underlie his liability to punishment.[33] Because of Saul's presumption in offering sacrifice, Saul's kingdom would not endure (1 Sam 13:14), a fact

[32] Mettinger, *King and Messiah*, 68.
[33] Halpern, *Constitution of the Monarchy*, 17.

symbolically portrayed in the rending of Samuel's robe (13:14ff.; cf. 19:24). The rejection of Saul as king is made complete when the *rûaḥ yhwh* departs from him (16:14). The *rûaḥ* which gave Saul authority and power to conquer the enemy is now transferred to David and replaced by the *rûaḥ rāᶜāh*, which is characterized by mental anguish, fear, and depression.

Whether the *rûaḥ rāᶜāh* is a demon or a powerful evil influence is not clear from the texts. An evil spirit from God is mentioned in other OT passages in addition to those in 1 and 2 Samuel (cf. Judg 9:23; 1 Kgs 22:21–23; 2 Kgs 19:7; Isa 37:7; Zech 13:2; 2 Chron 18:20–22). First Samuel describes Saul's suffering theologically and shows how all things in the end are under God's control. The evil influence on Saul affects the king in order to destroy his leadership capabilities and judgment. Rather than concerning himself with the vital needs of the nation, Saul seeks to kill David and is responsible for the slaughter of the priests of Nob (1 Sam 22:18–19).[34] This act in itself shows Saul's utter depravity and failure to understand the ways of God.

The narratives of Saul's downfall portray his unsuitability for the throne and highlight David's abilities and charisma as the heir to the throne. Saul's disposition and behavior affect his ability to rule. He loses his military courage and becomes "terrified" when the *rûaḥ rāᶜāh* comes on him (cf. Isa 21:4; Job 7:14). With David's rise to favor and fame, Saul becomes insecure, fearful, and inflamed with jealousy. Although the musical ability of David serves to soothe Saul and alleviate his suffering, the *rûaḥ rāᶜāh* drives Saul to try and kill David (18:10; 19:9). The presence of David, who becomes the bearer of the *rûaḥ,* causes Saul to consider David a threat to the throne. Saul's behavior and loss of ability is, therefore, attributed to the loss of the Spirit that had come on him and was initially symbolized by the anointing oil. Saul opens himself to the receive the *rûaḥ rāᶜāh* in place of the Spirit, which reverses the blessings that come with the Spirit of God. Subsequently, Saul is unable to carry out his divinely entrusted royal duties.

---

[34] See H. W. Hertzberg, *1 and 2 Samuel: A Commentary* (OTL; trans. J. S. Bowden; Philadelphia: Westminster, 1964) 140–41. Cf. L. J. Wood, *The Holy Spirit in the Old Testament* (Grand Rapids: Zondervan, 1976) 126–38, who claims that it was a demon that influenced Saul. Also see F. Lindström, *God and the Origin of Evil* (ConB 21; Lund: Gleerup, 1983) 74ff.

The Anointing Oil

Anointing with oil had a variety of purposes in the ancient Near East. Oil was used for its medicinal properties, for cleansing rites, and for the consecration of people or items for cultic use. An assortment of ingredients were concocted depending on the oil's use. On some occasions oil was used in an enthronement rite in which the people authorized the king to rule over them.[35] The OT has a variety of contexts in which anointing occurs, most often of persons, such as priests (Exod 28:41; 29:7), prophets (1 Kgs 19:16), and kings. However, tabernacle furnishings were to be anointed to indicate their transfer from ordinary profane use to that of sacred cultic use (Exod 40:9–15; Lev 8:10–13).

In Israel, the anointing oil was for sacred use and had to be made by a specific person, initially Bezalel, who was filled with the Spirit for his tabernacle-related duties (Exod 37:29). Later, Eleazar son of Aaron took on this task (Num 4:16). The oil required special ingredients such as liquid myrrh, fragrant cinnamon, fragrant cane, cassia, and olive oil (Exod 30:22–33). The anointing oil may have had some connection to the fragrant incense that filled the tabernacle in a similar manner as did the glory-cloud that filled the abode on occasion (Exod 30:34–38; cf. 37:29). In this sense, the oil and incense were symbolic of the divine presence and *rûaḥ* of God.

Although priests, prophets, temple implements, and kings are all referred to as those who experienced anointing, the majority of OT references refer to the anointing of kings. In addition to the fable of kingship in Judges 9:8–15 where anointing is practiced, specific kings who were anointed included Saul (1 Sam 9:16; 10:1), David (1 Sam 16:3, 12f.; 2 Sam 2:4; Ps 89:20), Absalom (2 Sam 19:10), Solomon (1 Kgs 1:34, 39), Hazael (1 Kgs 19:15), Jehu (1 Kgs 19:16; 2 Kgs 9:3–6), Joash (2 Kgs 11:12), and Jehoahaz (2 Kgs 23:30). Priests or prophets performed the anointing, but on occasion it is specifically stated that Yahweh did the anointing. In Saul's case, Yahweh anointed him as ruler over the divine inheritance (1 Sam 10:1; 15:17). In regard to David, his responsibility as king is underlined in Nathan's prophetic rebuke where

[35] See E. Kutsch, *Salbung als Rechtsakt: Im Alten Testament und im Alten Orient* (Berlin: Töpelman, 1963) 1–5, 39. See also W. Beyerlin, "Das Königscharisma Bei Saul," *ZAW* 73 (1962) 186.

God says, "It is I who anointed you" (2 Sam 12:7; cf. Ps 89:20a). Jehu was anointed by Yahweh for the precise task of destroying the house of Ahab (2 Kgs 9:3–12; 2 Chron 22:7). For the messianic servant, God would anoint him to preach and to deliver the nation, among other duties (Isa 61:1f.).

The term "anoint" *[māšaḥ]* gives rise to the concept of the messiah in OT theology (1 Sam 13:14; 25:30; 2 Sam 5:2; 6:21; 7:8; 1 Kgs 1:36) and indicates the special relationship of the anointed one to Yahweh. Anointing confers authority to act and is tied closely to the bestowal of *rûaḥ* for enablement. "The ceremony of anointing by means of oil was the sacramental sign and seal of the coming of God's Spirit."[36] The externally flowing oil represented the internal reality of the Spirit's filling. The imagery of the oil and dew, therefore, indicates the work of the Spirit in bringing about unity and blessing in the community (Ps 133). The anointed one is divinely enabled to fulfill royal and prophetic duties. In the anointing of the tabernacle and its furnishings, the oil marked out as sacred the dwelling place of God. This was ratified by the coming of the glory-cloud to fill God's earthly abode.

The four main messianic qualities connected to kingship and anointing are the (1) election of an individual; (2) anointing by priest or prophet; (3) Spirit-endowment; and (4) public demonstration of the gift in bringing about victory over the enemy.[37] All four of these qualities appear with the rise of kingship, and are evident in the experience of Saul and David. These qualities form messianic theology which supports kingship from its inception. The title *môšîᶜa yhwh* stands for the election, authorization, and protection of Yahweh's king. The connection of the title "anointed one" with the *rûaḥ yhwh* is so close that F. Hesse claims the two are probably identical.[38] The king is God's "anointed one" whom he protects in a special way (Pss 2:2; 18:50; 132:17). God's anointed individuals are also revered by the pious (1 Sam 12:3; 24:6; Ps 20:6). When kings fail to uphold the covenant, however, God sends anointed prophets to rebuke them (Ps 105:15). In the end, the kings are not as inviolable as the people thought: "The Lord's anointed, our very life breath, was caught

---

[36] Payne, *Theology,* 175.

[37] R. Knierim, "Die Messianologie des Ersten Buch Samuel," *EvTh* 30 (1970) 114–15.

[38] F. Hesse, "*chriō,*" *TDNT,* 9.502–3.

in their traps. We thought that under his shadow we would live among the nations" (Lam 4:20).

Concerning the role of the anointing, K. Seybold indicates that divine selection is affirmed by anointing. Also, through the representative of God, the anointing is a symbolic act of sending and commissioning. Furthermore, the anointing is followed by Spirit-reception through which the king experiences unique charismatic gifts.[39] Mettinger notes that an important aspect of the charisma is that it grants the king the ability to administer the kingdom. This relates particularly to the reign of Solomon, who was given great wisdom for his judicial tasks. Both the military charisma (evident in the service of the judges and Saul) and the charisma of wisdom are necessary for an effective rule.[40]

Although the *rûaḥ yhwh* is not specifically stated to come on Solomon, he was anointed as successor to the throne by Zadok the priest and Nathan the prophet (1 Kgs 1:32ff.). At the news of the impending ceremony of anointing, Benaiah son of Jehoida proclaims: "As the LORD was with my lord the king, so may he be with Solomon to make his throne even greater than the throne of my lord King David" (1:37). Through the anointing the Lord was indeed present with Solomon (cf. 1 Chron 29:23–25). His reign shows the results of the charisma of wisdom that gave him discernment in the administration of the kingdom. Solomon was not only an able administrator but a shrewd politician, diplomat, strategist, and organizer. His ability as a poet and wisdom preacher was also lauded in the ancient Near East (1 Kgs 4:32; ch. 10). Although Solomon suffered a serious moral lapse, the era of peace and prosperity that he ruled over became a significant illustration of the eschatological event where the nations will come to Israel for instruction and direction in their affairs (Isa 2:1–5; Mic 4:1–5). In this coming era, the anointed messiah will reign and fulfill God's intended design for kingship. With the presence of God on his chosen, anointed servant, the rule of God will be realized universally.

The Spirit and David

The narratives from 1 Samuel 16 to 2 Samuel 5:1–4 are usually referred to as the "history of David's Rise." These narratives

[39] K. Seybold, "*māšaḥ*," *TWAT*, 5.51.
[40] Mettinger, *King and Messiah*, 238–46.

justify David as Yahweh's chosen king who is to succeed Saul, and also exonerate David from any intrigue or desire to depose God's anointed one.[41] The fourfold sequence of motifs that give rise to Saul's kingship are also evident in the rise of David. He is elected by Yahweh (1 Sam 16:1ff.), anointed by Samuel, endowed with the *rûaḥ,* and prepared for the military battles to follow (cf. 16:13–14; ch. 17). An added feature is evident in 1 Samuel 16:13 following his anointing in that "the *rûaḥ* came upon David from that time onward." The passage implies a "perpetual attribute," not just a sporadic occurrence. This is the only time that the *rûaḥ* is said to come on David, but the military skills and charisma for his leadership responsibilities are evident throughout his reign. After his sin with Bathsheba, David fears for the loss of the *rûaḥ* that he knew would debilitate him as king. David pleads with God to not take the Holy Spirit from him (Ps 51:11). At the end of his reign as king, he attributes his successes to the *rûaḥ* on him (2 Samuel 22).

David's providential entrance to the king's court is recorded just as Saul's providential meeting with Samuel was (16:14ff.). David is brought to Saul's attention as a man with unusual qualities. He is a musician, a brave warrior, an eloquent speaker, is good looking, and above all, Yahweh is with him (16:18; cf. 18:12–28; 2 Sam 5:10). With the *rûaḥ yhwh* on David, he exhibits his military power by defeating Goliath and then credits the victory to Yahweh (1 Sam 17:45–47). In contrast, Saul lacks courage and is terrified at the Philistine threat (17:11).

Support for David as king grows, as is evident in the narratives following the account of David's anointing and Spirit-endowment. After the death of Saul, David's role as king is ratified with a public anointing at Hebron by the men of Judah (2 Sam 2:4), and then by all Israel (5:3). The transition from the leadership of Saul to that of David is similar to the transfer of authority from Moses to Joshua (Deut 34:9) and that from Elijah to Elisha. Samuel anointed each one for kingship at Yahweh's command. Yahweh reserves the right to dispose of one king and to replace him with another. The prowess of David in battle is vividly recorded in the historical literature, and under his reign the covenant borders expanded significantly.

---

[41] J. H. Grönbaek, *Die Geschichte vom Aufstieg Davids: Tradition und Komposition* (Copenhagen: Prostant Apud Munksgaard, 1971) 270ff.; See also Mettinger, *King and Messiah,* 39ff.

Lament for the Spirit: Psalm 51:11 [13 MT]

The superscription of Psalm 51 credits David with the authorship of this individual lament. Here the king repents of the sin committed with Bathsheba and ultimately recognizes that his sin is against God (Ps 51:4; cf. Exod 20:14). After he pleads for cleansing, David cries out: "Do not cast me from your presence or take your Holy Spirit from me" (Ps 51:11). This plea seems to be more than just a request for sanctification (which is evident in other verses in the psalm).[42] David is aware of his sin and fears being rejected as Saul was. Yahweh turned away from Saul because of his sin (1 Sam 16:14; 28:16–19), and now David fears the same consequences. Without the *rûaḥ*, David knows that his reign as king will not only be fruitless and unsuccessful, but his ability to reign as vice-regent with Yahweh will be over.[43]

The leadership of the kings shows that the necessary ingredient for kingship is the anointing and reception of the *rûaḥ*. Yahweh elects his representative, has him anointed, comes on him with the Spirit, and empowers him for rule in his kingdom.

The Spirit and the Leadership of the Messiah

The history of the monarchy indicates the failure of individual kings who do not rule according to God's expectations. Yahweh rules through chosen representatives, but the extent of rule through them is limited by their human failures. Nevertheless, the covenant of Yahweh is particularized in the oracle of Nathan to establish the Davidic dynasty forever. Yahweh will rule over Israel through the chosen and anointed king. Key elements of the Davidic covenant include a name (2 Sam 7:9), a place (7:10), a seed (7:12), a son (7:14), and a people

[42] A. Weiser claims, "The worshipper's true desire is that he may not be cast away from God's presence; that is to say that he may always enjoy the presence of God and through continuous contact may be able to partake of his Spirit so as to receive power for 'sanctification.' " *The Psalms: A Commentary* (OTL; trans. H. Hartwell; Philadelphia: Westminster, 1962) 407.

[43] Dumbrell, "Spirit and Kingdom," 5.

(7:23–24).[44] The surprising element in Nathan's oracle is the unconditional promise, "I will establish the throne of his kingdom forever" (7:13; cf. v. 16; cf. 23:5; Ps 89:29–38). An eternal covenant is made with the Davidic dynasty that promises that a descendant, called God's son, will have an everlasting kingdom. But numerous references indicate the punishment of individual kings in the lineage who default their position by failing to rule in accordance with the covenant obligations (cf. 2 Sam 7:14–15; Pss 89:31–32; 132:11–12; 1 Kgs 2:4; 8:25; 9:4–5).

Israel's failure to rule the kingdom of Yahweh in righteousness and with justice brings about the exile and the loss of kingship.[45] The prophetic response is not to give up hope but to look into the future for Yahweh to keep the divine promise. Yahweh will raise an ideal ruler to fulfill divine intentions for a righteous rule in the kingdom. As is common with other leaders in Israel, the coming Davidide will be endowed with the *rûaḥ* that will usher in the righteous reign of Yahweh.

The Anointed One to Come: Isaiah 11:2

Isaiah the prophet presents some of the characteristics of the ruler whom Yahweh will raise up (Isa 11:1). The charismatic endowment of the *rûaḥ* that characterizes his rule is emphasized by the fourfold use of *rûaḥ* in this passage. The *rûaḥ yhwh* will "rest" on him and qualify him for his task. This term for rest *(nûaḥ)* is reminiscent of the Spirit resting on the elders (Num 11:25f.) and on Elisha (2 Kgs 2:15). Just as the *rûaḥ* rested on them to qualify them for their tasks, so the *rûaḥ* will rest on the "root of Jesse."[46]

The first two qualities given by the Spirit are "wisdom" *[ḥoḵmāh],* which includes the skill necessary for the application of knowledge, and "understanding" *[bînāh],* which involves the discernment necessary for proper administrative functions. The paradigm of a wise king who exercises these functions is Solomon who is given a special endowment of wisdom after his anointing and request for this charisma (1 Kgs 4:29–32 [5:9–12

[44] W. C. Kaiser, Jr., "The Blessing of David: The Charter for Humanity," *The Law and the Prophets* (ed. J. Skilton; Philadelphia: Presbyterian and Reformed, 1974) 309.

[45] Kaiser, "Blessing of David," 318.

[46] Preuss, *"nûaḥ,"* 299.

MT]). The king also receives the *rûaḥ* of "counsel" to assist him with the intellectual ability and volition required to make correct judgments and to prepare for action. In addition, he has the "power" *[geḇûrāh]* to activate the necessary qualities for leadership. Thus, the *rûaḥ* is the motivating power of the king's rule that bestows the necessary virtues characteristic of ideal kingship.[47] He will also receive the *rûaḥ* of "knowledge," which is a trait of the promised day of salvation (cf. Hos 2:21f.). He will know the Lord through an intimate relationship with him and recognize him as the source of his authority. He will "fear" Yahweh and prove his fear by living uprightly before him as a moral paradigm for the people.

This ideal ruler will finally mete out judicial pronouncements with righteousness and justice. It is probable that Isaiah 11:1–9 brings the military charisma of the judges and the judicial charisma of the king together. Thus, the wisdom of Solomon for judicial administration (1 Kgs 15:23; 16:5, 27; 2 Kgs 18:20) and the martial charisma of Saul and David are merged to include the two main functions of the messianic role.[48] His reign is characterized by wisdom and compassion through which all may find help (Isa 11:3–5). The results of his reign have universal implications which anticipate a return to Edenic conditions (11:6–9). Peace and safety are the order of the day and will once again be a reality.

Although Isaiah 9:1–6 does not refer to the *rûaḥ yhwh* as coming on the "child" who will sit on David's throne, the passage does make allusions to the deliverance he would effect. The deliverance alludes to the victory of Gideon, the Spirit-endowed judge, who won the battle at Midian (Judg 8:22). As in the case of Gideon, God's will is to be done through the child (Isa 9:1–6). His reign will be characterized by peace, justice, and righteousness and will have no end (9:6). These characteristics are similar to those portrayed in the royal psalms. There the king is anointed by Yahweh and installed as regent over the kingdom. He is proclaimed a son who will uphold justice and righteousness in the land and who will mediate blessing, rain, and fertility to the people of God (cf. Pss

[47] Ringgren, "König und Messias," *ZAW* 64 (1952) 134. See also H. Ringgren, "*bînāh*," *TDOT,* 2.105–6; Müller, "*ḥoḵmāh*," 375; H. Kosmala, "*gebûrāh*," *TDOT,* 2.370.

[48] Mettinger, *King and Messiah,* 249.

2; 8; 21; 72; 110).[49] In the same way, the anointed king to come will possess the Spirit of Yahweh that will enable him to fulfill the righteous rule of the ideal king in a way that had not yet been realized in Israel's monarchy. He will be called a Wonderful Counselor, Mighty God, Everlasting Father, and Prince of Peace (Isa 9:6).

The Anointed Servant of the Lord

A number of texts stand out in the book of Isaiah which are usually referred to as the "Servant Songs." A variety of interpretations have been set forth to argue for a collective, an individual, a cultic, or a corporate-personality identification for the "servant."[50] Four "Servant Songs" are typically referred to: Isaiah 42:1–9; 49:1–6 (or 1–13); 50:4–9 (or 1–11); and 52:13–53:12, but Isaiah 61:1–3 should also be included in this category. Although we include Isaiah 61:1–3 in this category, it is mainly in Isaiah 40–55 that the prophet focuses attention on the servant of Yahweh. The significant themes reiterated in these chapters include the investiture of the *rûaḥ* (42:1), the proclaiming of good news (40:9; 41:27; 52:7), and various acts of mercy (42:5–9). These are the main themes needed to encourage and comfort the post-exilic community.[51]

The songs feature the character and functions of the servant. The title "servant" *[ᶜeḇeḏ]* as used in the OT refers to a variety of individuals ranging from slaves, to officers (1 Sam 19:1), officials (2 Kgs 22:12), and ambassadors (Num 22:18). It was also a title of honor for the king who rescued God's people from their enemies (1 Sam 3:18; cf. 7:8, 19; 1 Kgs 3:6). Moses is referred to as *ᶜeḇeḏ* at least forty times. The prophets are also considered Yahweh's servants who act as his messengers and warn the people of impending judgment (2 Kgs 17:13, 23; Jer 7:25).[52]

---

[49] Ringgren, "König und Messias," 129; see Kraus, *Theologie der Psalmen,* 150ff.

[50] See C. R. North, *The Suffering Servant in Deutero-Isaiah* (London: Oxford University Press, 1948), and H. H. Rowley, *The Servant of the Lord and Other Essays on the Old Testament* (Oxford: Basil Blackwell, 1965).

[51] See P. D. Hanson, *The Dawn of Apocalyptic* (Philadelphia: Fortress, 1975) 66; Ackroyd, *Exile,* 230.

[52] See W. Zimmerli, *"paîs theou," TDNT,* 5.654ff.

The prophet's words, in the context of the Servant Songs, are addressed to those who are in exile. Israel's punishment is now declared to be complete, and the threat of judgment is replaced by a message of hope and deliverance. Much of Isaiah 40–55 is filled with exodus typology where the situation of Israel in Babylon is paralleled to that of their bondage in Egypt (40:3–5; 41:17–18; 42:14–16; 43:1–3, 14–21; 48:20–21; 49:8–12; 51:9–10; 52:11–12). The exodus is the great paradigm of salvation and deliverance for Israel. For the exiles, a new way is prepared for them through the wilderness. Therefore, the prophet announces that preparation is to be made for the Lord because he will again act on behalf of his people. Isaiah 40:10ff. emphasize the greatness of God in order to encourage the brokenhearted. Yahweh has not left them and assures them that he has chosen a servant through whom salvation will surely come (41:8–10).

This salvation to come has several elements. To a degree it involves judgment upon the nations who have overstepped their boundaries as instruments of Yahweh to punish other nations (Isa 47). For Babylon, judgment will be meted out by Yahweh's servant Cyrus. He is the helper whom Yahweh summons and anoints for the task of subduing the nations (43:14ff.; 45:1ff.) and for bringing release to Israel. Through this event, the nations will realize that God is still with the exilic community (45:14b). But the main element is the salvation that comes through the Spirit-endowed servant, who brings not only physical deliverance but spiritual salvation. This is the focus of the Servant Songs.

The Spirit and the Servant: Isaiah 42:1–9

The first song opens with an expression reminiscent of a royal designation for Yahweh's choice of a king: "This is the man I spoke to you about; he will govern my people" (1 Sam 9:17; Zech 3:8). In Isaiah 42:1, the *ᶜeḇeḏ* is Yahweh's chosen one whom he will uphold for the task entrusted to him. The relationship between Yahweh and the chosen servant is intimate, as expressed by the term "delight" (cf. 1 Sam 29:4; 2 Chron 10:7). The means of upholding the servant for the task is through the agency and endowment of the *rûaḥ*. It is by Yahweh's power and presence that the success of the servant's mission is assured.[53]

The promise of the *rûaḥ* comes before the extent of his service is presented. His task includes the bringing of "justice" *(mišpāṭ)* to the nations that is a far-reaching agenda characterized by the real experience of justice and righteousness.[54] As the central term of the song, justice is the characteristic feature of the servant's role (cf. 1 Sam 8:5f., 20; Isa 9:6; Jer 21:11; 22:3, 15). Thus, the threefold reference to "justice" in Isaiah 42:2–4 points to a just state of affairs that the nation longs for and the order that the servant alone can bring through the enabling work of the Spirit.

The coming of the Spirit on the servant will be evident by his character and in the way he serves others. His calm and quiet disposition and the manner of his service contrast with that of the soldier (42:2). Through the *rûaḥ* he takes care to represent the helpless and brings forth justice in "truth" (42:2–3). He is kept faithful to his role, and regardless of the consequences, justice will be established. In his "*tōrāh*" the islands will place their hope and trust. The scope of the servant's task is broadened from that of a focus on the nations to a universal ministry (42:4; cf. 2:13). The task is further elaborated on in 42:6–7 where the servant will be made a "covenant for the people." Through the servant Yahweh will effectively transform others. The servant will be a covenant pledge for the world because he embodies the covenant and perpetuates it for Israel.[55] This far-reaching ministry is made possible by the Spirit-endowed servant.

A further consequence of the servant's ministry is the opening of blind eyes, the liberating of prisoners from dungeons, and the freeing of prisoners who dwell in darkness. The subject of these infinitives is not as immediately evident in Isaiah 42:7 as in 61:1–3. Both texts proclaim the salvation to come. To the exiles in prison who do not see the hand of God in history will come spiritual illumination. They will be liberated from their captivity through the work of the anointed servant of the Lord.

---

[53] See F. D. Lindsey, "Isaiah's Songs of the Servant, Part 1: The Call of the Servant in Isaiah 42:1–9," *BSac* 139 (1982) 16.

[54] See W. A. M. Beuken, "*mišpāṭ:* The First Servant Song in Context," *VT* 22 (1972) 7.

[55] W. J. Dumbrell, *Covenant and Creation* (New York: Thomas Nelson, 1984) 192–94. See Westermann, *Isaiah 40–66,* 100.

The Anointed Servant: Isaiah 61:1–3

Isaiah 61:1–3 opens with the announcement, "the *rûaḥ a'ḏōnāy yhwh* is upon me." In this context the prophet may be referring to his awareness that he is anointed for the task of proclamation. But the words in the prophet's mouth are more characteristic of the Davidic king whom Yahweh raises up as the royal servant. It is quite likely that the offices of prophet and king are here merged so that the proclamation of the good news and the actions performed are brought about by the same figure. The authority of the proclaimed message and the actions carried out by the servant are attributed to the inspiration and power given by the Spirit. The many allusions in Isaiah 61:1–3 to the other Servant Songs suggest that it is a reaffirmation that restoration and order will yet be realized through the work of the servant whose whole task is marked by the *rûaḥ*.

The servant has a twofold task before him. The first task involves the proclamation of "good news to the poor," of "freedom for the captives" and of "release from darkness for the prisoners." He is to proclaim "the year of the Lord's favor and the day of vengeance." The second task of the servant involves action. He is sent to "bind up the brokenhearted," to "comfort all who mourn," to "provide for those who grieve," and to "bestow on them a crown of beauty," "the oil of gladness," and "a garment of praise." The servant is endowed with the Spirit for this broad program of restoration. The exiles are not to abandon hope but are to look for the deliverance yet to come. Through the servant, whom Yahweh has chosen and equipped, the present and future concerns of the community will be addressed.

The Servant: Isaiah 49:1–6; 50:4–9; 52:13–53:12

Since the Servant Songs of Isaiah 42:1–9 and 61:1–3 frame the other three songs, it is fitting at this juncture to note the various attributes of the servant as described in them.[56] In the second Servant Song, the servant addresses the nations in order to account for his prophetic call. The servant's mouth is likened

[56] See F. D. Lindsey, "The Commission of the Servant in Isaiah 49:1–13," *BSac* (1982) 129–45; "The Commitment of the Servant in Isaiah 50:4–11," *BSac* (1982) 217–29; "The Career of the Servant in Isaiah 52:13–53:12," *BSac* (1982) 312–29 & *BSac* (1983) 21–39.

to that of a sharpened sword, indicating the prophetic nature of his speech. The imagery of the sword and the polished arrow seems to indicate the penetrating power of the message he speaks (cf. 50:4). The servant is also assured of the divine protection that he will receive and apparently requires.

Isaiah 49:3 is a paradox in that the servant will "display [the Lord's] splendor." This is a new feature in the prophetic task that seems impossible since the servant utters despair at not seeing more positive results in his task. "I have labored to no purpose; I have spent my strength in vain and for nothing." But rather than give in, the servant entrusts all results into the hands of God (49:4). His task is not only to restore Israel back to the Lord, but is extended to the Gentiles, in order to bring salvation to the ends of the earth (49:5–6).

The form of the third song is that of an individual lament that includes a note of confidence. The servant here views his task in much the same way as the prophets did, but in this case he fully accepts the suffering he endures. Using prophetic imagery, the servant acknowledges the divine enabling for his task. The Lord gives him an instructed tongue and makes his words effectual. He is obedient and fully cooperative with his master regardless of the consequences. The theme of suffering alluded to earlier is now expanded on. He accepts the abusive treatment at the hands of his enemies and trusts the Lord for intervention (50:6–7). Whereas his enemies may find him guilty, he knows that vindication will come in the court that matters (50:8). Though innocent, he does not retaliate but awaits vindication from the sovereign Lord, knowing that his enemies will ultimately be judged (50:9).

While the second and third songs allude to affliction, the fourth clearly portrays the servant's suffering. Two or more speakers are evident in the passage, with God initiating and concluding the oracle. The introduction parallels that of 42:1. "Behold" calls attention to the royal designation. We are immediately directed to the fact that the servant who "will act wisely" will be "highly exalted," a feature that seems impossible when the description of his appalling appearance is presented. Observers are astonished at his anguish and startled at the effects of his suffering that is to "sprinkle many nations" (52:15). The element of astonishment continues due to the description of the servant's life span. Though insignificant and isolated (53:2–4), his development indicates that he is the recipient of the divine blessing. But in his suffering, observers consider the servant devoid of blessing.

The words that refer to suffering in this passage indicate a wide range of meanings from that of physical infirmity to a violent experience of "piercing" and "crushing." It is this punishment which is now understood by the speaker to be suffering by one for another. As a result of the iniquity of others, the servant suffers (53:5, 6, 11; cf. Exod 28:38; Lev 16:22; Num 18:1). Those who now receive the benefits of the servant's suffering, namely peace and healing, view the servant as a representative or substitute for their guilt. His innocence is stressed throughout the passage, although he is oppressed, afflicted, and led to the slaughter. He is stricken for the "transgression" of the people (Isa 53:8), and in this sense is a guilt offering that brings pleasure to the Lord. But the servant is ultimately restored and exalted. He is rewarded for his far-reaching accomplishment and shares the victory with others.

In short, Israel's future existence and hope depend on a coming servant and messiah whom Yahweh selects, anoints, and sends in the power of the Spirit for the purpose of establishing a righteous rule as an example of the original expectations for the monarchy. The nature of the servant's work is diverse and unexpected. It includes humiliation, suffering, and travail in addition to exaltation and victory. But through his anointed ministry, he brings about the far-reaching benefits indicated in the Isaianic Servant Songs.

The Anointed Foreign Ruler: Cyrus

We have noted the crucial role which the servant of the Lord was to fulfill according to Isaiah. The complexity of the servant's identity, particularly in Isaiah 40–55 but also through chapter 66, is due to the different individuals or communities that filled the servant's role. At times the servant is definitely Israel, or a messianic ruler, but "the servant" may also be a foreign king such as Cyrus or Artaxerxes I. In some prophecies, Yahweh particularly wishes to assure the exiles of his care for them. The prophet indicates that divine care will include the services of Cyrus. The Chronicler notes specifically that the prophecy of Jeremiah was fulfilled when the Lord "stirred up" the *rûaḥ* of Cyrus for the service of Yahweh (2 Chron 36:22).

According to the OT, it is Yahweh who raised up Cyrus as ruler over Persia and Media (Isa 41:1ff.), in order that foreign policies would be reversed in favor of Israel. Whereas the Assyrians and Babylonians believed fervently in moving their captives away from their homeland, the law of the Medes and Persians promoted their repatriation. From 558 BC onward, Cyrus was used by God to fulfill the divine promises to God's people (Ezra 1:1ff.). Cyrus directs the return of exiles to their homeland and even instructs his subjects to assist Israel with the financial and physical needs they will have in their journey (Ezra 1:4; cf. *ANET,* 316).

The rise and exploits of Cyrus were abundantly recorded in the ancient Near East. In the Cyrus Cylinder, the king states: "I am Cyrus, king of the world, great king, legitimate king, king of Babylon, king of Sumer and Akkad, king of the four rims (of the earth), son of Cambyses, great king, king of Anshan, grandson of Cyrus, . . . of a family (which) always (exercised) kingship; whose rule Bel and Nebo love, whom they want as king to please their hearts" (*ANET,* 316). Isaiah records Yahweh's role behind the scenes: "This is what the Lord says to his anointed, to Cyrus, whose right hand I take hold of to subdue nations before him and to strip kings of their armor, to open doors before him so that gates will not be shut" (45:1). Yahweh chose a polytheistic king to bring about the divine purposes for God's people. In order to accomplish Yahweh's intentions, Cyrus is the "anointed one," the "enabled one," commissioned to accomplish the divine will. Cyrus begins the messianic work presented in 41:21–42:12 and acts as a shepherd to God's people (44:28). He is empowered for his far-reaching military and administrative roles by Yahweh, who anoints him and upholds him. Although Cyrus remains unaware of Yahweh's role in his successful rule (45:3–5), he is an instrument in God's hands to fulfill the promises to Israel.[57]

The Spirit and Artaxerxes I: Isaiah 59:15–21

As observed in the case of Cyrus, Yahweh at times turns to foreign rulers to help God's people in the return to and restoration of Jerusalem. In the context of Isaiah 59:15–21, Yahweh

[57] See Ackroyd, *Exile,* 131f., 140ff.; D. J. A. Clines, "Cyrus," *ISBE,* 1.845–49; J. D. W. Watts, *Isaiah 34–66* (WBC; Waco: Word, 1987) 146ff.

decides to intervene in a situation where apathy was the order of the day. Finally he determines that "his own arm" would work to bring about his design and plan for the exiles. Just as God employed Cyrus to assist with divine plans, so now God turns to Artaxerxes I to aid the restoration process (ca. 465 BC).[58] Part of the restoration will include military intervention. Thus, Yahweh uses a foreign military power to set things in order (59:17–19). Their motivation and zeal will be directed by Yahweh, who "will come like a pent-up flood that the *rûaḥ* of the Lord drives along" (59:19b). Whereas the NIV translates *rûaḥ* as "breath," Watts' translation fits the context better: "For he comes like a rushing stream. The spirit of Yahweh is the driving force in him."[59] Thus, God's sovereign purposes for the people will be brought to pass, even if the instruments God must use are other than initially desired.

God's promises to Zion will be fulfilled, and God now makes a covenant with the people. In the covenant context of Isaiah 59:21, the prophet encourages the people by assuring them that Yahweh's *rûaḥ* will not depart from them, even if the Spirit was assisting a foreign ruler. " 'As for me, this is my covenant with them,' says the Lord. 'My Spirit, who is on you, and my words that I have put in your mouth will not depart from your mouth, or from the mouths of your children, or from the mouths of their descendants from this time on and forever,' says the Lord." Thus, Yahweh pledges his support to the leader he raises up as his servant. In this case, "my words" may refer to God's decrees and plans for Israel (cf. Ezra 7:11–26; Neh 2:7–9).

The Spirit and the Leadership of the Prophets

In this section we briefly examine the role of the prophet in relation to the monarchy in Israel. The prophet's functions as they specifically relate to his leadership responsibilities will be surveyed here, but specific elements of the prophetic office and the nature of prophecy are addressed in chapter 5.

The transition from a predominately tribal administration with charismatic judges to that of the monarchy did not occur easily in Israel. Samuel initially opposed the call for a king

[58] Watts, *Isaiah 34–66*, 286.
[59] Ibid., 285.

because of the implications this request had on the theocratic rule of God and on the covenant with Israel. The reign of Solomon exemplified some of the abuses that Samuel warned the nation of when they called for a king (1 Sam 8). To check the threat of a king leading Israel in a manner corresponding to the ancient Near Eastern practices of kingship, God raised up the prophetic and royal offices together. Prophecy was the continuation of the Mosaic office in that it interpreted the covenant for the people and for the king. Whereas the king was to administrate the kingdom with justice and righteousness and protect the people from enemies, the prophet directed the spiritual matters of the kingdom and sought to maintain true Yahwism in the nation. The court prophets observed the activities of the king and ultimately held them responsible for actions out of step with their covenant obligations. The prophet was Yahweh's messenger who chose and deposed the king at the direction of the Deity. The prophet sought to keep the king and the nation loyal to Yahweh.[60]

Although the prophetic office arises with the ministry of Samuel, the role of "prophet" *[nāḇîʾ]* is already in evidence in the Pentateuch. The function of a prophet in Israel's early history is particularly related to mediation and intercession (cf. Gen 20:7; 18:17; Exod 20:19) but also to revelation (Gen 15:1ff.; Deut 34:10–12; Hos 12:13). The role of prophet calls for total allegiance to Yahweh and truthful utterance of his message (Deut 13:1–5; 18:22). Prophets after Moses were called to speak authoritatively for Yahweh.[61] Next to Moses, Samuel is the paradigm of the prophetic leader in the historical literature. He is described as engaging in several activities that will characterize the functions of the prophet in the period following Samuel's leadership. The main role of the prophet in the initial stages includes these aspects: "(1) He designated the chosen of Yahweh to be king by oracle and anointing, (2) He pronounced judgment on the king, the forfeit of kingship for breach of law or covenant, as well as the death of the king for like reasons, (3) He called Israel to battle in the authentic 'war of Yahweh' as well as determined the times for Israel to go to war (in victory or in defeat)."[62]

---

[60] See Dumbrell, *Covenant and Creation,* 136ff.
[61] See Zimmerli, "Der Prophet im Pentateuch," 197–211.
[62] See Cross, *Canaanite Myth,* 223–24.

The tension between the prophetic movement and the monarchy is due to the mediated rule of Yahweh through the prophets that transcends the political rule of the kings. This is particularly evident in the predominant association of *rûaḥ* with the prophets after the time of David.

The Spirit and Elijah and Elisha

Few prophetic figures match the character and power exhibited by Elijah and Elisha. In the midst of grave religious apostasy, the battle for Yahwism was mainly carried on by these two prophets and the "remnant" of seven thousand faithful (1 Kgs 19:14). With the marriage of Ahab to Jezebel, Baalism threatened to replace Yahwism in the north (cf. 1 Kgs 18:4–19; 19:10–14). During the period of the judges the threat to Israel's faith derived from the slow infiltration of Canaanite religion. During Ahab's reign, however, Jezebel made the bold attempt to replace Yahweh with a foreign deity. Jezebel's hostility toward the prophets increased to the point that their extermination was threatened. Prophets of Baal were given official status (1 Kgs 18:19) while prophets of Yahweh were forced to seek refuge. It was in this difficult situation that Yahweh raised up the tenacious prophets called Elijah and Elisha.

The call of Elisha by Elijah is symbolized in the throwing of the mantle over the prospective prophet (1 Kgs 19:13, 19). Such mantles were usually made of animal hair (Gen 25:25), and could be quite beautiful (Josh 7:21–24) and elaborate (Jonah 3:6). The mantle made of hair identified the wearer as a prophet (Zech 13:4). By throwing his mantle onto Elisha, Elijah was indicating that the burden of his office would fall on Elisha in the future. This symbolic gesture is similar to the coming of the Spirit of God in some passages and analogous to the "hand of Yahweh" that comes on the prophet during prophetic functions. This is illustrated in the experience of Ezekiel who claims, "The Spirit then lifted me up and took me away, and I went in the bitterness and in the anger of my spirit, with the strong hand of the LORD upon me" (Ezek 3:14). The mantle was also used in the miraculous parting of the water (2 Kgs 2:8, 13), and in the experience of Elijah and Elisha, it was like the enveloping or clothing of the individual by the Spirit (Judg 6:34).

The narratives concerning these two prophets indicate that the power for their zeal and miraculous deeds originated in the *rûaḥ yhwh*. When Elisha is given a last request by Elijah, the prophet asks for a "double portion" of Elijah's *rûaḥ* (2 Kgs 2:9, 15). Although this request is not explicitly for the *rûaḥ yhwh,* Elisha must certainly refer to the *rûaḥ yhwh,* whose power and influence he had observed in the ministry exploits of Elijah. The whole of Elijah's ministry was characterized by the *rûaḥ yhwh,* that could carry him away at any time (1 Kgs 18:12; 2 Kgs 2:16). Only Yahweh was able to accomplish the miracles performed by Elijah through the Spirit. Only Yahweh could bestow this power. This narrative, therefore, shows the charismatic nature of the prophetic office where the choice of a prophet is not hereditary but left to the prerogative of Yahweh who chooses (1 Kgs 19:10, 19–21) and empowers the prophets for service. After Elisha receives the *rûaḥ,* he begins to do similar miracles as Elijah did.

The Commissioned Prophet: Isaiah 48:16

The context of Isaiah 48:12–22 takes place during the exile and at the point of return to Jerusalem. Ezra and Nehemiah record at least four expeditions to Jerusalem, and the response among some Israelite communities is pathetic. This particular oracle seems to fit into the context of the return under the leadership of Sheshbazzar during the reign of Cyrus (ca. 525 BC). In this passage, Yahweh laments the apathy of the people, whom he tried to awaken to divine activity by announcing historical events and then bringing about their fulfillment. "I foretold the former things long ago, my mouth announced them and I made them known; then suddenly I acted, and they came to pass" (Isa 48:3). This is the particular work of the Spirit that inspires the prophetic word and then brings it into reality. Yahweh did this to vindicate the divine name from being profaned by people, who did not heed his voice. Yahweh even resorts to using a foreign ruler to deliver the people of God. Now, Yahweh's Spirit that anoints Cyrus commissions the prophet to speak to the nation.[63]

In this text, the prophet is conscious of the Spirit's presence with him and is confident of the authority he possesses in his prophetic ministry. He proclaims, "And now the Sovereign LORD

[63] Watts, *Isaiah 34–66,* 178.

has sent me, with his Spirit" (48:16). The message the prophet underlines is that the Lord teaches the nation what is best for them and he directs them in the paths they should take. Though they are reluctant to return to Jerusalem, and though they seem oblivious to God's acts on their behalf, the prophet tries to awaken them to Yahweh's plan. He desires that they recognize their Creator, Savior, and Redeemer, and in obedience return to Jerusalem for the rebuilding of the temple and ruins. As they were led by the Lord during the exodus, so now he will lead them by his presence.

Man of the "Spirit": Hosea 9:7

In the judgment oracle of Hosea 9:1ff., the prophet warns the people of imminent punishment. The people's perception of the prophet's role, however, is quite different from that of Hosea's understanding. The people express their irritation at the presence of the prophet at their festival. In their view the *nāḇîʾ* is a "fool" and an "inspired maniac" *[mešuggāʿ ʾî hāraḥ]*. The caricature of the prophet according to the people is one who babbles unintelligibly (2 Kgs 9:11; Jer 29:26) and is out of control. As a "fool," they perceive the prophet as one who does not know how to live life skillfully or behave normally. By referring to Hosea as a "man of the Spirit," they place him in the same category as Elijah (1 Kgs 19:11), Micaiah (1 Kgs 22:21f.), and Elisha (2 Kgs 2:9, 16), but they probably refer to Hosea derogatorily for his ecstatic behavior.[64] In S. Mowinckel's view, this was the main conception not only of the people but of the writing prophets as well.[65] For them, possession by the *rûaḥ* was undesirable and therefore rarely mentioned by the prophets. But Hosea is referring to the people's conception rather than to a fair or accurate evaluation of the prophetic role. The prophets avoid featuring ecstatic behavior due to the similar correspondences in the cultic practice of Baalism.

Hosea sets the record straight in 9:8. Contrary to the popular view, the prophet is deeply concerned for the spiritual health of the nation and thus is the watchman over them (cf. Jer 6:17; Ezek

---

[64] H. W. Wolff, *Hosea: A Commentary* (trans. G. Stansell; Philadelphia: Fortress, 1974) 157.

[65] S. Mowinckel, "The 'Spirit' and the 'Word' in the Pre-exilic Reforming Prophets," *JBL* 53 (1934) 199ff.

3:17; 33:2, 6, 7; Isa 56:10). The prophet "watches" over the people in the sense of evaluating their relationship with Yahweh. Rather than being a raving and irrational maniac, the prophet knows Yahweh and abides with him—the very thing that the people failed to do (cf. Exod 34:28; Deut 18:13). The warnings of the prophet and his persistent confrontations with the people concerning their sin bring on the harsh opposition of the populace.

Filled with Power and Might: Micah 3:8

The prophecy of Micah is a strong censure of the leaders who abused their positions of authority. The prophets are rebuked for prophesying "weal" rather than the true word of "woe" in order to obtain monetary benefits (cf. 3:5f.; 9:10; 2:6–11; Lam 2:14). Because of their indiscretion they will be punished. Visions will no longer come to them, nor will Yahweh answer their requests. In contrast, however, the prophet Micah has credentials that qualify him as the true representative of God, who gave him authority to speak.[66] "But as for me, I am filled with power, with the Spirit of the LORD [*rûaḥ yhwh*], and with justice and might, to declare to Jacob his transgression, to Israel his sin" (Mic 3:8). Micah is full of "power" *[kōaḥ]* given to him by Yahweh, who fills him with the presence and inspiration of the Spirit. The prophet is enabled to bring Yahweh's message of Israel's sin to the people. Power and might are two necessary qualities for the prophet that strengthen him in the difficult task of exposing the sins of those who do not feel they are guilty. Thus, Micah is sustained by the Spirit to stand in the midst of opposition and courageously proclaim the word of the Lord to a rebellious people. Micah speaks boldly against the injustice of his day and speaks for justice rather than for monetary gain.[67] The mark of a true prophet is to call sin evil and to uphold the law within the covenant.

Spirit-Commissioned Prophets: Zechariah 7:12

Similar to the message of the prophet Micah, Zechariah is called to speak to the people regarding their obligations to the

---

[66] See Allen, *The Books of Joel, Obadiah, Jonah and Micah,* 313.

[67] See J. L. Mays, *Micah: A Commentary* (OTL; Philadelphia: Fortress, 1976) 85; Mowinckel, " 'Spirit' and the 'Word,' " 223.

covenant as well as in regard to the administration of true justice (7:9). In summary of the response of the populace to the prophets, Yahweh says: "But they refused to pay attention; stubbornly they turned their backs and stopped up their ears. They made their hearts as hard as flint and would not listen to the law or to the words that the LORD Almighty had sent by his Spirit through the earlier prophets. So the LORD Almighty was very angry" (Zech 7:11–12). The authority of the prophets is evident in their endowment of the *rûaḥ* by which they are inspired to call the people back to covenant loyalty. Rejecting the words of Yahweh's emissaries resulted in the hardening of their hearts against God—not just against their fellow prophets. Thus, the community was encouraged to heed the prophetic word of Zechariah lest they incur the wrath of Yahweh.

Administration by the Spirit: Daniel 4:5–15[5–6 MT]; 5:11–14

Although the book of Daniel is placed in the Writings of the Hebrew canon, much of the material is prophetic. Daniel has numerous roles but among them he is referred to as "the man greatly loved" by God (or "highly esteemed"; cf. 9:23; 10:11, 19). To some degree this title may be higher than the title of prophet. It is possible that this title is given because of the perception of the Babylonian kings who believed that "the spirit of the holy god(s)" dwelt in Daniel (Dan 4:8, 18; 5:11–14). K. Koch claims that, "The possession of that spirit elevates Daniel above the abilities of all other wise men and makes him an outstanding seer announcing the mysteries of the end of days (2:2–3) or the time of the end (11:35–40; 12:4–13)."[68] Daniel's great abilities and piety are set forth from the beginning of the book. On five occasions the ability of Daniel to interpret dreams is attributed to the *rûaḥ* within him.

Initially, Daniel's ability to interpret Nebuchadnezzar's dream is simply credited to the God in heaven (2:28). Before Daniel interprets the dream, he makes clear that this skill is not given to wise men, enchanters, magicians, or diviners, but is granted by God to his chosen agent. In this sense the narrative

[68] K. Koch, "Is Daniel Also Among the Prophets," *Interpreting the Prophets* (ed. J. L. Mays and P. J. Achtemeier; Philadelphia: Fortress, 1987) 244.

has many affinities to the episodes of Joseph. After Daniel tells Nebuchadnezzar the dream and the interpretation the king exclaims, "Surely your God is the God of gods and the Lord of kings and a revealer of mysteries, for you were able to reveal this mystery" (2:47).

In the second instance, Daniel participates in a court contest and interprets the king's dream. Nebuchadnezzar reports in a letter that Daniel is able to do what the others could not do. Daniel interprets the king's dream because the *rûaḥ* of the "holy gods" is in him (4:8–9, 18). This perception by the Babylonian king concerning the *rûaḥ* could be construed as typical polytheistic language.[69] But Daniel's previous statement that his ability comes from God makes it probable that the *rûaḥ* here is understood as the *rûaḥ* of Daniel's God.

In the last instance, Daniel is summoned by King Belshazzar to interpret the enigmatic writing on the wall, which the king's wise men could not read. The queen refers the king to Daniel "in whom is the spirit *[rûaḥ]* of the holy gods" (5:11). Daniel is summoned and is enabled by the *rûaḥ* to interpret the writing. The king understands that the *rûaḥ* in Daniel gave him insight, intelligence, and outstanding wisdom (5:14). In recognition that the *rûaḥ* of the holy gods was in Daniel, and that Daniel's ability to interpret dreams came from the *rûaḥ,* the king promoted Daniel to the third highest position in the kingdom (5:29). In this respect, the account of Daniel's leadership abilities has affinities with the Joseph narratives. Both men attribute their skills to the special gift of God. They interpret dreams but are also capable stewards and administrators. Because of their accomplishments, they are both elevated in recognition of the presence of the "*rûaḥ* of the gods" in them (cf. Gen 41:38). Daniel's abilities for the variety of leadership roles he exercises are therefore credited to the Spirit of God that is present with him in his administrative capacities.[70]

---

[69] See A. Lacocque, *The Book of Daniel* (trans. D. Pellauer; Atlanta: John Knox, 1979) 76.

[70] The form of the Joseph, Esther, and Daniel narratives shows how leaders are elevated to positions of power. They often include a pattern where: (1) a king cannot understand a dream; (2) his wise men are unable to interpret; (3) God's servant has the ability to understand; and (4) the servant is exalted to a high position. See J. J. Collins, "The Court-Tales in Daniel and the Development of Apocalyptic," *JBL* 94 (1975) 220–27.

Spiritual Instruction: Nehemiah 9:20, 30

Nehemiah 9 is a prayer of instruction and petition complete with a historical recital of Israel's history. The historical review of Yahweh's dealings with the nation highlights the preservation and guidance of Yahweh.

> Because of your great compassion you did not abandon them in the desert. By day the pillar of cloud did not cease to guide them on their path, nor the pillar of fire by night to shine on the way they were to take. You gave your good Spirit to instruct them. You did not withhold your manna from their mouths, and you gave them water for their thirst. For forty years you sustained them in the desert; they lacked nothing, their clothes did not wear out nor did their feet become swollen (Neh 9:20). For many years you were patient with them. By your Spirit you admonished them through your prophets. Yet they paid no attention, so you handed them over to the neighboring peoples (9:30).

In the wilderness, they were not abandoned but were guided by the pillar of cloud and fire. Also, Yahweh gave his "good *rûaḥ* to instruct them," to provide for them, and to sustain them on their journey. The nature of their instruction included the sending of prophets, the greatest of whom was Moses, to warn them through the *rûaḥ*. The recital makes clear that although the nation continually rejected God's rule through the emissaries sent to them, Yahweh patiently instructed Israel. The prophets endowed with the Spirit were inspired and authorized to call the people back into a covenantal relationship, but "they did not listen" (9:8b; cf. 1 Kgs 18:4, 13; 19:10, 14; 2 Chron 24:21).

The Spirit and the Leadership of the Priests

The importance of the priesthood in Israel is partially indicated by the length of their leadership duties in the nation. The leadership role of the priests preceded the office of both prophet and king and lasted beyond their services. Yet, the goal of all three of these positions was the maintenance of the covenant relationship between Yahweh and Israel.

In the light of the importance that the priesthood held, it is not surprising that priests, like kings and prophets, should be anointed for their functions (Exod 30:22–29; 40:9–11; Lev 8:10f.;

Num 3:2–4). The ritual of anointing consecrated the priests and Levites for their sacred ministries. The Levites were in charge of dismantling, carrying, and erecting the sacred tabernacle (Num 1:47–54). They camped around it and served the priesthood (Num 1:51–53; 3:5–10). They were substitutes and representatives of the firstborn of other tribes (Exod 4:22; 13:12–13). The responsibilities of the priesthood entailed the discerning of oracles (Deut 33:8–11; 1 Sam 14:41–42), the offering of sacrifices (Exod 30:10; Lev 1:14–15; 5:8; 16:29–34), and the teaching of the law *[tōrāh]*, that is, both practical and theological instruction (Deut 31:9, 26; Ezra 7:10). Although there is some evidence that the priests gave oracles to petitioners at the temple (1 Sam 1; Pss 20; 21; 50), because of the dearth of materials it is difficult to set forth specific details concerning private prophetic utterances. What is evident, however, is that priests on occasion prophesied under the inspiration of the *rûaḥ*.[71]

The Hand of the Lord: Ezekiel and Ezra

Perhaps the main paradigm of a priest who ministered under the *rûaḥ* was Ezekiel (I discuss his prophetic ministry more fully in ch. 5). The *rûaḥ* was manifested in a variety of ways in his ministry. Thus, one might anticipate that even the Levitical priests manifested prophetic characteristics when the Spirit came upon them. This phenomenon is mainly recorded in 1 and 2 Chronicles.

A particular phrase that is evident in a number of OT books occurs often in the books of Ezekiel and Ezra, namely, "the hand of the Lord" or "the hand of God." Because of the particular ecstatic aberrations of some prophets, and also among the prophets of Baal, there is some reluctance to refer to the *rûaḥ* of God in Jeremiah, Amos, Habakkuk, and Zephaniah. Therefore, they use other terms to refer to the presence and enabling of God. Ezekiel does not have a problem in referring to the Spirit of God, but in his prophecy he uses both the "Spirit of the Lord" and the "hand of the Lord" to indicate God's work through his ministry that helps him in his particular leadership duties. In the

[71] See de Vaux, *Ancient Israel,* 1.273–86; F. M. Cross, "The Priestly Houses of Early Israel," *Canaanite Myth and Hebrew Epic* (Harvard University Press, 1973), 195ff.; W. O. McCready, "Priests and Levites," *ISBE,* 3.965–70.

case of David, both the Spirit of God and the hand of the Lord are involved in transmitting and inspiring the plans for the temple (1 Chron 28:12, 19). A similar merging of this concept occurs in the NT Gospels where the "hand" or "finger" of the Lord may refer to the Spirit of God (Luke 11:20; Matt 12:28), and signifies the mighty acts of God.

At the river Kebar the hand of the Lord first comes upon Ezekiel the priest (Ezek 1:3). From that time onward he is commissioned and continually "controlled" by the divine presence as indicated by the Spirit and the hand of the Lord (3:14, 22; 8:1–4; 33:22; 40:1). "The hand of the LORD was upon me, and he brought me out by the Spirit of the LORD" (37:1). This experience of being under the "hand of the Lord" was also realized by Elijah (1 Kgs 18:46), Elisha (2 Kgs 3:15), Isaiah (Isa 8:11), and Jeremiah (Jer 15:17). In the two hundred OT references to the "hand of the Lord/God," most refer to the power of God by which he demonstrates his ability to fulfill his word, deliver, inspire, or create (cf. 1 Kgs 8:15, 24; Isa 45:12; 48:13; 48:2).[72] The "hand of the Lord" also protects those whom he holds (1 Kgs 18:46; Ezra 8:22). For Ezekiel, the hand of the Lord moves him according to the divine will to convey dramatically and verbally the word of the Lord to the exilic community.

Ezra does not take on a prophetic role as such, but the "hand of the Lord his God" plays a prominent role in his responsibilities. We have noted the pronounced place of the Spirit of God during the restoration process, and find ample testimony in the books of Ezra and Nehemiah that the Lord directs the restoration according to his design. First God "stirs up" the spirit of Cyrus and motivates the Persian king to initiate a new foreign policy in favor of all exiles who desire to return to their land (Ezra 1:1). Then he selects prominent leaders to take charge of the restoration process. Ezra is not only a priest in the lineage of Aaron (7:1–6), but a scribe and an administrator in the royal court (7:6, 11). In summary of his role, Ezra 7:10 concludes, "For Ezra had devoted himself to the study and observance of the Law of the LORD, and to teaching its decrees and laws in Israel." Ezra was not only a proficient scholar of the law, but he applied it practically to his life and ministry, and therefore was an able

[72] W. Zimmerli, *Ezekiel 1: A Commentary on the Book of the Prophet Ezekiel Chapters 1–24* (Hermeneia; trans. R. E. Clements; Philadelphia: Fortress, 1979) 42, 117f.; see also P. R. Ackroyd, "*yād*," *TDOT*, 5.418–26.

teacher of the word. In all his successes, Ezra gives credit to the presence of God in his life.

One of the benefits experienced by Ezra because of the presence of God was favor with the Persian administration. "The king had granted him everything he asked, for the hand of the Lord his God was on him" (Ezra 7:6, 28; cf. Neh 2:8, 18). Also, God granted Ezra a safe and speedy journey (7:9). In fact, Ezra was reluctant to accept an armed escort because he had claimed divine protection: "the gracious hand of our God is on everyone who looks to him" (8:22; cf. v. 31). In addition, God helped them in the selection of personnel for the return to Jerusalem and the work there (8:18). Although no inspired prophetic utterances are recorded in Ezra, the equipping for his crucial ministry is attributed to the divine presence of God.

The Levitical Priests: Inspired Oracles

In some exilic passages, the coming of the *rûaḥ* on the priests was mainly to inspire an oracle or to give a word of encouragement. These prophetic sermons have several similar elements: (1) the quotation of an ancient or prophetic source; (2) the selection of a theological principle with corresponding application to Israel's circumstances in the past; and (3) a call to the present community to act on the word of the Lord.[73]

Amasai is "clothed" with the *rûaḥ* that inspires him to offer David an eloquent word of reassurance, "We are yours, O David! We are with you, O son of Jesse! Success, success to you, and success to those who help you, for your God will help you" (1 Chron 12:18 [MT 12:19]). In this case Amasai helps David in the selection of leaders in a manner similar to the practice of some prophets who gave directions in holy war. Azariah is inspired by the *rûaḥ yhwh* to exhort Asa to enforce cultic reforms (2 Chron 15:1). The authority of his prophetic word is recognized by the king and results in the removal of detestable idols from the land. Subsequently, Asa leads the people in a rare covenant renewal where the people are encouraged to seek the Lord with all their heart and soul (15:12ff.).

[73] See G. von Rad, "The Levitical Sermon in 1 and 2 Chronicles," *The Problem of the Hexateuch and Other Essays* (trans. E. W. Trueman Dicken; London: Oliver & Boyd, 1965) 271ff.

Jahaziel is inspired by the *rûaḥ yhwh* to speak forth an oracle of salvation (2 Chron 20:14–17). Zechariah is inspired to preach a word of exhortation to the people when the *rûaḥ yhwh* comes on him (24:14). In these examples, the inspiration of the prophets is associated with the *rûaḥ yhwh* that directs reforms in the nation and guides Israel according to the plan and purposes of Yahweh. The importance of the prophetic word that is inspired by the Spirit and set in the context of the exile concerns the future reign of Yahweh through his leaders. In fact, as J. D. Newsome, Jr., claims, "The Chronicler goes to great lengths to affirm his belief that the kingdom came into being in response to the prophetic word and that the word was active in guiding and sustaining the kingdom."[74]

Charismatic Leadership

We have observed a wide range of leadership styles and functions in this chapter. The common denominator is the influence of the Spirit of God on chosen leaders to fulfill specific purposes in the life of the nation. In order to fulfill these purposes, God gives the *rûaḥ* to provide the necessary charisma, with the necessary energy and resources required for a task. In this sense, the leadership provided by God for Israel is not only charismatic but supernatural. That is, in God's estimation, the natural skills and resources inherent in chosen leaders are insufficient for the accomplishment of the divine purposes. Therefore, God intervenes by endowing them with the Spirit. It is the Spirit who enables and makes the leadership roles of those who are endowed successful.

As noted, charismatic leadership may involve a variety of experiences and results. For some individuals, such as the Messiah, the gifts are numerous and provide for a wide range of responsibilities. In the case of the judges and some kings, the gifts pertain mainly to military prowess, the ability to motivate people to battle, and the ability to organize. For others, dreams and visions, together with the ability to interpret them, are part of the gifts required for administration. Others have unusual

[74] J. D. Newsome, Jr., "Toward a New Understanding of the Chronicler and His Purposes," *JBL* 94 (1975) 203.

wisdom and knowledge that enable good administration. For the prophets, the influence of the Spirit causes them to receive revelation, inspiration, and illumination. Through the Spirit they are empowered to deliver difficult messages within hostile circumstances. Prophets, priests, and on occasion kings proclaim oracles to the nation. Thus, leadership in every era of Israel's history includes the presence and direction of the Spirit that assists Israel throughout their spiritual pilgrimage.

5

The Spirit of God in Prophecy

And afterward, I will pour out my Spirit on all people. Your sons and daughters will prophesy, your old men will dream dreams, your young men will see visions. Even on my servants, both men and women, I will pour out my Spirit in those days. (Joel 2:28–29 [3:1–2 MT])

Numerous OT passages refer to the *rûaḥ* in relation to the gift of prophecy. While the office of prophet seems to have arisen in conjunction with kingship, prophetic activity was evident even before the monarchy era. The influence of the *rûaḥ* on the prophets resulted in a variety of manifestations, such as prophesying, reception of both auditory and visual revelations, inspiration, and the proclamation of messages. In this chapter we examine passages referring to the *rûaḥ* that indicate the nature of prophecy in Israel. Various issues regarding prophecy are discussed as they arise from texts mentioning the *rûaḥ*. Also, the larger context of prophecy in the ancient Near East as it relates to Israel is considered as a background to the OT theology on the subject. The main personalities in this overview are Moses, the seventy elders, Balaam, Saul, David, Elijah, Elisha, Micaiah, Ezekiel, and Micah.

Prophecy in the Ancient Near East

In recent years the framework for understanding prophecy in the ancient Near East and in Israel has significantly broadened.

Literature from different sites and royal courts has been discovered that sheds some light on Israel's own experience of prophetic inspiration. Although many aspects concerning the development, content, character, and significance of prophecy remain obscure, a number of similarities between Israel's experience and that of the surrounding cultures will provide background knowledge of the origins of prophecy. The main elements of prophecy in the ancient Near East, as characterized by H. B. Huffmon, include a communication from the divine world, normally for a third party through a mediator (prophet), who may or may not be identified with the deity. The prophet may be inspired through an ecstatic experience, dreams, or what may be called inner illumination. It is an immediate message that does not require a technical specialist to interpret it, nor is it solicited. The message is usually exhortatory or admonitory.[1]

Some literary materials from cultures surrounding Israel indicate both similarities and dissimilarities to Israel's prophetic literature. For instance, the "Prophecy of Nefer-rohu" purports to be a prophetic tract in the sense of foretelling particular events during the reign of King Snefru of the Fourth Dynasty. In apocalyptic terms, the main section details the depravity and chaos that would come on the land. It forecasts a period of social decadence and foreign domination that leads to the downfall of the Old Kingdom. With messianic overtones, the named king will right the wrongs, restore justice and order over a united kingdom, and repatriate the foreigners.[2]

This document is considered to be representative of propaganda writing that assumes the style of "prophetic utterance" to proclaim Amenmehet I as the deliverer of Egypt. It also serves to present his program of administrative and social reform.[3] This type of prophecy is used to authorize and advance the political and religious views of the leadership. In addition, it is motivated

---

[1] H. B. Huffmon, "Prophecy in the Mari Letters," *BA* 31 (1968) 103; See also H. B. Huffmon, "The Origins of Prophecy," *Magnalia Dei: The Mighty Acts of God* (ed. F. M. Cross et al; Garden City: Doubleday, 1976) 172; H. Ringgren, "Prophecy in the Ancient Near East," *Israel's Prophetic Tradition* (ed. R. Coggins et al; Cambridge: Cambridge University Press, 1982) 1–11.

[2] J. A. Wilson, "The Prophecy of Nefer-rohu," *ANET,* 446.

[3] See R. K. Harrison, *Old Testament Times* (Grand Rapids: Eerdmans, 1970) 110; Also J. A. Wilson, *The Culture of Ancient Egypt* (Chicago: University of Chicago Press, 1951) 125ff.

by a period of historical upheaval and seeks to provide an agenda for change. Often the political directions are given after the crisis begins, whereas in Israel the crisis lies in the future and may be averted if a right response to Yahweh is effected.[4]

From Phoenicia, a text possibly dating from 1100 BC describes an occurrence of prophetic frenzy. An official from the temple of Amon at Karnak is sent to Byblos to purchase lumber but is treated poorly by the prince. When the official is continually told to leave empty-handed, a youth, presumably from the prince's court, is seized with prophetic frenzy. "Now while he was making offering to his gods, the god seized one of his youths and made him possessed. And he said to him: Bring up [the god]! Bring the messenger who is carrying him! Amon is the one who sent him out! He is the one who made him come!"[5] A prophetic function of some kind is practiced and appears to carry some influential authority in the court.

Some of the main correspondences to Israelite prophecy have been found in tablets at Mari, an influential center in Mesopotamia during the third and early second millennia BC. Prophetic literature, discovered along with other documents, illustrate some interesting similarities with biblical prophetic functionaries (ca. 1828–1758 BC). Within the Mari prophetic texts, a number of designations are applied to various functionaries.[6] Some refer to the *āpilu,* which generally means "to respond or to answer," and may indicate the result which the functionary receives as a response to questions put to a god or solicited by him in some way. The servant then passes on the message of the god and leaves it to the king to consider what actions to take. Another professional functionary is referred to as the *muḫûm,* the root of which means "to rave" or "become frenzied" or ecstatic. They convey messages to the king concerning details of

---

[4] See R. R. Wilson, "Early Israelite Prophecy," *Int* 32 (1978) 10; S. Herrmann, "Prophetie in Israel und Agypten," VTSup 8 (Leiden: Brill, 1963) 53–64.

[5] Wilson, R. R., "The Journey of Wen-Amon to Phoenicia," *ANET,* 26.

[6] See J. F. Craghan, "Mari and Its Prophets: The Contributions of Mari to the Understanding of Biblical Prophecy," *BibTheoBul* 5 (1975) 32–55; A. Malamat, "Prophetic Revelations in New Documents from Mari and the Bible," VTSup 15 (Leiden: Brill, 1966) 207–27; W. Moran, "New Evidence from Mari on the History of Prophecy," *Bib* 50 (1969) 15–56; J. F. Ross, "Prophecy in Hamath, Israel, and Mari," *HTR* 63 (1970) 1–28.

sacrifices or buildings. The *assinnu* is another functionary who serves as a male eunuch cult prostitute. He delivers messages from the goddess, at times accompanied by ecstatic behavior, and usually warns the kings of plots against them.

The main content of the messages brought by these functionaries regards matters of the cult and the royal administration. In one instance the king is admonished for his failure to recognize the gods and their needs, usually in matters of cultus and temple. A sacrifice may have been neglected or the maintenance of a temple may have been avoided. These admonitions are designed to move the king to actively pursue his duties.[7] Political relations are also addressed in oracles. The king may be encouraged by the oracle where the foe is denounced and victory is proclaimed for Mari. The salvation oracle is often contingent on the king's response to the prophetic word, both in matters of cultus and social concerns, where he is encouraged to rule with justice and equity.

It is from the OT itself that we have evidence of Canaanite prophetic practices. Although Israel is warned to rid itself of the Canaanite influence, the culture and practices of the people are a constant temptation to Israel (cf. Deut 7–8; 13:1–5; 18:9–15; Lev 18:3). The tendency for the population in the north towards Baalism increases until finally, with Ahab's marriage to Jezebel, the Baal cult threatens to replace Yahwism completely (1 Kgs 18:4–19; 19:10–14). The main inroads of Canaanite practice become prominent during the Omride dynasty (ca. 876–869 BC). Altars and cultic personnel, mainly priests (1 Kgs 18:19) and prophets (2 Kgs 10:19), are introduced.[8] Jezebel's hostility towards the prophets of Yahweh increases to the point where she seeks to exterminate them and replace them with prophets of Baal and Asherah who enjoy official status (1 Kgs 18:19).

Though many prophets remain faithful to Yahweh during this period, others compromise their trust and prophesy by Baal in support of the apostate kings of the north (1 Kgs 22).

---

[7] The building of temples and their maintenance as well as cultic responsibilities like sacrifices and the feeding of the gods were duties of the king in Mesopotamia. A king was often censured and evaluated by his disposal of this duty. See A. L. Oppenheim, *Ancient Mesopotamia* (Chicago: University of Chicago Press, 1964) 183–197.

[8] See L. Bronner, *The Stories of Elijah and Elisha As Polemics Against Baal Worship* (Leiden: Brill, 1968).

Into this situation comes Elijah, who confronts the claims of the prophets of Baal and tells them to solicit proof of Baal's deity by sending fire (1 Kgs 18:24ff.). The prophets of Baal cry out, "O Baal, answer us!" Their cries are accompanied by self-mutilation and frantic prophesying, all to no avail. This kind of frantic prophesying has given rise to speculation that Israelite prophecy was influenced by the prophets of Baal. Although some prophets are said to "prophesy by Baal" (Jer 2:8; 23:13), and others exhibit ecstatic behavior (1 Sam 10:9ff.; 18:10; 19:20–24), it is unclear how this influences prophecy in Israel. Since there are no specific texts from Canaanite/Ugaritic prophetic oracles, it is speculative at best to see this as a determinative influence in Israel.[9]

The Rise of Prophecy in Israel

Whereas the office of the prophet *[nāḇîʾ]* first arises along with kingship, the role of a prophet is already set forth in the Pentateuch. The term "prophet" occurs fourteen times in the Pentateuch and refers to Abraham (Gen 20:7), Aaron (Exod 7:1), and predominately Moses (Deut 34:10).[10] In connection with this title, Abraham is told to make intercession for Abimelech as he did earlier for Sodom (Gen 18:17). Like the latter prophets, he receives divine revelation and speaks with God personally (Gen 15:1ff.). Aaron was Moses' prophet in the sense of being his spokesman. The request of Israel for a prophet in the sense of a mediator arises in connection with the theophany at Sinai. Expressing fear and awe for Yahweh's presence, Israel responds to Moses, "Speak to us yourself and we will listen. But do not have God speak to us or we will die" (Exod 20:19; cf. Deut 5:23–27).

---

[9] Some maintain that ecstasy was typical of Israelite prophecy once inherited from the Canaanites. See the summary in D. L. Petersen, *The Roles of Israel's Prophets* (Sheffield: JSOT, 1981) 26; Also see M. Fishbane's perceptive article on the uniqueness of prophecy in Israel as compared to that of the ancient Near East (especially pp. 67–69); "Biblical Prophecy as a Religious Phenomenon," *Jewish Spirituality* (ed. A. Green; London: SCM, 1989) 62–81.

[10] Other occurrences of the term *nāḇîʾ* are in Num 11:29; 12:6; and Deut 13:2–18; 18:22; See Zimmerli, "Der Prophet im Pentateuch," 197–211.

Thus, mediators become a vital factor in conveying God's revelation to Israel.

Because of his great responsibilities in leadership, Moses requests help from the Lord with his task. Seventy elders are chosen and given the Spirit, by which they prophesy. This characteristic functions to legitimize their role as leaders. The desire of Moses that "all the Lord's people were prophets" has an eschatological dimension to it in which the hope refers implicitly to the individuals' intimate relationship with Yahweh and a serious undertaking of their covenant obligations.

The threat of illegitimate means of receiving revelation and of communicating falsehood was a concern requiring specific guidelines. False prophecy is due to human nature and the possibility of deterioration in the communication process. Abusing one's office as prophet by promoting idolatry was against God's revealed commandment (Deut 13:1–6). Thus, the message and the person need constant evaluation. Two fundamental criteria for evaluation involved that of total allegiance to Yahweh and the fulfillment or nonfulfillment of a prophetic word (18:22). Yahweh reveals his sovereign omniscience by foretelling future events to the prophets and then brings about those events through his omnipotence. This is clearly illustrated in the former Prophets. First Samuel marks a new beginning in the prophetic movement and all that it involves. A bleak picture of the religious climate in Israel is presented at Shiloh, but the piety of Elkanah and Hannah, who maintain their faith in Yahweh, provides hope. In answer to Hannah's prayer, Yahweh providentially provides this barren woman with a son. The unique circumstances of the narrative prepare the reader for Samuel's call and rise as prophet (1 Sam 3:19–20). He is contrasted with Eli and shown to be Eli's rightful successor (2:11–27). The prophecy ending this section foretells the end of the Elides and indicates a reversal of the wickedness and apostasy of that generation. With Samuel, a turning point in the prophetic history is evident.

Reference to the word of Yahweh as "rare" (1 Sam 3:1) makes clear that oracles or messages from Yahweh to Israel were infrequent during the period of the judges. Samuel is the vessel through whom Yahweh speaks to Israel. He is recognized as a prophet whose word is substantiated and sure (3:19–21). The term for "prophet" in the OT is generally *nāḇîʾ*, referring to "the called one." Other terms relating to prophetism are "seer" *[rōʾeh]* and "visionary" *[ḥōzeh]*. In Samuel the seer seems to be connected to a city where he is esteemed as one who responds to inquiries for a fee (1 Sam 9:9–19). The context of the text indicates that seer may be an archaic term referring to one who enacts his role in the setting of the sacrificial system.[11] The distinction between these terms could be that the prophet stressed the objective work of the messenger in speaking God's word while the seer emphasized the subjective element of receiving the revelation.[12]

Moses and the Seventy Elders: Numbers 11:25

The first narrative indicating the influence of the *rûaḥ* in relation to prophecy occurs in Numbers 11:16–30. Moses gathers the seventy elders in obedience to Yahweh's direction so that Yahweh could "take" from the *rûaḥ* on him and bestow some of the *rûaḥ* on each of the elders. The verb *ʾâṣal* indicates the "withholding" of a portion of the *rûaḥ* that is on Moses for his leadership duties and is then distributed among the elders for their new responsibilities. The term emphasizes the great endowment of Spirit on Moses and is conceived of materially and quantitatively.[13] This event occurs at a crucial point in the history of Israel when the leadership burden on Moses becomes unbearable. By virtue of the Spirit-endowment, the elders are now equipped by the *rûaḥ* to function in a leadership capacity alongside Moses. The transfer of the Spirit is therefore both paradigmatic and programmatic for leadership in Israel.

The immediate consequence of the *rûaḥ* resting on the seventy elders is their spontaneous expression of "prophesying" *[wayyitnabbʾû]* (Num 11:25). Not only do the elders "prophesy" at the Tent of Meeting, but Eldad and Medad, who are in the camp, also "prophesy" (Num 11:27). The nature of this ecstatic activity and what it consists of is difficult to determine. But the external manifestation of ecstatic behavior serves to indicate the internal reception of the Spirit. The supernaturally influenced

---

[11] Petersen, *Roles of Israel's Prophets,* 44.

[12] W. White, "*rōʾeh,*" *TWOT,* 1.823.

[13] See G. B. Gray, *Numbers: A Critical and Exegetical Commentary* (ICC; Edinburgh: T. & T. Clark Ltd., 1903) 110f.; cf. Neve, *Spirit of God,* 18.

prophesying is an indicator of the divine commissioning and enabling for public office. The coming of the *rûaḥ* and the subsequent prophesying is a public and tangible event indicating to both the elders and the people that the seventy are set apart and equipped for a vital role of leadership in the community. Through this experience, the elders are assured of Spirit-reception. The ecstatic nature of the prophesying is not uncontrolled nor is it viewed in a negative way in this passage. Although it is evident in some OT passages that raving and "being beside oneself" are associated with "prophesying" (1 Sam 18:10; 19:18f.), this kind of expression is not evident in the activity of the seventy elders.[14] A similar public manifestation occurs on the day of Pentecost (Acts 2:1ff.).

Joshua immediately understands that the bestowal of the *rûaḥ* indicates new leadership responsibilities for the elders and for some reason he fears that this impinges on the authority of Moses (cf. Num 11:28). The incident following this event does indicate a threat to Mosaic leadership (cf. ch. 12). But the Eldad and Medad pericope anticipates Moses' statement regarding the programmatic hope that all God's people will be prophets. Moses assures Joshua that this event is divinely orchestrated and part of Yahweh's programmatic plan. All those selected by Yahweh are eligible for Spirit-reception.

From the Pentateuchal understanding of what it means to be a prophet, Moses' hope for all God's people refers to the reception of revelation as well as to various aspects of mediation and intercession. For Moses, the experience of prophetism begins with a call (Exod 3:1–4), and includes intimate "face-to-face" communication with Yahweh (Exod 33:11; Deut 34:10). Moses is, therefore, the paradigmatic prototype of a prophet (Deut 18:15–18). His relationship with Yahweh and his power in ministry are unequaled. "For no one has ever shown the mighty power or performed the awesome deeds that Moses did in the sight of Israel" (Deut 34:12). Implicit in Moses' desire for the people to be prophets is the removal of the fear that gripped the people when they heard directly from Yahweh (Exod 20:19). These elements are part of Yahweh's intention for all of his

[14] See H. H. Rowley, "The Nature of Old Testament Prophecy in the Light of Recent Study," *The Servant of the Lord and Other Essays on the Old Testament* (Oxford: Basil Blackwell, 1965) 97ff.; A. Guillaume, *Prophecy and Divination* (London: Hodder and Stoughton, 1938) 114, 293.

people. Reception of the *rûaḥ* moved them one step closer to Yahweh's goal of making a kingdom of priests and a holy nation of his people (Exod 19:6).

Ecstatic Prophecy and the Spirit

Negative statements concerning prophets are often made in reference to ecstatic behavior. Hosea serves in a period when prophets are considered fools and those with ecstatic behavior ("inspired men," Hos 9:7; cf. 2 Kgs 9:11) are called maniacs. In Jeremiah's time, such "madmen" who act like prophets are placed in stocks (Jer 29:26). In both early and late prophetic literature, the relationship of the Spirit to ecstatic experiences is noted. Perhaps because of the Spirit-ecstasy association, particularly in the eighth century, there is evidence of a growing disdain for Spirit-induced ecstatic behavior. Although ecstatic behavior is downplayed and restrained by the predominance of the "word" in the writing prophets, the association of Spirit and ecstasy always remained a factor in Israel's prophetic circles.[15] In both the OT and the ancient Near East, ecstatic behavior is evidenced within prophetic communities. For example, functionaries at Mari, referred to as the *muḫḫûm*, are considered part of the cultic personnel. Limited references are made to singers and beer, which are provided for the ecstatics and allude to the practice of inducements used to promote an "ecstatic" state.[16] The significance of the ecstatic behavior at Mari appears to be a way of legitimizing the functionary's message.

The distinctive features of ecstatic prophecy that M. Haran claims are typical of preclassical prophecy in the ancient Near East are: (1) collective ecstasy as a mode of activity in prophetic bands (cf. 1 Sam 10:5–6, 10–13; 19:20–24; Num 11:24–30), (2) the use of instruments to awaken ecstasy and inspiration (2 Kgs 3:15; 1 Sam 10:5; cf. Exod 15:20), (3) the propensity to special places of oracular activity (e.g., Sinai—the mountain site was sacred), (4) an attraction to permanent institutions of oracular activity in which group ecstasy and inspiration take place (e.g., the Tent of

---

[15] Kraus, *Worship in Israel*, 102.
[16] Huffmon, "Prophecy in the Mari Letters," 112.

Meeting; cf. Exod 33:5–11; Num 11:16–17, 24–30; 12:4–10; Deut 31:14–15), and (5) a connection to the house of God or temple as the place of revelation (1 Sam 3:3–10; Isa 6).[17]

Haran and others are correct in observing ecstasy as part of the early preclassical experience of the prophets, but they do not go far enough in showing that ecstatic activity is not common to all of Israel's early prophets. The many similarities of ecstatic experiences in various cultures indicate that this is a sociological and anthropological tendency.[18] Whereas the nature of ecstatic prophecy is not completely clear from the biblical data, anthropological studies show that ecstasy may have a variety of manifestations, ranging from dancing dervishes, mantic frenzy, and trances to controlled utterance. From a sociological perspective, the revelatory or auditory condition is an experience characterized by unnatural activities that serve to externally indicate supernatural influences.

Some clues regarding the nature of prophesying are evident in the terms used. The hithpael and niphal forms of the root *nbʾ* convey the thought of one acting or behaving like a *nābîʾ* (the experience of trances, verbal prophesying, etc.). The nature of this prophetic activity is often "ecstatic." The root *nbʾ* is most likely to be understood in the passive sense of "the called one" rather than the more active sense of "proclaimer."[19] This conclusion is usually arrived at because the hithpael form occurs frequently in contexts where ecstatic behavior is observed (1 Sam 10:5ff.; 19:20ff.; 1 Kgs 22:10). But R. R. Wilson claims that the semantic development theory where the hithpael form indicates ecstatic activity and the niphal form comes to be associated with intelligible speech is oversimplified.[20] A. G. Auld sees no distinction between the two verbal themes and claims that the variation of the forms in the same context is entirely stylistic.[21] The latter observation is mainly made from passages in Jeremiah and Kings, but it is generally true that the verbal themes are used inter-

---

[17] M. Haran, "From Early to Classical Prophecy: Continuity and Change," *VT* 27 (1977) 385–97.

[18] See J. Lindblom, *Prophecy in Ancient Israel* (Philadelphia: Muhlenberg; Oxford: Basil Blackwell, 1962) 6ff.

[19] R. Rendtorff, "*prophetes*," *TDNT*, 6:797.

[20] R. R. Wilson, "Prophecy and Ecstasy: A Reexamination," *JBL* 98 (1979) 329–30.

[21] A. G. Auld, "Prophets and Prophecy in Jeremiah and Kings," *ZAW* 96 (1984) 67.

changeably. However, the ecstatic nature of prophecy is often more explicit in passages which use the hithpael forms.

Characteristics that follow the coming of the Spirit on prophets include orgiastic prophetic ecstasy (verbal utterances; Num 11; 1 Sam 5–10). This type of ecstasy is apparently contagious (1 Sam 19:20ff.) and causes Saul to strip naked and prophesy for a day and a night. Visions and auditory revelations are also transmitted by the Spirit or by the hand of the Lord (Ezek 3:1ff.; cf. 2 Kgs 3:15). When the power of the Lord comes on Elijah after his victory over the priests of Baal, he runs all the way to Jezreel (1 Kgs 18:46). Supernatural revelatory knowledge is imparted to the prophets on occasion that gives them special insights into the spirit world and into events that are not seen in the natural realm (2 Kgs 6:12, 17, 32). Elisha's *rûaḥ* could even discern what his servant was doing. He asks, "Was not my spirit with you when the man got down from his chariot to meet you?" (2 Kgs 5:26). Whereas these features of Spirit-induced, ecstatic-revelatory activity are positive, the danger of ecstatic behavior as exhibited in the activities of priests and prophets in other groups threaten pure Yahwism. This is illustrated by the activity of the prophets of Baal in response to Elijah's taunts: "So they shouted louder and slashed themselves with swords and spears, as was their custom, until their blood flowed. Midday passed, and they continued their frantic prophesying until the time for the evening sacrifice. But there was no response, no one answered, no one paid attention" (1 Kgs 18:28–29).

Jeremiah specifically denounces the prophets of Samaria who prophesy by Baal and lead Israel astray (Jer 23:13). According to him, these prophets, who are probably associated with syncretistic cults at the high places, are inspired by Baal and exhibit ecstatic behavior in seeking inspiration and answers from their deity. Some writers, such as J. Blenkinsopp, claim that there is little to distinguish this type of ecstasy, including the slashing and frantic behavior, from that of the sons of the prophets who are associated with Samuel, Elijah, and Elisha.[22] But there is not much OT evidence to show that Israel's prophets exhibit the more negative features of ecstatic prophecy. In fact, they seem to avoid this association in their materials. It is particularly this perceived notion that led to the silence among

[22] J. Blenkinsopp, *A History of Prophecy in Israel* (Philadelphia: Westminster, 1983) 55.

many prophets in relation to Spirit-reception and inspiration. They feature mainly a direct relationship with Yahweh and the inspiration of the word that comes to them. Lindblom claims: "The reason for the infrequent references to *rûaḥ* in the accounts of the revelatory experiences of the great prophets was essentially theocentric. In every situation they were in the presence of Yahweh and under His constraint. What they uttered was the word of Yahweh, and what they saw and heard in their visions came from Him. Yahweh had sent them, consequently Yahweh Himself dictated to them the oracles and messages they had to deliver. Accordingly, they had no need of intermediary power such as the spirit."[23] Rather than complicate the issue, the writing prophets identify the reception of the word in other ways than simply through the Spirit. What seems to be clear from the OT accounts is that in Israel the prophets who experience ecstasy do so as a by-product of the conscious reality of God's presence and Spirit. The OT focus is on the verbal utterances of the prophets.

Balaam: Numbers 22:1–24:25

The *rûaḥ ʾelōhîm* is not restricted only to individual Israelites but also comes on a Gentile named Balaam. The Balaam narratives present an important aspect of the role of the *rûaḥ* in prophecy. The events leading up to the inspiration of the *rûaḥ ʾelōhîm* are integral to this discussion which sheds light on the prophetic elements involved.

The growing threat of Israel's presence along the Jordan caused fear to arise in those dwelling in Canaan. Moab saw Israel's encroachment as a serious problem calling for action. Balak, king of Moab, sent for the services of Balaam, son of Beor, in order to hire his talents as a "diviner" (*qōsem;* Num 22:7). In the ancient Near East divination was a popular technique of communication with supernatural forces that was believed to provide direction for a group or individual regarding their destiny. Large collections of omens, clay models, and records testify to the importance of divination in the Near East. Various technical means were devised that were thought to have magical

[23] Lindblom, *Prophecy in Ancient Israel,* 178.

potency in manipulating the actions of the gods for the benefit of human beings.[24] The diviner devised operational or magical means of communication. Operational means involved the casting of lots or smoke from a censor to indicate a yes or no answer by the deity. Magical conceptions held that the deity produced changes in natural phenomena such as the weather, stars, or animal viscera based on a code acceptable to both the deity and the diviner. This elaborate code took much learning within a guild where apprentices were taught by their masters.[25]

Divination was prohibited in Israel (Lev 19:26; 20:27; Deut 18:9–14; 2 Kgs 17:17), especially when associated with magic and sorcery. Lots and dreams were often considered valid forms of direction, but Yahweh was recognized as sovereignly involved in providing direction through such means (cf. Prov 16:33). When dreams are given (Gen 40:5–8; 41:1–8; 44:4, 15; Dan 1:17; 2:1–11), it is Yahweh who provides the interpretation and meaning through Spirit-filled servants (e.g., Joseph and Daniel). It is the prophetic word inspired by the Spirit that provides direction for Israel. Diviners were usually associated with the false prophets (Jer 27:9; 29:8; Ezek 13:6–9, 23; Mic 3:6f.; Zech 10:2).

Some scholars try to align the Near Eastern view of a diviner with some Israelite prophetic practices, and in particular with Balaam. In this view, the terms visionary, seer, man of God, and prophet are technical terms from Israel's early history. Connections between the prophet and diviner or seer are sought in the phenomenon of ecstasy. Both diviners and prophets were considered proponents of God's word and received directions from God through dreams, objects, and sounds.[26] The OT character who gives rise to such claims is Balaam, who is not only called a diviner (Josh 13:22) but one who tries to reverse God's blessing of Israel by means of a curse. The Near Eastern concept of the power of the spoken word is reflected in the narratives of Balaam. The word was

---

[24] Guillaume, *Prophecy and Divination,* 107ff.

[25] Oppenheim, *Ancient Mesopotamia,* 208. Various forms of operational means included augury (interpreting the flight of birds), hepatoscopy (the formation of livers), extispicy (the formation of viscera), astrology, leconmancy (smoke from the censor), libonomancy (oil in water), and the interpretation of dreams. Based on these forms of divination predictions concerning the future were made. Reports were made and records kept of the events that preceded and followed a technique.

[26] H. M. Orlinsky, "The Seer in Ancient Israel," *Oriens Antiquus* 4 (1965) 154–55.

considered a mighty and terrifying power that could prove effective in all spheres of life when spoken by the "right" functionary.[27] Although Balaam's curse was believed to be effective, it was thwarted by the sovereignty of God, who in the end has Balaam speak divinely inspired words (Num 22:35, 38; 23:5, 16, 26). It is because of the words he speaks, and not his practice of divination, that Balaam is aligned with the prophets.

Numbers 22–24 presents Balaam as a seer who is capable of receiving divine revelations from "his" God (Num 22:18). The term "seer" *[rōʾeh]* is used in reference to Samuel (1 Sam 9:9), who responds to inquiries for a fee. The seer is not necessarily one who dreams and sees visions for revelations but one who is allowed by Yahweh to perceive a divine communication for specific situations. The term "seer" is related to the word "visionary" and "prophet" and mainly indicates one of the functions of the prophet. This becomes clear from the predominant use of the *leitwort rāʾāh* ["to see"], which occurs over twenty times in the narrative.[28] The role of Balaam was to look into the future or into the unseen reality behind a situation for direction. The paradox of the Balaam episode is that the professional seer cannot perceive the reality of the situation, while the ass does, until God opens his eyes (Num 22:31). The "opening of the eyes" is something God must do and is what occurs subsequent to the coming of the *rûaḥ ʾelōhîm* on Balaam (cf. 24:1ff.).

Balak's main purpose in hiring Balaam is to have him speak a curse over Israel. This is a dominate theme in the narrative. Two words for "curse" are used, the first of which appears seven times *(ʾārûr)* and the second nine times *(qāḇaḇ)*. The curse was perceived to have inherent power to effect a reversal of the state of blessing or to set into effect misfortune. A magical understanding of the spoken word that could bring about the destruction of Israel and safety for Moab is evident in Balak's request.[29] The narrative makes clear that Balaam was unable to curse the people of God. Moreover, the curse would fall on those who

---

[27] B. Albrektson, *History and the Gods* (Lund: Gleerup, 1967) 67.

[28] See R. Alter's perceptive analysis of the Balaam pericopes in *The Art of Biblical Narrative* (New York: Basic, 1981) 104ff.; See also A. Jepsen, "*ḥāzāh*," *TDOT*, 4.283; D. Vetter, "*rʾh, sehen*," *THAT*, 2.694–702.

[29] J. Scharbert, " *ʾrr*," *TDOT*, 1.412–25; cf. Num 22:6 (3x), 12; 23:7; 24:9 (2x) for *ʾārûr;* Num 22:11, 17; 23:8 (2x), 11, 13, 25, 27; 24:10 for *qāḇaḇ*.

curse Israel. Balaam was sovereignly constrained to say only what God permitted (cf. Num 22:23; 23:12, 26; 24:13). Therefore, the Abrahamic promises of blessing will not be reversed through divination or curse. Indeed, the curse would fall back on those who curse Israel (Gen 12:3).

Balaam speaks four oracles, the first two after he performs three sets of sacrifices with Balak. Each sacrifice consists of offering seven rams and seven bulls on seven altars. The offering was probably a ritual to predispose the deity toward the petitioner and to bring the deity near in order to effect the curse.[30] But to the growing dissatisfaction of Balak, the oracles of Balaam fall short of cursing Israel. Balak's reaction of mounting anger is similar to Balaam's anger over his disobedient ass. The repetition of events in the narratives serves to emphasize Balaam's inability to see what his ass could see and Balak's inability to subvert Yahweh's promise of blessing to the chosen people. It takes the unveiling of Balaam's eyes by the *rûaḥ ʾelōhîm* for the seer to realize that God's will could not be altered by technical manipulation or cursing.

When Balaam realizes God's desire to bless Israel, he turns from his sorcery and looks toward Israel, who is encamped in the desert (Num 24:1–2). At this point the *rûaḥ ʾelōhîm* comes on Balaam and he is inspired to speak his third and fourth oracles. The coming of the Spirit of God on him indicates the difference in reception and inspiration from that of the first two oracles. The claim of Balaam at this juncture is that he "hears the words of God," he "sees a vision from the Almighty," he "falls prostrate," his "eyes are opened" (24:4, 16). Balaam is now presented as a prophet who perceives God's message, that is inspired by the Spirit rather than by technical means. His fourth oracle includes some positive and extensive prophecies: "I see him, but not now; I behold him, but not near. A star will come out of Jacob; a scepter will rise out of Israel. . . . A ruler will come out of Jacob and destroy the survivors of the city" (Num 24:17, 19). The blessing of Israel is reasserted and a coming king is announced. R. Alter's perceptive statement summarizes the force of the narrative: "Paganism, with its notion that divine powers can be manipulated by a caste of professionals through a set of carefully prescribed

[30] Lindblom, *Prophecy in Ancient Israel*, 91.

procedures, is trapped in the reflexes of a mechanistic worldview while from the biblical perspective reality is in fact controlled by the will of an omnipotent God beyond all human manipulation."[31]

The Spirit and the Power of the Prophetic Word

Both the Former and the Latter Prophets stress the resilience and effectual power of the prophetic word (1 Sam 2:27–36; Isa 40:8; cf. Deut 8:11; 30:14ff.). The word of God is neither empty nor unfruitful (Deut 32:47; Isa 55:11). Moreover, we have noted in chapter 1 the relationship between the spoken word of God and the Spirit of God which brings that word into reality. This relationship is particularly evident in Genesis 1:2 and also in Psalm 33:6. There the *rûaḥ* of God is the active, creative, and vital presence of God which functions to fulfill the spoken word [*dāḇar*] or commandment. This relationship is vividly portrayed in Isaiah where the word of God is like a messenger that goes forth and subsequently becomes effectual. "As the rain and the snow come down from heaven, and do not return to it without watering the earth and making it bud and flourish, so that it yields seed for the sower and bread for the eater, so is my word that goes out from my mouth: It will not return to me empty, but will accomplish what I desire and achieve the purpose for which I sent it" (Isa 55:10–11). This simile illustrates the efficacy of the word, which like a prophet goes out to proclaim and accomplish the will of God (cf. Isa 45:23; Jer 23:29). The specific relationship between the word and the Spirit is featured in Isaiah 34:16: "For it is his mouth that has given the order, and his Spirit will gather them together." The implementation of the word is further implied in verse 17: "He allots their portions; his hand distributes them by measure." The prophetic word was effective, creative, and charged with energy.[32]

Israel held this belief in common with the ancient Near East, that "the word of the god was a mighty and terrifying power which could prove effective in all spheres of life, a dynamic force bringing about the death or victories of kings as well

[31] Alter, *Biblical Narrative,* 106–7.

[32] Lindblom, *Prophecy in Ancient Israel,* 51ff., 113–15.

as the growth or withering of the crops."[33] Particularly in Mesopotamia, the divine word was conceived as a physical-cosmic power, the giver and sustainer of life, creative, irresistible, irrevocable, and constant energy.[34] It must be emphasized here that the OT does not have a magical or mantic conception of the word of God. The potency of the word has to do with the one who speaks the word, not with the speaking of formulas or the manipulation of forces to fulfill the words of functionaries. Even the utterance of blessings and curses and their fulfillment depended on whether the utterance was inspired and condoned by Yahweh (cf. Num 22–24).

Israel emphasized specifically that God could foretell his great deeds in history through the prophets. Numerous verbs indicate the accomplishment, fulfillment, establishment, confirmation, and truth of the divinely inspired word.[35] Israel believed that history was shaped and directed by the word of the Lord, who had the power to bring divine plans and foretold events into reality. Yahweh's word to Samuel illustrates: "At that time I will carry out against Eli everything I spoke against his family—from beginning to end" (1 Sam 3:12). This feature in the Former Prophets is abundantly portrayed in the prophetic word that is presented and then brought to fulfillment in the life of the nation.[36] One purpose of the historical literature is to record the faithfulness of God in fulfilling divine promises in history to the covenant people. The prophets play a substantial role as the emissaries sent by God to foretell the word and to act as those who direct history by anointing and deposing kings. The Spirit's role in this process is often illustrated in the commissioning, inspiring, motivating, and guiding of the prophets (cf. Ezek 3). The relationship between the word and the Spirit in the prophet's estimation was very intimate. W. Eichrodt summarizes: "As a cosmic power of God, therefore, the word takes very much the

[33] Albrektson, *History and the Gods,* 67.

[34] Schmidt, "*dāḇar,*" 120, cf. 91ff.

[35] Ibid., 115f.

[36] Note the following prophetic declarations (P) and their fulfillment (F): (Josh 6:26 (P) 1 Kgs 16:34 (F); 1 Sam 2:27–36 (P) 1 Kgs 2:26–27 (F); 2 Sam 7:13 (P) 1 Kgs 8:20 (F); 1 Kgs 11:29ff. (P) 1 Kgs 12:15b (F); 1 Kgs 13 (P) 2 Kgs 23:16–18 (F); 1 Kgs 14:16ff. (P) 1 Kgs 15:29 (F); 1 Kgs 16:1ff. (P) 1 Kgs 16:12 (F); 1 Kgs 22:17 (P) 1 Kgs 22:35 (F); 2 Kgs 1:6 (P) 2 Kgs 1:17 (F); 2 Kgs 10:30 (P) 2 Kgs 15:12 (F); 2 Kgs 22:15ff. (P) 2 Kgs 23:20 (F). See G. von Rad, *Studies in Deuteronomy* (SBT; trans. D. Stalker; London: SCM, 1961) 74–91.

place for these men which in popular thinking was occupied by the *rûaḥ,* and enables them to discern God's direct control of history."[37] The prophetic word is thus a guiding force in history, and the Spirit is the active presence of God that implements it and causes the spoken word to live.

In the Latter Prophets, this conception is evident in passages where the judgments of God are spoken by prophets and implemented by God (Isa 9:7ff.; Ezek 2:4ff.). Jeremiah's prophetic ministry included the destruction of false beliefs and the replacement of them with divine truth. The divine "hand" inspires the prophet and the message instructs God's people through the divine word. "Then the Lord reached out his hand and touched my mouth and said to me, 'Now, I have put my words in your mouth. See, today I appoint you over nations and kingdoms to uproot and tear down, to destroy and overthrow, to build and to plant' " (Jer 1:9–10). We have noted the relationship of the divine hand and the Spirit in connection with the leadership of Ezra (ch. 4). In addition, the expression "hand of Yahweh" is often used in prophetic texts to describe Yahweh's possession, inspiration, and empowering of a prophet. The phrase often occurs concerning the revelation of divine visions and the activity of the Spirit (see below on Ezekiel).

Through the word of the prophets, therefore, the operation of the Spirit is realized in the community. Unfortunately Israel often rejected the word and thereby grieved the Spirit, as indicated by Zechariah. "They made their hearts as hard as flint and would not listen to the law or to the words that the Lord Almighty had sent by his Spirit through the earlier prophets. So the Lord Almighty was very angry" (Zech 7:12; cf. Isa 63:10; Neh 9:30; also note Ps 95:7–8 and Heb 3:7–8). As Eichrodt says, "It was the spirit which gave rise to the word of God uttered in times past and now of normative significance in the present, and which is at the same time the power giving life to the community."[38] The word becomes a living reality in the life of the community as the Spirit, that inspired the prophet and motivated him to speak, also applies it to the spiritual life of the nation. In this sense, the OT function of the prophetic word together with the Spirit is similar to the NT role as signified by

---

[37] Eichrodt, *Theology,* 2.73.
[38] Ibid., 64.

Jesus: "All this I have spoken while still with you. But the Counselor, the Holy Spirit, whom the Father will send in my name, will teach you all things and will remind you of everything I have said to you" (John 14:25–26).

Is Saul among the Prophets?

We have noted the role of Saul and his anointing for kingship in chapter 4 but now address the nature of Saul's prophesying with the prophets. Saul is privately anointed by Samuel as leader over Israel. The rhetorical question of Samuel, "Has not Yahweh anointed you leader *[nāḡîḏ]* over his inheritance?" (1 Sam 10:1) is followed by three signs that would confirm to Saul that he indeed was Yahweh's chosen leader. The third sign is perhaps the most crucial for Saul. He is to meet a procession of "prophesying" *[mitnabbᵓîm]* prophets playing musical instruments (10:5). The use of musical instruments was employed at times to awaken ecstasy or inspiration (2 Kgs 3:15). The *rûaḥ yhwh* would then come on Saul and cause him to prophesy with the prophets. In accordance with Samuel's word, Saul meets the prophets at Gibeah, the *rûaḥ ᵓelōhîm* comes on him in power, and Saul joins with the band in their prophetic activity (10:10). Implicitly, the prophetic band prophesies by the same Spirit that comes on Saul.

An immediate result of Saul's prophesying was the public observance of Saul's prophetic activity by "all those who formerly knew him." Not only does this occurrence confirm to Saul the words of Samuel regarding his anointing as leader, but the Spirit-endowment associated with all prophecy is now recognized by others to be upon Saul. This event gave rise to the saying, "Is Saul also among the prophets?" A variety of views regarding the intent of this saying is held by commentators ranging from positive to negative. The most interesting is perhaps by E. Ruprecht, who paraphrases the question, "Can Saul continually provoke the Spirit of Yahweh for Yahweh war as the ecstatic prophets provoke the Spirit of God so that he would be fit for a leadership office?"[39] Although this interpretation may be close to the intent, the passage does indicate a

[39] Quoted in Albertz and Westermann, *"rûaḥ, Geist,"* 745.

positive occasion where Saul and the prophets share in the Spirit of God which is a sign that God is with the newly selected king.[40] Therefore, the coming of the Spirit of God on Saul and the subsequent activity of prophesying serve as a public indicator of Saul's charismatic endowment for leadership. Saul's leadership is then affirmed and ratified by the people at Mizpah (10:17–24) who shout, "Long live the king!" It is also possible that at this key transition period in the leadership of Israel, the prophetic activity of Saul, which in essence overcomes him, is to establish the fact that the king is subject to the prophetic word and to the prophetic office. Thus, Samuel instructs Saul to meet him at Gilgal and expects the new leader to be obedient to his command (10:8).

Saul Is Overcome by the Spirit of God: 1 Samuel 18:10; 19:9

A number of passages refer to the Spirit of God as overcoming Saul, while others indicate the influence of an evil spirit on him. A negative consequence of the coming of the evil *rûaḥ ʾelōhîm* on Saul occurs on two occasions. In the first instance it is recorded: "The next day an evil spirit of God came forcefully upon Saul. He was prophesying in his house, while David was playing the harp, as he usually did. Saul had a spear in his hand and he hurled it, saying to himself, 'I'll pin David to the wall.' But David eluded him twice" (1 Sam 18:10).

In the second instance, Saul again tries to kill David when he is overcome by the evil spirit sent by God (19:9f.). On both occasions David escapes danger. F. Lindström claims that Saul's ailment has to do with an attitude of the mind, not a demon or God's Spirit. He claims it is a way of indicating judgment and the consent of God to allow evil to affect humankind.[41] But there is more than a psychological disturbance indicated here. Saul is unable to shake the evil affects upon him. He tries to hold on to his former experience of the Spirit and the positive influences that the presence of God gives to him. The interesting phenome-

[40] See J. Sturdy, "The Original Meaning of 'Is Saul Also Among the Prophets?' (1 Samuel 10:11, 12; 19:24)," *VT* 20 (1970) 207–9; B. C. Birch, "The Development of the Tradition on the Anointing of Saul in 1 Sam 9:1–20:16," *JBL* 90 (1971) 55–68.

[41] See Lindström, *God and the Origin of Evil,* 74ff.

non is that although Saul is influenced by the evil spirit, he still has the ability to prophesy while David plays the harp. But his ability to lead the nation as intended is diminished. Saul seeks to hang on to the only tangible element that initially indicated his relationship to the presence of God, namely, the verbal utterances of his lips.

The persistent attempts to kill David grow in intensity and number as Saul's mental condition deteriorates. After David escapes the hand of Saul who tries to kill him with his spear, David seeks refuge with Samuel and the prophetic band at Ramah and then at Naioth. Saul, however, manages to locate David and sends a number of men to capture him. Each of the three groups are overcome, however, by the *rûaḥ ᵓelōhîm* as they near the prophetic group that prophesies. "But when they saw a group of prophets prophesying, with Samuel standing there as their leader, the Spirit of God came upon Saul's men and they also prophesied" (1 Sam 19:20). The men of Saul "prophesy" [*(wayiṯnabbᵓû)*] (cf. 1 Sam 19:20, 21 [2x]) and are unable to take David. Finally Saul himself goes to Naioth but is overcome by the Spirit of God, causing him to walk along prophesying. Upon arrival at Naioth, Saul stripped off his clothes and prophesied before Samuel all that day and night (19:23–24)! As indicated in this narrative, the presence of the Spirit of God at Naioth was inescapable.[42] The nature of the prophetic activity at Naioth seems to include not only verbal utterance but a trance-like experience that incapacitates those who seek to capture God's anointed king. Contact with the prophesying band presided over by Samuel was in this instance contagious.

The account of Saul and his men who were overcome by the Spirit of God serves a number of functions. The first and more obvious function is that Saul and his men are restrained. Their desire to capture David is thwarted as the Spirit of God comes on them. David is protected by the *rûaḥ* and Saul is rendered harmless. Saul's uncontrollable actions before Samuel present the king as a weak and pitiful character. A different role of the Spirit is indicated in this passage from that of 1 Samuel 10:10–12, where Saul's election as leader is confirmed by the Spirit of God. In 19:23-24, Saul is constrained by the Spirit of

---

[42] See Hertzberg, *Samuel,* 167.

God. Also, Saul lies helplessly before Samuel the prophet and "king maker," stripped not only of his kingly robes but of his dignity and ability to function as ruler over the people. This is the last occasion that Saul sees Samuel. The context confirms the necessity of the king to submit to the prophetic word. The passage also highlights the difference between Saul, who tried to kill the anointed of the Lord, and David, who attempted to uphold the anointed of the Lord (24:10).

The Spirit of God and the Spirit of Yahweh

It is interesting to note that Samuel tells Saul that the *rûaḥ yhwh* will come on him (1 Sam 9:6), but in 10:10 it is the *rûaḥ ʾelōhîm* that inspires Saul to prophesy. Moreover, it is the Spirit of God which influences Saul in 11:6 concerning the war. The evil spirit of God affects him in 16:14 (2x) and 16:15 (2x), but it is the evil spirit of Yahweh that was to come over him (16:14). In 16:13 the Spirit of Yahweh comes on David for his role as king, and at the same time the Spirit of Yahweh departs from Saul (16:14). In 2 Samuel 23:2, David is inspired by the Spirit of Yahweh and then articulates his last psalm. In 1 Samuel 19:19, 23 the Spirit of God causes Saul to prophesy with the prophets.

From this brief overview it is evident that the "Spirit of God" is used in reference to the ecstatic behavior of the prophets and in reference to Saul's malady (8x). The "Spirit of Yahweh" is used five times in 1 and 2 Samuel but the theological significance of this variation in the light of all the OT references is limited. Examining all twenty-one occurrences of the "Spirit of God" and the twenty-seven occurrences of the "Spirit of Yahweh," one notices a fluctuation and variation in phraseology in a diversity of contexts. The divine names associated with the Spirit may often refer to similar details such as inspiration (cf. Ezek 11:5; Num 24:2). But the "Spirit of Yahweh" appears most often where Israel's covenant faith is threatened (cf. the period of the judges and the Elijah cycles).[43]

[43] See Albertz and Westermann, "*rûaḥ, Geist,*" 742–43.

David the Prophet: 2 Samuel 23:2

David's final words are those of a prophet. He is introduced as the man whom the Most High exalted and anointed to be king. His last words are inspired by the Spirit of Yahweh. "The Spirit of the Lord spoke through me; his word was on my tongue" (2 Sam 23:2). In addition to being the anointed one of the Lord, David was also the "sweet singer of Israel" (23:1). As the anointed one, David was not only inspired as a prophet but also equipped with the skill of writing poetry. Thus, David was "qualified to be the bearer of the divine spirit and the mediator of the divine word."[44] David received the revelation of God concerning the ideal king to come who would rule by the fear of God. The oracle he proclaimed presented the theological program for his future dynasty.

The Chronicler presents the role of David as prophet to an even greater extent. David is viewed as one who receives the word of the Lord and then passes it on to others as one who receives answers to his requests. At times he is viewed as functioning in the capacity of both priest and prophet. He offers sacrifices and calls on the Lord. "David built an altar to the Lord there and sacrificed burnt offerings and fellowship offerings. He called on the Lord, and the Lord answered him with fire from heaven on the altar of burnt offering" (1 Chron 21:26; cf. 1 Kgs 19). David receives not only the word of the Lord (1 Chron 22:8; 28:6), but through the Spirit he receives the plans for the temple and presents them to Solomon. "He gave him the plans of all that the Spirit had put in his mind for the courts of the temple of the Lord and all the surrounding rooms, for the treasuries of the temple of God. . . . 'All this,' David said, 'I have in writing from the hand of the Lord upon me, and he gave me understanding in all the details of the plan' " (1 Chron 28:12, 19).

Some of the Davidides also have this privilege. In the case of Solomon, he receives revelations from God who also responds to his prayer and fills the temple with his glory (2 Chron 1:7–12; 7:1, 11–22; cf. 13:4–12; 32:20–23). Therefore, not only is the king the regent of Yahweh over the kingdom but he is capable of receiving Yahweh's inspired messages. Although David is not identified with the prophetic bands, he did at times receive

[44] Hertzberg, *Samuel*, 400.

messages from the court prophets such as Nathan and Gad (2 Sam 12). Even though David was capable of receiving the word of Yahweh, he was still subject to the prophetic word of the court prophets.

Elijah and Elisha: 1 Kings 17–2 Kings 9

The narratives of Elijah and Elisha are perhaps the most intriguing of the prophetic materials and take a prominent place in 1 and 2 Kings, stressing the prophetic nature of the books. The uniqueness of these narratives lies in the numerous supernatural feats included in them. These supernatural miracles were accomplished by the *rûaḥ* that was active in the ministry of Elijah and then transferred to his successor, Elisha. Just as Numbers 11 and Isaiah 63 make explicit that the leadership of Moses was charismatic, so 2 Kings 2 makes explicit that the leadership of Elijah and Elisha was charismatic.

The struggles of Elijah and Elisha for Yahwism occur during the reigns of Ahab (869–850 BC), Ahaziah (850–849 BC), Jehoram (842–840 BC), Jehu, Jehoahaz, and Joash. The context of the narratives is that of the Omride dynasty (876–869 BC) during which the conflict between Baalism and Yahwism greatly intensified. During this period, the importation of Baalism escalated through the marriage of Ahab and Jezebel, daughter of the Tyrian king. Jezebel was a zealous devotee to the Tyrian Baal cult. The danger during this period is concisely stated by Elijah, "The Israelites have rejected your covenant, broken down your altars, and put your prophets to death by the sword" (1 Kgs 19:10).

These narratives must be read in the light of the covenant, that stipulates that obstinate disregard for Yahweh would result in drought, famine, and adversity. In the midst of this religious conflict, Yahweh raised up the two outstanding prophetic figures of Elijah and Elisha to fight for Yahwism in Israel (1 Kgs 19:16). These narratives refer to Elijah not only as "lord" *[ʾăḏōnay]*, but also a "prophet" (1 Kgs 18:36; 19:16), and "a man of God" (1 Kgs 17:18, 24). This last reverent title refers to a number of men in the OT, many of whom were charismatic servants of Yahweh. The man of God was commissioned and sustained by Yahweh for a task. His words were often accompanied by miracles, which underscored his authenticity and power (cf. 13:7ff.; 2 Kgs 5:5).[45]

The first association made between Elijah and the *rûaḥ yhwh* occurs when Elijah meets Obadiah. Due to the persecution of the prophets by Jezebel, Obadiah hid one hundred prophets and supplied them with provisions (1 Kgs 18:4). Upon meeting Elijah, Obadiah greets him with the title "my lord Elijah" (18:7). Elijah then sends Obadiah to Ahab with the message that he has found Elijah the "troublesome prophet." Obadiah, however, is fearful that Elijah will disappear from sight as he had when sought by Ahab's men. "I don't know where the Spirit of the Lord may carry you when I leave you" (18:12), he exclaims. This illustrates why the prophet could not be found in any kingdom or nation by Ahab. Obadiah's fear that Elijah might disappear was warranted, and he could be left before the king with a false report. The prophets, therefore, understood that the *rûaḥ yhwh* could not only hide and protect the prophets (cf. 19:18) but that the *rûaḥ* could supernaturally transport the prophet out of sight or to another location (*nāśāʾ*, "carry"; cf. 2 Kgs 2:16). In the prophetic understanding, Elijah's power and ability to withstand the threat posed by Ahab and Jezebel was associated with the Spirit of Yahweh. The coming and going of the prophet were related to the Spirit that was the power behind the extraordinary miracles that Elijah performed.

The miracles performed by Elijah and Elisha are usually connected to a tenet of faith attributed by Baal worshipers to their deity. Thus, Elijah's miracles are often a polemic against beliefs attributed to Baal. The miracles in these narratives are not just rendered for the sake of dramatization but to counter the claims of a pagan religion and culture—a context where prophetic words had to be accompanied with signs and wonders (similar to the religious conflict between God and Pharaoh). Examples of things said of Baal that in the Elijah/Elisha account are credited to Yahweh include the provision of fire (1 Kgs 18:39; 2 Kgs 1:10–17), rain (1 Kgs 17; 18:4ff.), oil and corn (1 Kgs 17:14; 19:16; 2 Kgs 4:1ff.), life and healing (1 Kgs 4:12; 2 Kgs 4:28–31; 5:10ff.; 13:20–22).[46] Although the parallels between the Baal

[45] See N. P. Bratsiotis, "*ʾîsh*," *TDOT*, 1.234; J. A. Holstein, "The Case of *ʾîš hāʾelōhîm* Reconsidered: Philological Analysis Versus Historical Reconstruction," *HUCA* 49 (1977) 77ff.

[46] See Bronner, *Stories of Elijah and Elisha.*

myths and the biblical narratives are sometimes stretched, the polemical framework provides a necessary background through which to view these narratives whose purpose is to reveal Yahweh as the true God who provides, sustains, gives life, and keeps his covenant with the faithful remnant.[47]

The Call of Elisha and the Transfer of the Spirit

The call of Elisha as prophet was directed by Yahweh, who instructed Elijah to anoint Elisha (1 Kgs 19:16). The actual ritual of anointing is not recorded in the narrative, but the practice of anointing with its typical function of indicating Yahweh's choice for a position of leadership is implied. Elijah added another form of conveying Yahweh's choice and call of Elisha by throwing his "mantle" *[ʾadderet̠]* on Elisha (19:19). Elisha immediately comprehended the import of this action and left his vocation to become Elijah's attendant.

The significance of the mantle is mainly indicated in the succession narrative of 2 Kings 2. Elijah told the sons of the prophets that he was about to be taken away by Yahweh (2:2, 5). At one point in the sequence Elijah used his mantle to strike the Jordan, which subsequently parted for the prophets as it had for Joshua and as the Reed Sea had for Moses. The use of the mantle is similar to that of Moses using his rod. In the Joshua pericope the water parts when the feet of the priests touch it (Josh 3:7–17). In 1 and 2 Kings, however, the mantle also becomes a sign of authorization and confirmation that Elisha is Elijah's rightful successor. It is a sign of Yahweh's choice for prophet and of Yahweh's power on an individual. It portrays the enveloping of an individual with the Spirit of the Lord.[48]

---

[47] See B. S. Childs, "On Reading the Elijah Narratives," *Int* 34 (1980) 128–37; F. C. Fensham, "A Few Observations on the Polarisation Between Yahweh and Baal in 1 Kings 17–19," *ZAW* 92 (1980) 227–36.

[48] An interesting feature in the Mari prophetic texts is the mention of hair and the fringe of a garment (*ANET,* letters a, b, m, n, p, and w). In these texts, a message was sent with a piece of garment and hair in order to identify the person sending the message. This seems to be a checking system to verify a message, and indicates that the oracle was subjected to technical means for verification. In some way the hair and garment fringe were used to identify the person and guarantee his veracity. In the case of Elijah and Elisha, the mantle did identify the prophets as those empow-

Elisha's last request before his master's departure was for a double portion of Elijah's *rûaḥ*. "When they had crossed, Elijah said to Elisha, 'Tell me, what can I do for you before I am taken from you?' 'Let me inherit a double portion of your spirit,' Elisha replied" (2 Kgs 2:9–10). This request has a twofold implication. The first has to do with the meaning of "a double portion." The phrase comes originally from the practice of a father giving the firstborn son twice the inheritance of the other sons (cf. Deut 21:17). The giving of a double portion indicated the greater responsibility that the son had for meeting the family needs and for giving leadership to the family when the father died. Elisha's request differs slightly in that he desires a double portion for the right of succession to the position of leadership over the sons of the prophets, and the commanding role in the battle against Baalism. Elijah indicates that this office could only be held by the person who had the same *rûaḥ* resting on him as experienced by Elijah. The difficulty in honoring the request is demonstrated by Elijah, who makes the right of succession depend on Elisha seeing his departure. Elijah indicates that it is not his prerogative to grant this request but God's prerogative. Thus, the request for a "double portion" is not his to give but depends on Yahweh permitting Elisha to witness his departure and "open his eyes" to God's selection. Only God could choose a successor to Elijah and transfer his Spirit to the chosen prophet.

The phrase "sons of the prophets" *[bene hanneḇîʾîm]* refers most likely to groups of prophets who separated themselves from society for special devotion to Yahweh's service under a prophet who may be referred to as a "father" in the sense of a spiritual mentor.[49] A leader presided over the activities of such groups that at times included ecstatic prophesying (cf. 1 Sam 10:5, 10). Elisha's request for a "double portion" of Elijah's *rûaḥ* is a request to assure his position as rightful successor to Elijah in the place of honor over the prophetic community.

---

ered by Yahweh for their tasks. See Malamat, "Prophetic Revelations in New Documents from Mari and the Bible," 225–26. Moran, "New Evidence from Mari," 21–23; Craghan, "Mari and Its Prophets," 42.

[49] See J. G. Williams, "The 'Prophetic Father': A Brief Explanation of the Term 'Son of the Prophets.' " *JBL* 85 (1966) 344. The conclusion that the sons were lay supporters of Elisha after the persecution during the time of Ahab is speculative. See T. R. Hobbs, "Excursus: On the Term 'Sons of the Prophets,' " *2 Kings* (WBC; Waco: Word, 1985) 25–27.

The second implication of Elisha's request for a double portion of Elijah's *rûaḥ* has to do with the power associated with the prophet for his difficult task. The battle against Baalism could not be fought without the power of the *rûaḥ*. It is no coincidence that after the *rûaḥ* of Elijah is transferred to Elisha the latter begins to perform miracles. After Elijah is taken away by God, Elisha picks up the mantle that fell from Elijah, symbolizing the transfer of authority. The association between the mantle and the *rûaḥ* is here evident. It is this mantle that was thrown on Elisha that conveyed to him his call. The mantle is also the "rod" in the hands of the prophets that parts the waters. Just as the mantle falls from Elijah, so the *rûaḥ* falls from Elijah to empower his successor for the prophetic work that must be done. That the prophets understood that Elijah's miraculous deeds were done by the Spirit of Yahweh is clear from their association of the parting of the Jordan with the *rûaḥ* of Elijah. In order to test if his desire had been granted, Elisha struck the Jordan and cried, "Where is Yahweh, the God of Elijah?" Elisha's hopes are confirmed by the parting of the Jordan. The prophets who witnessed this event exclaim, "The spirit *[rûaḥ]* of Elijah is resting on Elisha" (2 Kgs 2:15). It is clear, therefore, that the prophets understood Elisha's power for miracles to be a result of the *rûaḥ* that was transferred from one prophet to the other. Elisha himself realized that the parting of the Jordan was possible only if Yahweh was present to part it.

The prophets of Yahweh take special care not to associate the practices of Baalism with the *rûaḥ yhwh* (cf. 1 Kgs 19). The sparsity of references to the *rûaḥ yhwh* in the Elijah/Elisha narratives may be explained by the tension resulting from the ecstatic practices of the prophets of Baal. Some writers think that ecstatic activity had negative connotations during some periods of Israel's history and that biblical writers took special care not to associate the *rûaḥ* with ecstatic behavior. This accounts for the silence regarding the *rûaḥ yhwh* in the prophecies of Jeremiah, Amos, Habakkuk, Zephaniah, and others, until the time of Ezekiel. This also may be the reason for the association of the mantle with the *rûaḥ* and for the tendency to describe the coming of the *rûaḥ* with the phrase "the hand of the Lord" (cf. 1 Kgs 18:46). Where used, this latter term indicates the effective power of Yahweh through the ministry of the prophet.

The transfer of the Spirit to Elisha becomes another episode highlighting the OT emphasis on the need for charismatic leadership. Just as Joshua and the seventy elders received the Spirit for leadership, so also Elisha required the Spirit for his ministry. This motif is also featured in the NT when Jesus, the anointed one, transfers the Spirit to the disciples after his ascension. Luke alludes specifically to the transfer episodes in 1 and 2 Kings when emphasizing the disciples' need for Spirit- reception (Luke 9:57–62; Acts 1:6–11).[50]

Micaiah and Prophetic Conflict: 1 Kings 22

The nature of the Spirit's involvement in the process of prophetic inspiration is presented in a narrative that introduces prophetic conflict. In 1 Kings 22 the *rûaḥ* is featured as an agent who brings about the divine will but does so in an unconventional manner. Before examining the details concerning the activity of the Spirit, we review the setting of the narrative.

First Kings 22 records the events leading up to the third battle between Israel and the Syrians (cf. ch. 20). In this account, the king of Israel and the king of Judah come together and plan to retake Ramoth Gilead from the Syrians.[51] Before aligning himself with the king's proposal, however, Jehoshaphat makes a demand: "First seek the counsel of the Lord" (22:5). The typical method of seeking Yahweh's counsel was through the prophetic word. The court prophets were readily available to provide the king with an oracle as was common in the royal court, particularly in relation to holy war (2 Sam 7:4–17; 24:11). Sometimes the king would call for a prophet (1 Sam 28:5–6; 1 Kgs 22), and on other occasions he would go to the prophet for direction (2 Kgs 3:11f.). In this instance, the king of Israel was able to bring together four hundred prophets supported by the king's court, who encouraged the king to enter into battle with the positive

---

[50] Blenkinsopp notes a number of parallels: "The disciples are to be clothed with power and work miracles, reminiscent of the miraculous cloak of Elijah, and it is emphasized that they see Jesus being taken up, as Elisha must see his master, in order to receive the spirit" (*History of Prophecy*, 79).

[51] See S. J. De Vries, *Prophet Against Prophet: The Role of the Micaiah Narrative (1 Kings 22) in the Development of the Early Prophetic Tradition* (Grand Rapids: Eerdmans, 1978) 93ff., on the identity of the two kings and the historical problems associated with this chapter.

claim that Yahweh would deliver Ramoth Gilead into his hand. Oracles often were solicited in relation to battle plans (1 Kgs 20:13–15, 35–45; 2 Kgs 6:8–10, 15–23). Oracles by independent prophets, however, were frequently unfavorable (cf. Isa 30:3; Jer 21:2; 23:33–37; 38:14–23; Ezek 20:1) and often went against the policies and designs of the monarchy.

Jehoshaphat was not satisfied with this overwhelmingly positive response, however, and he requested the services of a *nāḇîʾ* of Yahweh. He doubted the inspiration, motivation, and veracity of the popular oracle. Micaiah son of Imlah was then introduced into the narrative as one hated by the king of Israel because of his typically unfavorable prophecies—those that went against the king's interests (1 Kgs 22:8). The four hundred prophets were prophesying as one voice before the two kings. The oracles that the prophets gave were intelligible responses to the king. Zedekiah stepped out from the crowd and emphatically summarized the consensus of the prophets. Using iron horns to illustrate his prophecy, Zedekiah declared, "With these you will gore the Arameans until they are destroyed" (22:11). The anticipated victory of the king was vividly dramatized and the positive direction was meant to encourage the king to embark on his battle plan.

Micaiah came into this situation and delivered a much bleaker picture of future events. The prophet agreed initially with the others but he did so sarcastically. This original statement was understood by Ahab as a lie. "Attack and be victorious," he answered, "for the Lord will give it into the king's hand" (22:15). Perhaps the intention of Micaiah was to reveal and emphasize the emptiness of the majority counsel. In disbelief of Micaiah's statement, the king demanded that the prophet tell him nothing but the truth. The import of Micaiah's second prophecy was that Israel would soon be without a master, that is, the king would be killed in battle (22:17). His authority for this negative message and his understanding of why the four hundred prophets had a different message was then presented: Micaiah had access to the heavenly court where he saw Yahweh and his host around the throne.

Micaiah's claim of access into the heavenly court served to indicate his authority not only for his oracle but also for his interpretation of the events occurring in the king's court (cf. Jer 23:22; Isa 6:1ff.; Amos 3:7). Access into the heavenly council was presumably of greater importance for the authority of a message than the claim of the *Heilspropheten* to possession of the *rûaḥ* Yahweh.[52] In this court scene, Micaiah was a silent observer who then became Yahweh's mediator of the divine word. He overheard the council discuss Yahweh's plan of how he might lure the king into battle and thereby end his reign. In the midst of the discussion in the heavenly court, the *rûaḥ* stepped forward and volunteered to "lure" Ahab into battle. In this reference, *rûaḥ* has the definite article before it *(hārûaḥ),* indicating that only the one Spirit is capable of working out the divine plan. Many advisers in the royal court reasoned together but only the *rûaḥ* was able to implement the plan and bring to fulfillment the divine purpose. The *rûaḥ* inspired a message which was characterized as a "lying spirit" in order to deceive the king and accomplish the divine plan. Yahweh is presented as the one who inspires the prophets and although the word they speak is wrong, the purpose of God to thwart the wicked king is effected.

Micaiah's claim that the *rûaḥ* that inspired the prophets was a lying *rûaḥ* infuriates Zedekiah. From his perspective, he was inspired by the *rûaḥ* from Yahweh that he considered to be genuine. To show his indignation, Zedekiah strikes Micaiah and asks, "Which way did the *rûaḥ* from Yahweh go when he went from me to speak to you?" (22:24). Zedekiah cannot believe that two prophets who speak different messages can be inspired by the same *rûaḥ*. Micaiah's only answer to this perplexing problem is basically that the future outcome of the spoken word will vindicate his oracle. He emphasizes his prophetic word: "Mark my words, all you people!" The fulfillment of Micaiah's prophecy is brought to pass just as he said and validates its authenticity (22:33–34).

This narrative gives rise to some perplexing questions concerning the role of the *rûaḥ,* who may inspire a false message in order to deceive the wayward king but may also inspire a prophetic word that comes to pass (cf. 1 Kgs 13). The paradox of the narrative is that it takes both the false message and the genuine oracle that is inspired by the same *rûaḥ* to bring about the intended purpose (cf. Jer 20:7; Ezek 14:9). Ahab cannot prevent an unfavorable oracle from coming to pass and he follows the counsel of the majority of prophets that leads to his death. The narrative shows that Yahweh is able to control the prophets by

[52] De Vries, *Prophet Against Prophet,* 7, 50f.

inspiring them with his *rûaḥ* to accomplish the divine plan. Thus, the irony of the narrative in J. L. Crenshaw's words is that "the agents of the state are transformed into instruments of God without their knowledge or volition."[53] This passage also indicates the different perspectives of the prophetic office in Israel and in Judah. For Ahab, his prophets are to serve the goals of the state, whereas for Jehoshaphat, the prophets of Yahweh must communicate the divine word in the interests of their God.

True and False Prophecy

The prophetic conflict depicted in 1 Kings 22 is an indicator of the spiritual forces involved in the communication of the divine message. OT abuses of prophecy are just as relevant to our contemporary situation as they are in the OT context and in the early church. Consideration of the characteristics of false prophecy helps to expose contemporary abuses in relation to the veracity of inspired messages and the moral behavior of the messenger. The spread and practice of false prophecy is evident in a number of periods in Israel's history. In some incidents, part of the problem is laid at the feet of so-called "spirit men" who are often accused of external, behavioral abuses. This is partially due to the mode of inspiration through which God reveals his word to the prophets. Significantly similar formulas indicating the inspirational activity experienced by the prophets include the phrases "the Spirit of the Lord came upon" (Num 24:2; 1 Sam 19:20), "the hand of the Lord came upon" (Ezek 3:14), and "the word of the Lord came to" the prophet (1 Kgs 19:9; Zech 7:1, 8).

A growing concern for the people of God in the OT is the question of the authentic message of God. How do we know that this is what Yahweh says? The problem arises due to the mediation process. Israel's response to the theophany at Sinai is a call for mediation. "Speak to us yourself and we will listen. But do not have God speak to us or we will die" (Exod 20:19). Yahweh's reaction to this request is generally favorable (Deut 18:17–18). Mediators, including priests, kings, and prophets, are called to stand between God and humankind. The nature of humankind

[53] J. L. Crenshaw, *Prophetic Conflict: Its Effect upon Israelite Religion* (*BZAW;* New York: Walter de Gruyter, 1971) 84.

lends itself to the possibility of a communication breakdown in the mediation process. Two major areas of breakdown involve the character of the prophet and the content of the prophetic message. The OT emphasizes the necessity of the prophetic word to speak only what Yahweh inspires. Failure to do so is potentially fatal. "But a prophet who presumes to speak in my name anything I have not commanded him to say, or a prophet who speaks in the name of other gods, must be put to death" (Deut 18:20). Some prophets did not take this admonition seriously. Thus, it was vital for Israel to evaluate accurately and to recognize the true prophetic word and to reject the presumptuous word.

The problem of discerning authentic prophecy is highlighted in the enigmatic narrative of 1 Kings 13. This narrative is placed in a strategic place in First and Second Kings in order to highlight the prophetic word as a guiding force in the history of the monarchy, as well as the requirement of prophets to walk in obedience to God's instructions.[54] The confrontational incident between the man of God from Judah and Jeroboam occurs after the significant religious reforms that Jeroboam institutes in the north (1 Kgs 12). Featured in the narrative is the immediate power of the prophetic word against the altar which symbolizes the religious reforms. The spoken word is followed by signs that verify the word and within the context of Kings are ultimately fulfilled in detail (2 Kgs 23:15–20). The text also shows the potency of the prophet's intercession (13:1–6).

The second and more pronounced conflict in the passage is between the man of God from Judah and the old prophet in the north. The old prophet hears about the events that have taken place at Bethel and determines to test the veracity of the man of God. Implicitly, the old prophet supported the new cult at Bethel and was intrigued by the strong prophetic word of

---

[54] See R. L. Cohn, "Literary Technique in the Jeroboam Narrative," *ZAW* 97 (1985) 24, on the chiastic structure of the narrative, and the following articles on the importance of the passage in the historical literature; T. B. Dozeman, "The Way of the Man of God From Judah: True and False Prophecy in the Pre-Deuteronomic Legend of 1 Kings 13," *CBQ* 44 (1982) 382–93. U. Simon, "1 Kings 12: A Prophetic Sign—Denial and Persistence," *HUCA* 47 (1976) 81ff.; W. Gross, "Lying Prophet and Disobedient Man of God in 1 Kings 13," *Semeia* 15 (1979) 100ff.; W. E. Lemke, "The Way of Obedience: 1 Kings 13 and the Structure of the Deuteronomistic History," *Magnalia Dei: The Mighty Acts of God*, 302ff.

denunciation from the south. Although the man of God had resolved to follow the instructions of God, not to partake of hospitality but to return directly to Judah (indicating God's wrath on the nation), he succumbed to the old prophet's claim to secondary revelation. "I too am a prophet, as you are. And an angel said to me by the word of the Lord: 'Bring him back with you to your house so that he may eat bread and drink water' " (13:19). The note in the text indicates that this is a lie. After accepting this change of instruction as being from Yahweh, the man of God is rudely confronted in the midst of a meal with the words, "You have defied the word of the LORD and have not kept the command the LORD your God gave you" (13:21). Punishment for this action results in death for the man of God but a powerful lesson to the old prophet.

Through this episode, the old prophet realizes that the word of the man of God against the cult at Bethel is true. Apparently no prophet in the north is prepared to denounce the new religious system. The man of God had to come from Judah, demonstrating that the political divisions are also evident among the prophets of Israel. No other chapter in Kings emphasizes the word of God to the extent that 1 Kings 13 does. The narrative indicates the tension between the monarchy and the prophets, as well as the struggle between true prophets and those supporting an apostate monarchy. It shows the nature of prophetic inspiration and the requirement for complete obedience. The narrative addresses the prophetic community and calls for prophets to take their stand against a perverse monarchy and religious cult. Those who do are forced to gather in monastic groups or stand against the tide of apostasy as individuals (Shemiah, Elijah, Elisha, et al.).

Crenshaw notes that the prophetic conflict in Israel was inevitable because of the nature of prophecy itself. His accounting of the four stages that the prophetic message undergoes is informative. First, there is the secret experience with God that is sometimes followed by an ecstatic reaction. Second, the prophet interprets his encounter according to his faith and past experiences with Yahweh. Third, there is the stage of intellectual revision. The last stage involves the artistic development and adaptation of the message to ancient rhetorical form. He concludes, "Within the twofold task of the reception of the word of God in the experience of divine mystery, and the articulation of the word to man in all its nuances and with persuasive cogency, rest multiple possibilities for error and disbelief."[55]

This problem was exacerbated because of the conflicting interests between the king and the prophet as well as the tensions between prophet and priest. Samuel clearly presented the temptations of the king who would be on the take (1 Sam 8:10ff.). The prophet charged with the role of confronting the flagrant abuses of kingship during the monarchy would be hard-pressed to keep his place in the royal court for denouncing the false practices of the king. This led to the numerous tensions between supporters of the king and individual prophets who went against the status quo, such as the man of God from Judah (1 Kgs 13), Elijah (1 Kgs 19), and Jeremiah. In relation to the sacrificial system, the prophetic word denounced flagrant abuses of the cultus that subsequently brought the prophets into disputations with the priests, not only in Bethel and Dan but also in Jerusalem (Isa 1:10–20; Jer 7:6ff.; Amos 5:21–24; Hos 8:11–14; Mic 6:6–8; Mal 1:6ff.).

In addition to the pressure on the prophet to speak messages that facilitated the interests of the king (1 Kgs 22; Amos 7:10–17), prophets were tempted to generalize their words so that they might come true. The criterion of fulfillment was a pressing reality on them according to Deuteronomy 18:22. "If what a prophet proclaims in the name of the Lord does not take place or come true, that is a message the Lord has not spoken." Furthermore, the fulfillment of their word was an important factor contributing to their level of success in the community. Also, the problem of "popular theology" was a difficult factor to stand up against. The interpretation of God's revelation in the light of changing historical situations, as well as the interpretation of calamities in nature, often went against popular hopes and conceptions.

Due to the breakdown between the theory and practice of covenant obligations, the prophets had difficulties in reconciling the disparity between the promises of God and their realization. Part of the problem involved the "power of tradition," which stressed the election of Israel and the inviolability of the temple and Zion. It was difficult for the people of God to comprehend the threats of judgment and exile. Inherent in these two issues

[55] Crenshaw, *Prophetic Conflict*, 3.

was the rise of syncretism and idolatry that the prophets could not always distinguish from true Yahwism.[56] Moreover, the problem of timing for a prophetic word also indicated whether it was true or false. In the dispute between Jeremiah and Hananiah, the word spoken by the latter had been theologically correct in another historical moment but was now incorrectly applied to a different situation and context (Jer 28). This conflict led to the characterization of Hananiah as a "cultic, nationalistic pseudoprophet, a fanatic demagogue, a libertine in morals, illiterate of spirit, and indeed an offender against the Holy Spirit."[57] However, consideration of the context and theology of the message shows that Hananiah was merely wrong about the application of his prophetic word.

Jeremiah finds himself in a quandary as he seeks to call a generation having a false conception of security back to covenant loyalty. The LXX uses the term *pseudoprophētēs* as a label for those prophets who contradict the message of Jeremiah. In an age where a division of political loyalties is evident, conflict arises between pro-Egyptian factions and pro-Babylonian factions. In the midst of it all stands Jeremiah, who opposes the message of other prophets. In most cases, the content of a message is repudiated although at times the moral conduct of the prophet is condemned (Jer 27–29). T. Overholt summarizes the nature of the false prophets and their characteristics:

> While Yahweh appoints the true prophet (1:5), who then speaks in his 'name' (26:16), he does not 'send' the false prophet (14:14; 23:21; 27:15; 28:15; 29:9). The erring prophets may be pictured as prophesying 'by Baal' (2:8; 23:13) or serving 'other gods' (2:26f.). They prophesy 'peace,' or speak of Yahweh's unconditional protection, or his inaction (6:13f.; 8:10f.; 14:13–16; 23:17; chs. 27–29). They are sometimes accused of being immoral (23:14f.; 29:21–23), or speaking their messages on the basis of auto-inspiration (the visions of their own minds, 23:16; dreams, 23:25–32; traffic in oracles, 23:30f.).[58]

---

[56] See Crenshaw for elaboration, *Prophetic Conflict,* 65ff.

[57] J. A. Sanders here refers to the study of G. Quell who highlighted this problem (p. 90). Sanders deals with the hermeneutics of false prophecy and historical context in "Canonical Hermeneutics: True and False Prophecy," *From Sacred Story to Sacred Text* (Philadelphia: Fortress, 1987) 87–105.

[58] T. W. Overholt, *The Threat of Falsehood* (SBT; London: SCM, 1970) 37.

The conflict between the prophets is presented clearly in Jeremiah 23:9ff. Jeremiah is consumed with grief at the state of the land and the abuse by both prophet and priest of their respective offices. Judgment is portrayed as looming over them for their prophesying by Baal and leading Israel astray. Immorality reveals their true character and their message, and the mode of its revelation tells of their falsehood. They fail by not having an immediacy with God and the heavenly council (23:22). The prophets in 1 Kings 22 also receive a mediated message, and the prophet in 1 Kings 13 claimed to be inspired by an angel. Genuine revelation comes to Micaiah through the heavenly council, just as Moses also received messages directly from God (Num 12:6–8).

Although some writers disparage the possibility of finding adequate criteria for the discernment of true prophecy, the above factors and principles indicate crucial concerns for evaluating true messages from God. Quenching the Spirit, a common practice in some communities, is not featured as an option because it is through the Spirit that the prophetic word is often conveyed. Whether visionary or auditory revelation, the Spirit's role in transmitting the prophetic word is affirmed, as the experience of Ezekiel demonstrates.

Ezekiel: Prophet of the Spirit

The noun *rûaḥ* occurs fifty-two times in the book of Ezekiel, and its translation covers the full semantic range that the word signifies throughout the OT. The frequent use of the term *rûaḥ* in Ezekiel indicates a change of perception regarding the role and activity of the Spirit. A number of references to the *rûaḥ* relate specifically to the activity of the Spirit in relation to prophecy.

Ezekiel is taken into exile with a large number of deportees (ca. 597 BC). Ezekiel serves initially as a priest, but after the judgment of God on Israel he is called to be a prophet. The prophet's call occurs five years into the exile at the river Chebar (cf. Ezek 1:1; 3:15, 23; 10:15, 22; 43:3). As a priest, Ezekiel may have been involved in conducting some religious services or in teaching, but with the call to the prophetic office he is sent to Israel with powerful messages of judgment and interpretations regarding Yahweh's imminent punishment.[59] His prophetic ministry as divine messenger includes the dramatic portrayal of the word that depicts the punishment to come on the people of God (cf. 4:1–2, 9-11; 5:1ff.). Ezekiel is indeed a "sign" of Yahweh's word to the community in exile (12:6, 11; 24:24). His prophetic calling also includes the grave responsibility of "watchman." This aspect of his call entails warning the people of God's impending judgment (3:16–21; 33:1–9). Ezekiel is responsible for the very lives of individuals whom he is obligated to stimulate to heed the word of Yahweh.[60]

Ezekiel and the Moving Creatures

The book of Ezekiel is partially structured around the three main visions revealed to Ezekiel (cf. Ezek 1–3; 8–11; 40–48). The main focus of these visions is related to temple concerns that emphasize the theme of divine kingship.[61] Ezekiel's inaugural vision sets the ominous tone for his whole prophetic ministry. He is given access to the throne room of God and is overwhelmed by the transcendent nature of the Deity. In 1:4 Ezekiel sees an approaching "wind" *[rûaḥ]* coming from the north which is described as a brilliant theophany. Featured in this theophany are the four composite creatures who apparently bear the throne of Yahweh (1:6–11, 15–16). These creatures move directly toward Ezekiel and are guided by the *rûaḥ*. "Wherever the *rûaḥ* would go, they would go" (1:12). Thus, their motivating power is solely described as coming from the *rûaḥ*. Zimmerli states that the "identity of movement between the creatures and the wheels is brought about by means of the *rûaḥ*." The power permeating the phenomenon "cannot be understood apart from the will of the One who is enthroned above the creatures."[62]

---

[59] Although W. Eichrodt claims that Ezekiel was only 25 years of age and on the verge of entering the priesthood when the exile occurred, his age and induction to the priesthood are unknown. Cf. Zimmerli, *Ezekiel 1,* 111f.; Eichrodt, *Ezekiel: A Commentary,* 52.

[60] See R. R. Wilson, "Prophecy in Crisis: The Call of Ezekiel," *Interpreting the Prophets* (ed. J. L. Mays and P. J. Achtemeier; Philadelphia: Fortress, 1987) 167–68.

[61] See Dumbrell, *The Faith of Israel,* 127ff.; Ackroyd, *Exile,* 103–17.

[62] Zimmerli, *Ezekiel 1,* 130.

This inaugural vision sets the tone for the whole book. Concerning our focus here, however, it is evident that the *rûaḥ* is active in bringing the creatures toward Ezekiel in his vision. Just as the *rûaḥ* actively moves the creatures, so also the *rûaḥ* will move and motivate Ezekiel in his prophetic office.

Ezekiel: "Moved" by the Spirit

After Ezekiel's inaugural vision he is commanded by Yahweh to stand but seems unable to do so. As Yahweh spoke, however, Ezekiel reports: "the Spirit *[rûaḥ]* came into me and raised me to my feet, and I heard him speaking to me" (2:2). This extraordinary experience occurs often in the book of Ezekiel and underlines the strong enabling of the prophet by the *rûaḥ* for his difficult task. The task of Ezekiel as presented in 2:3–8 is clearly a difficult one that will bring much opposition and thus requires much divine help. In 2:2 the *rûaḥ* is described as coming into Ezekiel, implying possession by the Spirit for the completion of his role (3:1–11). In 3:12 the *rûaḥ* "lifts" Ezekiel up contrary to his desire. "The Spirit *[rûaḥ]* then lifted me up and took me away, and I went in bitterness and in the anger of my spirit *[rûaḥ]*, with the strong hand of the LORD upon me" (3:14). The difficulty of the prophetic task is here underlined in a subjective manner. It is quite possible, judging from Ezekiel's experiences as a prophet, to conclude that without the strong motivation of the *rûaḥ*, Ezekiel would have preferred another vocation and another responsibility. Verse 24 again asserts the forceful nature of his motivation. "Then the Spirit came into me and raised me to my feet. He spoke to me and said: 'Go, shut yourself inside your house.' "

A further element indicating the sovereign hold of Yahweh on the prophet occurs in 8:1 and 8:3. The first reference is to Ezekiel's experience where "the hand of the LORD" comes on him (cf. 3:22). This phenomenon occurs in conjunction with 8:3 where the prophet experiences supernatural transportation. "He stretched out what looked like a hand and took me by the hair of my head. The Spirit lifted me up between earth and heaven and in visions of God he took me to Jerusalem" (8:3).

Prophetic texts often use the expression "hand of Yahweh" to describe Yahweh's possession and empowering of a prophet. The phrase occurs seven times in Ezekiel, often in concert with the revelation of divine visions and the activity of the Spirit.[63] The *rûaḥ* in this passage transports Ezekiel by way of vision to prepare the prophet for his prophetic proclamation. This same intention is evident in 11:1, where the prophet is lifted by the *rûaḥ* and transported to convey Yahweh's message to the leaders of Israel. The *rûaḥ* in this passage also inspires the prophet with the very words he is to speak (11:5). Furthermore, the same *rûaḥ* that moved the cherubim (cf. 11:22–24), now moves Ezekiel and reveals to him visions by the *rûaḥ ᵓelōhîm*. "The Spirit lifted me up and brought me to the exiles in Babylonia in the vision given by the Spirit of God" (11:24). Thus, the Spirit of God reveals supernatural visions to the prophet.

Two other passages have a similar understanding of the *rûaḥ* in relation to the prophet's ministry. In 37:1, "the hand of Yahweh was upon me, and he brought me out by the Spirit of the LORD *[rûaḥ yhwh]* and set me in the middle of the valley." This experience was preparatory to Ezekiel's prophesying to the bones. In 43:5 the prophet is again lifted up by the Spirit and brought into the inner court of the temple, which was filled with the glory of the Lord. In this vision Ezekiel is again inspired with the message he is to proclaim to the community.

The various workings of the *rûaḥ* in the life of Ezekiel characterize him as a man of the Spirit. His whole prophetic experience is portrayed as one motivated and directed by the *rûaḥ*. Through the *rûaḥ* Ezekiel received visions, was often "transported," and was inspired to prophesy.

Prophet of Righteousness: Micah 2:7

The prophet Micah was a contemporary of Isaiah who prophesied during the reigns of Jotham, Ahaz, and Hezekiah (742–686 BC). As we have seen in chapter 4, Micah was a man of

[63] See Ezekiel 1:3; 3:14, 22; 8:1; 33:22; 37:1; 40:1. See Zimmerli, *Ezekiel 1*, 117ff., for a complete survey of this phrase as it is used in the OT. Cf. W. E. Lemke, "Life in the Present and Hope for the Future," *Interpreting the Prophets*, ed. J. L. Mays and P. J. Achtemeier (Philadelphia: Fortress, 1987) 200; J. J. M. Roberts, "The Hand of Yahweh," *VT* 21 (1971) 244–51.

conviction who courageously spoke the word of the Lord by the *rûaḥ* that inspired and strengthened him (3:8). Perhaps the most difficult task Micah had to deal with was the corruption among the leaders of Israel (cf. 3:1–3; 7:1–4) and among the priests and prophets themselves (2:6, 11; 3:5–7).

Micah's harshest words are reserved for the prophets who preferred to speak messages of weal rather than the true word of Yahweh. J. L. Crenshaw concludes that the *vox populi* of the prophets that Micah and other true prophets confronted consisted of (1) confidence in God's faithfulness, (2) satisfaction with traditional religion, (3) defiance in the face of prophets who hold a different view, (4) despair when hope seems dead, (5) doubt as to the justice of God, and (6) historical pragmatism.[64] To this perspective that often included the wrong emphases, Micah presents a radically different approach. In response to Micah's message of judgment and woe, the prophets exclaimed, "Do not prophesy. Do not prophesy about these things; disgrace will not overtake us" (2:6). The prophets were incredulous at Micah's suggestion that the *rûaḥ yhwh* was indeed angry. "Should it be said, O house of Jacob: 'Is the Spirit of the LORD angry? Does he do such things? Do not my words do good to him whose ways are upright?' " (Mic 2:7).

The main problem that confronted Micah was the prophet's theology. The content of their prophecies showed that they expected Yahweh's blessings without adherence to his ethical imperatives. For this reason, the *rûaḥ yhwh* was angry and grieved. Those in positions of power abused their trust and were leading the people astray. Micah's words are a fitting warning to prophets in every generation who are tempted to abuse their prophetic responsibilities. "Therefore night will come over you, without visions, and darkness, without divination. The sun will set for the prophets, and the day will go dark for them. The seers will be ashamed and the diviners disgraced. They will all cover their faces because there is no answer from God" (Mic 3:6–7). Persistent disrespect for God's intention for leadership and the morality of the priests and prophets would result in the quenching of the Spirit and the lack of inspiration and guidance.

---

[64] Crenshaw, *Prophetic Conflict,* 24ff.; See also Amos 5:14; 9:10; Isa 29:11–12; Jer 5:12; 11:21; 23:17); A. S. van der Woude, "Micah in Dispute with the Pseudo-Prophets," *VT* 19 (1969) 244–60; Mowinckel, " 'Spirit' and the 'Word,' " 205–6.

To counter this trend and to address this grievous situation, Micah required the strength and power of God to rebuke his wayward generation. To this end he gives credit to the Spirit of God: "But as for me, I am filled with power, with the Spirit of the LORD, and with justice and might, to declare to Jacob his transgression, to Israel his sin" (Mic 3:8). Filled with the Spirit, Micah is empowered to attack the root of sin in his fellow prophets.

6

Pneumatological Reflections

You know what has happened throughout Judea, beginning in Galilee after the baptism that John preached—how God anointed Jesus of Nazareth with the Holy Spirit and power, and how he went around doing good and healing all who were under the power of the devil, because God was with him. (Acts 10:37–38)

Our pilgrimage through the OT reveals a number of crucial theological facets in regards to the work of the Spirit of God. In the foregoing Chapters, a number of major and minor themes became evident from the analysis of texts that refer to the *rûaḥ* of God. This concluding chapter presents some observations and applications relevant to this subject. The same broad OT categories and pneumatological themes are used to inform and develop NT pneumatology. The NT expands the scope of the Spirit's work, influence, and functions. Although space does not allow a detailed presentation here (many excellent monographs do so), some basic foundational correspondences for further investigation are presented.[1]

---

[1] For further reading on NT pneumatology into issues raised in this chapter refer to: C. K. Barrett, *The Holy Spirit and the Gospel Tradition* (London: S.P.C.K., 1947); G. M. Burge, *The Anointed Community: The Holy Spirit in the Johannine Tradition* (Grand Rapids: Eerdmans, 1987); J. D. G. Dunn, *Jesus and the Spirit* (Philadelphia: Westminster, 1975); E. E. Ellis, *Pauline Theology: Ministry and Society* (Grand Rapids: Eerdmans, 1989); M. R. Mansfield, *Spirit and Gospel in Mark* (Peabody, Mass: Hendrickson, 1987); E. Schweizer, *"pneuma," TDNT,* 6.332–455; J. E. Yates, *The Spirit and the Kingdom* (London: S.P.C.K., 1963).

The Spirit of God in Creation and Temple Building

The first few verses of Scripture introduce the creative involvement of the Spirit in bringing about the directives of God. In this respect, the analogy of invisible wind that acts upon matter and brings about change is conspicuous. The meaning of the term *rûaḥ* as wind helps to describe the Spirit's activity. That is, just like wind which in the hands of God may bring about a variety of effects, the Spirit as a powerful force brings about the plan, design, and will of God concerning his kingdom. God operates through the invisible Spirit and effects transformation, not only in human beings and nature but in regards to all creation. As chapter 2 portrays, the Spirit makes the word and design of God a tangible and physical reality. The Spirit is the determining influence in making the invisible become real matter. That which is chaotic, unformed, and uninhabitable is transformed into the ordered, fashioned, and habitable cosmos. God brings about his order over chaos through the Spirit. Darkness is transformed into light. In this respect, the design, word, and Spirit of God have a significant role to play.

Isaiah 40:13 features the *rûaḥ* as capable of communicating the design for creation as well as the implementation of it (cf. Prov 1:23). The creation acts as recorded in Genesis were in the mind of God before they were articulated in the commands of God and brought to fulfillment by the Spirit of God. What is evident in the establishment of the macrocosmic creation of the earth and of Eden is also true of the microcosmic creation of the tabernacle and temples in which the presence of God is manifest.

When Moses is selected to oversee the building of the tabernacle, God reveals the specific design for his abode. "Then have them make a sanctuary for me, and I will dwell among them. Make this tabernacle and all its furnishings exactly like the pattern I will show you" (Exod 25:7–8, 40; cf. 26:30; Acts 7:44; Heb 8:2–5). Once the design is revealed, special artisans are selected and filled with the Spirit to carry out the creative work of assembling the tabernacle (Exod 31:1ff.). Special skills are imparted through the Spirit for the craftsmen that enable them to do the work. God also inspires the temple design to David which he in turn transfers over to Solomon for implementation.

"He gave him the plans of all that the Spirit had put in his mind for the courts of the temple of the LORD and all the surrounding rooms" (2 Chron 28:12–19). The exilic temple is also revealed to the prophet Ezekiel (Ezek 40:1ff.). In this respect, God through the Spirit achieves the architectonic work of revealing plans that are then creatively brought into reality through Spirit-enabled artisans. When the creative work is complete, God enters into the earthly dwellings through his powerful presence and glory (Exod 40:34–35; 2 Chron 7:1–3; Ezek 43:4–5; Hag 2:5–7).

In the NT, the temple analogy is transferred to the believing individual and to the corporate body of believers. First, the Gospels witness to Jesus as the new temple in which the glory and presence of God reside (John 2:19–21; cf. Matt 16:21; 26:61; 27:40; Mark 14:58). Not only is Jesus anointed for his ministry (Matt 3:16–17; 8:16; 12:28; Mark 1:10–11; Luke 3:22; Acts 10:38), but the glory of God transfigures him (Matt 17:1–8; Mark 9:2–8; Luke 9:28–36). God was present in Jesus' earthly body. "The Word became flesh and made his dwelling among us. We have seen his glory, the glory of the One and Only, who came from the Father, full of grace and truth" (John 1:14). Second, the NT bears witness that believing individuals are the residence of the Spirit (1 Cor 3:16ff.), but more predominately, the Church is like a building under construction in which the Spirit resides (2 Cor 6:16–17; cf. 1 Pet 2:4–10).

The nature of the building and its various corporate dimensions are revealed by the Spirit. The Spirit not only reveals the mysteries of Christ to the apostles and prophets, but also imparts the nature of the dwelling of God where all believing Jews and Gentiles are members of the one body (Acts 2:14–47; Eph 3:2–6; cf. 4:3ff.). Now Jesus and all believers are united as one body in which the Spirit resides. "Consequently, you are no longer foreigners and aliens, but fellow citizens with God's people and members of God's household, built on the foundation of the apostles and prophets, with Christ Jesus himself as the chief cornerstone. In him the whole building is joined together and rises to become a holy temple in the Lord. And in him you too are being built together to become a dwelling in which God lives by his Spirit" (Eph 2:19–22).

Furthermore, grace and ministry gifts are apportioned to the "craftsmen" who work together in the building of the church (Eph 4:14–16; cf. 1 Cor 12:3–13). Apostles (Acts 4:8, 31; 9:17), prophets (Acts 21:4–11; 1 Cor 14; 1 Thess 5:19), evangelists (Acts

8:29, 39), pastors and teachers (Acts 20:23, 28), as well as deacons (Acts 6:3–10; 7:55), are Spirit-enabled functionaries in the church. Just as Jesus is anointed for his earthly ministry, so are the leaders of the church (Acts 1:4–8; 2:4, 38; 4:8, 31; 9:17; 13:1–5). Their instructions and direction for church-related work and expansion of the kingdom of God come through Spirit-inspired revelation, prophecy, and visions (Acts 11:12; 13:24; 10:44–47; 16:6–7). Through the spiritual ministry of the NT leaders, the church is built up and prepared for the bridegroom. As the leaders each do their part, the church is "assembled" into the edifice of God's design (1 Cor 3:10–15; cf. Acts 9:31). Gifts, abilities, and power are given to them for the express purpose "to prepare God's people for works of service, so that the body of Christ may be built up until we all reach unity in the faith and in the knowledge of the Son of God and become mature, attaining to the whole measure of the fullness of Christ" (Eph 4:12–13).

The Spirit of God in the Creation of Humankind and in the Conception of God's Son

In chapter 2 we surveyed the OT material indicating the Spirit's vital part in the creation of humankind. A number of texts feature the Spirit of God as the animating principle of life, which when imparted by God to humankind makes men and women living beings created in the image of God (Gen 2:7; Ps 104:30; Job 32:8; 33:4; 34:14). When the Spirit of God is removed from a human being the body returns to its lifeless, inanimate state. In the OT, the Spirit of God participates in the primal act of creation as well as in the ongoing production of human life by imparting the breath of life. Although this same conception continues into the NT, the focus there changes from the physical to the spiritual dimensions of life.

The New Birth

With the giving of the Spirit by Jesus, individuals may be translated into the spiritual family of God through rebirth. Whereas all humans are alive by virtue of physical animation, spiritual life is experienced by those who have the Spirit of God in them through their experience of the new birth. This is emphasized in the Johannine literature, which specifies that those who wish to participate in the kingdom of God must be "born again" (John 3:3, 7). "I tell you the truth, no one can enter the kingdom of God unless he is born of water and the Spirit. Flesh gives birth to flesh, but the Spirit gives birth to spirit" (John 3:5–6; cf. 6:63). Therefore, individuals must experience a "new creation" through the Spirit in order to enter into the Christian community.[2] In this respect, John employs water as a metaphor for the new life, which Jesus dispenses (4:10, 14; 7:37–38). This experience initiates a new life whereby the believer lives and walks in the Spirit (Rom 8:4–8). The Spirit of God becomes a powerful presence to assist in controlling one's behavior and in transforming one's character (Rom 8:9; Gal 5:16–25). To belong to Christ one must have the Spirit of Christ, that not only gives new life but bestows everlasting life (Rom 8:9–17; 1 John 5:11–12). Through the Spirit, men and women become a "new creation," which is then transformed and renewed continually (2 Cor 3:17–18; cf. 5:17).

The birth of the Christ child is divinely initiated and miraculously brought about by the Holy Spirit (Matt 1:18, 20; Luke 1:35). Although many find the Holy Spirit's activity surrounding the Christ child's birth difficult to substantiate, NT believers realized that this was possible since OT theology also featured the Spirit's supernatural action in bringing invisible things into reality. The Holy Spirit's action does not refer to spiritual rebirth but to God's divine intervention in history in order to bring about the incarnation. The miraculous activity of God was expected, particularly since OT prophecy foretold the anticipated Messiah's coming. The world of Judaism generally expected renewal through the Messiah's arrival. "Just as the Spirit of God was active at the foundation of the world, so that Spirit was to be expected also at its renewal."[3] Whereas the OT attributes the opening of the barren womb to the work of God (Gen 17:15, 22; 18:9–15; 21:1–7; 25:21; 29:31; Judg 13:2–25; 1 Sam 1), the NT claims specifically that the Messiah is conceived through the overshadowing of Mary by the Spirit. The opening of Elizabeth's womb follows the OT examples, but the conception of Jesus through the Holy Spirit is unique in Scripture and other ancient literature.

---

[2] Burge, *Anointed Community*, 158–71.
[3] Barrett, *Spirit*, 23.

The Spirit and God's People in the NT

Sonship

As in the OT, the Spirit of God is active in the formation and establishment of God's people. Although the terms may be different, God actively calls a people to himself and assures them of the fact that they belong to him. Jesus experiences sonship in a unique way (Luke 3:22; John 3:34–36; Acts 13:33) but indicates that all who believe in him can experience the same dimension of sonship (Matt 11:27).[4]

In the OT, God called Israel out of Egypt and by his Spirit established them as his people (Exod 14–15; Isa 43:1). The book of Isaiah particularly develops the exodus typology to show God's deliverance of his people. In the NT Jesus calls disciples to follow him. Jesus makes a distinction between his physical family and those who receive him by faith (Matt 12:46–50; Mark 3:31–35; John 7:1–9). The Gospels indicate that the true family of God exhibits a life-style in keeping with the family characteristic of holiness. Friends of Jesus obey him. In the Epistles, Paul presents catalogues of sins that the children of God must avoid. Therefore, the characteristic of being a true child of God in the NT is indicated by one's allegiance to Jesus and the Father. "Because you are sons, God sent the Spirit of his Son into our hearts, the Spirit who calls out, 'Abba, Father.' So you are no longer a slave, but a son; and since you are a son, God has made you also an heir" (Gal 4:6–7).

Similar to the exodus event, the child of God is said to undergo a baptism. "For we were all baptized by one Spirit into one body—whether Jews or Greeks, slave or free—and we were all given the one Spirit to drink" (1 Cor 12:13). Individuals are not only baptized into the body, but also anointed or baptized by the Spirit for service (Acts 2:1–4; 10:44–46) and incorporated into the body—both Jew and Greek. Pentecost marks the birthday of the people of God as the church. Not only does the Spirit transfer the individual from the family of humankind to the family of God, but the Spirit serves to assure family members of sonship (2 Cor 1:22; 5:5; Eph 1:13; 2 Tim 1:14; 1 John 3:24; 4:13). "For you did not receive a spirit that makes you a slave again to

[4] See Dunn, *Jesus and the Spirit*, 22–39, 62–67.

fear, but you received the Spirit of sonship. And by him we cry, 'Abba, Father.' The Spirit himself testifies with our spirit that we are God's children" (Rom 8:15–16; cf. Gal 3:26–27). The gift of the Spirit transfers an individual into the body of Christ (Rom 8:9).

Provision and Guidance

As in the OT, God providentially sustains and guides his people in the NT era. But the focus in the NT is not so much on the physical provisions but on the spiritual inheritance. Jesus makes the spiritual emphasis clear from the general to the particular. In the analogy of fatherly care for children, he emphasizes, "If you then, though you are evil, know how to give good gifts to your children, how much more will your Father in heaven give the Holy Spirit to those who ask him!" (Luke 11:11–13). Although there are several examples of Jesus and the church providing for the physical needs of people (Matt 14:13–21; Mark 8:1–9; Acts 4:32–37), the focus is on the spread of the gospel. The director and implementor of the mission is the Spirit. The Spirit leads Jesus from the initiation of his ministry (Matt 4:1). Jesus tells the disciples not to worry during times of testing, for the Holy Spirit will inspire them as to what to say (Mark 13:11). Individuals such as Simeon are led by the Spirit (Luke 2:27), but the predominate involvement of the Spirit in the spread of the kingdom is his work as director. "With the movement out from Jerusalem after Stephen's death, the Spirit becomes much more regularly understood as the power of mission, directing the evangelists into the new developments that continually opened up before them" (Acts 8:29, 39; 10:19; 11:12; 13:2–4; 15:28; 16:6f.; 19:21; 20:22; 21:4; Rom 8:14; Gal 5:18).[5]

Judgment

Both John the Baptist and Jesus were active in calling sinners to repentance (Matt 3:6–10; 4:17; 10:34–36; Mark 9:49; Luke 9:54; 12:49f.). Both Jews and Gentiles are called to repentance in the light of the impending judgment. Whereas John's baptism was an external demonstration of repentance, Jesus' baptism involved the baptism of the Holy Spirit and fire (Matt

[5] J. D. G. Dunn, "Spirit, Holy Spirit," *NIDNTT,* 3.700.

3:11). According to the OT, fire symbolized the judgment of God through which he would purify his people (Isa 4:4; Amos 7:4; Mal 3:1–4; 4:1). The import of this in Dunn's words is that, "Those who acknowledged their liability to judgment by submitting to the symbolized judgment of John's baptism would experience the messianic woes as a cleansing by a spirit of judgment and by a spirit of burning (Isa 4:4). Those who denied their guilt and did not repent would experience the Coming One's baptism in Spirit and fire as the bonfire which burned up the unfruitful branches and chaff."[6] Whereas this judgment is restricted to those who reject the invitation to be part of the kingdom of God, the Holy Spirit can also be grieved by the community or by individuals who sin (Eph 4:30). This is dramatically illustrated shortly after Pentecost in the case of Ananias and Sapphira, who lie to the Holy Spirit (Acts 5:1–11). Moreover, in the strongest terms, Jesus warns people not to grieve the Spirit. "But whoever blasphemes against the Holy Spirit will never be forgiven; he is guilty of an eternal sin" (Mark 3:29). In other words, rejection of the Holy Spirit closes the door to his effectual work of convicting sinners and leading them into truth through his ministry of teaching (John 16:5–16). Thus, both unbelievers and believers are called to heed the voice of the Spirit. "He who has an ear, let him hear what the Spirit says to the churches" (Rev 2:7, 11, 29; 3:6, 13, 22).

Restoration and Renewal

The work of the Spirit in the believer's life effects an ongoing renewal and transformation. "And we, who with unveiled faces all reflect the Lord's glory, are being transformed into his likeness with ever-increasing glory, which comes from the Lord, who is the Spirit" (2 Cor 3:18). The process of transformation involves a commitment to live life "in the Spirit," an expression Paul uses to refer to the observation and practice of ethically established norms (Rom 8:4–14; Gal 6:8). The Spirit provides the power that enables the individual to refrain from "the lusts of the flesh" and submit to the rule of the Spirit in one's life (Rom 2:29; 8:1–27; Gal 5:16ff.; 1 Pet 3:18). Paul exhorts believers to be filled with the Spirit (Eph 5:18) who is the controlling factor in

---

[6] Ibid., 695.

their lives. The Spirit effects a separation between the sacred and profane. "But you were washed, you were sanctified, you were justified in the name of the Lord Jesus Christ and by the Spirit of our God" (1 Cor 6:11; cf. 2 Cor 3:18). Both elements of faith and holy living are necessary for salvation. According to Paul, "from the beginning God chose you to be saved through the sanctifying work of the Spirit and through belief in the truth" (2 Thess 2:13; cf. 1 Pet 1:2). Renewal is also effected through worship and prayer, which are inspired by the Spirit (Phil 3:3; Eph 6:18), who strengthens believers (Eph 3:16).

The Spirit of God and Leadership

In chapter 4 we observed that the Spirit of God enabled selected leaders for the various roles and functions required in the leading of God's people. Whether for providential roles in supplying physical needs, for encouragement or rebuke, for deliverance from enemies, or for guidance, divinely equipped functionaries were essential in the development of the nation. It was God's purpose through leadership to prepare the nation for their role of blessing the nations (Gen 12:1–3). Although Israel was not entirely successful in this venture, even the limited successes were due to the Spirit's influence. Just as the Spirit of God brought order out of the chaos of the creation event, so the Spirit of God sought to bring order within the nation of Israel and humanity. In the OT, God through the Spirit sought to preside theocratically over his people through selected, anointed leadership to bring order out of chaotic situations. Whether in famine or wilderness (Joseph, Moses), siege or oppression (judges), kingdom expansion, shepherding, delivering (kings), or seeking to provoke a right response to God (prophets), the Spirit of God was involved. The Spirit strove through leadership to sort out confusion, to make a way, to bring administrative order to the nation. Through the blessing of the Spirit, God made human efforts fruitful.

The OT focus is on the Spirit's enabling of specific individuals for specific situations and particular needs. Group leadership roles are seldom portrayed, and even among the prophetic bands distinct individuals dominate. Jesus is the model of exemplary individual leadership in the Gospels (Matt 12:18–21; Luke

4:18–19). He functions as teacher, preacher, prophet, exorcist, messiah, and rejected king. He not only represents the type of leadership longed for in the OT but is extremely effective and powerful in his task. Jesus experienced no limitation of the Spirit. "For the one whom God has sent speaks the words of God, for God gives the Spirit without limit" (John 3:34). The spiritual gifts noted in 1 Corinthians 12 are often evident in his ministry. Frequently Jesus brings supernatural wisdom to bear in a difficult situation (Matt 10:16–20; 22:15–22; John 8:1–11). Supernatural knowledge is expressed (John 1:48; 4:17–18). Incredible faith is exhibited in the face of impossible situations (Matt 8:10; 17:20; 21:21; Mark 8:1–13). His healing abilities free many from sickness and disease (Matt 8:1–17; Mark 1:21–2:12). Miraculous powers are used to supersede ordinary laws of nature (Matt 14:15–21; Mark 6:45–56; John 11:43–44). Prophetic statements are often uttered (Mark 8:31ff.; 10:32–34; ch. 13). Discernment is exercised in order to distinguish external influences of behavior (Mark 5:1–13). Although no examples can be given regarding Jesus' use and interpretation of tongues, he indicates that they are to be expected (Mark 16:19).

In the NT church, however, the focus is on group expressions of individual gifts, which are diverse and require group participation and the pooling of resources in a unified, harmonious expression. Leadership, gifts, abilities, and individuals must function together for the benefit of all members and their effectiveness in the church. Divisions and the elevating of individuals or gifts is discouraged (1 Cor 3). Team ministry is advocated and practiced among the NT leaders from the inception of the early church. Although difficulties arise, the Holy Spirit helps to resolve thorny issues and disputes (Acts 11:1–18; 15:1–21). Just as temple artisans required tools to accomplish the construction of God's dwelling, so NT leaders require spiritual gifts to accomplish the "construction" of God's people (1 Cor 12).[7]

In the book of Acts, the Spirit is given to all present on the day of Pentecost (Acts 1:4–8; 2:4) and continues to be given to leaders and believers alike (2:38–39; 10:44). Believers prayed for God to continue the ministry of Christ through his church. "Stretch out your hand to heal and perform miraculous signs and wonders through the name of your holy servant Jesus." God

[7] See Dunn, *Jesus and the Spirit*, 199–258.

answered their prayer. "After they prayed, the place where they were meeting was shaken. And they were all filled with the Holy Spirit and spoke the word of God boldly" (4:30–31). But leadership has specific responsibilities and functions that the Spirit gives to particular individuals. Apostles are inspired and directed by the Spirit (4:8; cf. 2:14–36; 9:17). Prophets also receive direction and inspiration through the Spirit (21:10–11). Philip the evangelist is not only directed by the Spirit (8:29) but is transported like Ezekiel by the Spirit of the Lord (8:39). Pastors and teachers were selected and placed as overseers of the flock by the Spirit (20:28). Deacons are selected on the criterion that they be filled with the Spirit and wisdom for their administrative roles (6:1ff.).

When the serious dispute arose over the Gentile issue, the Spirit's work among the Gentiles was the deciding factor that convinced leaders that God's work was not only for the Jewish community but for all. Peter claimed that the Spirit directed him to the Gentiles and that the Holy Spirit in fulfillment of Jesus' words, "John baptized with water, but you will be baptized with the Holy Spirit," provided the necessary evidence by coming upon them as he did on the day of Pentecost (Acts 11:12–16). The council of elders also arrived at this verdict. "God, who knows the heart, showed that he accepted them by giving the Holy Spirit to them, just as he did to us" (15:8).

Therefore, all that is necessary for the "construction" of the church is provided through Spirit-selected, anointed, and gifted leadership (Rom 12:6ff.; 1 Cor 12; Eph 4:8–11; 2 Tim 1:6). The Spirit distributes and empowers gifts for the expansion of God's kingdom, the growth of the church, and the proper administration of God's people. Apostles (Acts 4:8, 31; 9:17), prophets (21:4–11; 1 Cor 14; 1 Thess 5:19), evangelists (Acts 8:29, 39), pastors and teachers (20:23, 28), as well as deacons (6:3–10; 7:55), labored together for the benefit of the church. The result of Spirit led leadership in the early church is apparent. "Then the church throughout Judea, Galilee and Samaria enjoyed a time of peace. It was strengthened; and encouraged by the Holy Spirit, it grew in numbers, living in the fear of the Lord" (Acts 9:31; cf. Eph 4:14–16).

But what can be said about the examples of failure in charismatic leadership? Thus far we have asserted the necessity of Spirit-enabled leadership within the kingdom of God. In the light of the evidence we must affirm that all positive results and successes were predominately due to Spirit-enabled, cooperative, and obedient leadership. Throughout Scripture however, we are confronted with situations where different individuals grieved God. The glory of God eventually departed from his people largely because of the failure of leaders to direct the nation in their relationship with God.

From both the OT and the NT we have examples of serious deficiencies even among selected, anointed, capable leaders. Kingship for the most part ended in disaster. Among the prophets, whether they exhibited ecstatic activity or not, some were considered false prophets. Many priests behaved deplorably. In the NT Paul warned of false teachers and some who would have evil intentions for the flock. Even Moses, some judges, David, and others had their setbacks. But perhaps the greatest example of failure was Saul, Israel's first anointed, charismatic king.

Saul seems to have everything going for him, but the first sign of trouble occurs in his assignment against the Amalekites. Saul and the army spare the best of the "banned" livestock. They are unwilling to destroy it. To a degree, Saul's reasoning and excuses seem "reasonable." But God's judgment is that Saul turned away from him, that Saul did not carry out explicit instructions (1 Sam 15:11, 22). Saul also fails to take responsibility for his actions (15:15, 21). Therefore, God is grieved that he made Saul king. Saul argues initially against the verdict of God and Samuel, blaming the army for the breach of instruction (15:20–21). In spite of his charismatic ability and repentance, he becomes an example of failure in leadership. He begs for Samuel to attend the public meeting with him that he may not be disgraced. But the result of his failure is the loss of the Spirit with its attendant implications. Saul becomes a tormented individual who tries to compensate his loss by surrounding himself with anointed music and the "charismatic" David. He becomes an insecure, anguished person who tries to fill the void left by the Spirit. His authority and ability diminished, Saul totally abdicates his responsibility as king and wastes his time pursuing David. In Saul's case, failure to obey explicit instructions and to accept responsibility for actions, leads to an ineffective leadership experience.

A similar example of failure is Solomon, who increasingly concentrated on external supports. Army and allies, reputation, wisdom, wealth, and power slowly undermined his dependence on God and the charismatic wisdom he was given. Lack of care and eventual turning from God resulted in kingdom disintegration (1 Kgs 11:9–14).

The Spirit of God and Prophecy

As surveyed in chapters 4 and 5, the office of the prophet and the nature of prophecy are important features in OT theology. Prophets pursued spiritual matters and sought to keep God's people in line with their covenant obligations. Through the Spirit, prophets received revelation, inspiration, direction, strength, and motivation for their ministry of promoting true allegiance to Yahweh. Through their efforts the kingdom of God was greatly influenced. But prophecy has a forward anticipatory outlook to a period where God would have immediate and intimate communication with all his people (Num 11:29; Joel 2:28). This period would be inaugurated with God's exemplary prophet. Jesus as prophet comes in fulfillment of the word given to Moses. "I will raise up for them a prophet like you from among their brothers; I will put my words in his mouth, and he will tell them everything I command him" (Deut 18:15–18). This anticipation was heightened during the intertestamental period when the synagogue considered the Spirit of God to be quenched. J. Jeremias summarizes this conviction: "In the time of the patriarchs, all pious and upright men had the spirit of God. When Israel committed sin with the golden calf, God limited the spirit to chosen prophets, high priests and kings. With the death of the last writing prophets, Haggai, Zechariah and Malachi, *the spirit was quenched* because of the sin of Israel. After that time, it was believed, God still spoke only through the 'echo of his voice' (*bat qōl* = echo), a poor substitute."[8] Therefore, the key ingredient to divinely inspired prophecy was considered to be the Spirit of God. "In the Judaism of the time, the imparting of the spirit almost always means prophetic inspiration."[9] Prophetic inspiration makes the ministries of John the Baptist and Jesus so dynamic. As prophetic voices crying out in the wilderness, they

---

[8] J. Jeremias, *New Testament Theology* (trans. J. Bowden; London: SCM, 1971) 80–81.

[9] Jeremias, *Theology,* 52. Jeremias goes on to say that Jesus definitely included himself in the ranks of the prophets, not only in specific instances where the term "prophet" is used, but also in texts where he claims to possess the spirit. "For the synagogue regarded the possession of the holy spirit, i.e. the spirit of God, as the mark of prophecy. To possess the spirit of God was to be a prophet" (p. 52).

usher in the eschatological age which the people of God anticipated and yearned for.

Some of the similarities between Jesus and the OT prophets are apparent in the Gospels. C. H. Dodd lists a number of similarities including that of special authority, the use of OT forms, the reception of vision/audition or pneumatic traits, the pronouncement of predictions, the use of symbolic actions, the call to repentance, the intimate relationship with God, a special knowledge of God as well as the focus of mission to Israel.[10] Indeed, Jesus had a reputation as a prophet (Mark 6:15; Luke 7:16, 39; 24:19). He himself was aware of his prophetic ministry (Luke 13:33) and functioned as a prophet in various ways (Matt 13:16ff.; chs. 23–24).[11]

According to Luke, the early church also exhibited similar prophetic characteristics. Although all of God's people could be considered prophets in fulfillment of the OT programmatic statements of Numbers 11:29 and Joel 2:28, some individuals functioned as prophets in a greater capacity. By receiving the Spirit of God and giving evidence of the same by inspired utterances, people indicated their possession by the Spirit (Acts 2:38; 5:32; 10:45–46; 19:6; Rom 8:9–12; 2 Cor 1:22; 5:5; Titus 3:5–6). But some who functioned as prophets in the church had divinely inspired insights (Acts 11:27ff.; 21:4–10). Others were inspired speakers who gave direction to the church (13:1; 15:28; 16:6f.), and generally encouraged the flock (11:23, 15:32).[12] Aune notes, "There is little reason to deny that both conceptions of the presence of the Spirit—as a general endowment of all Christians and as an exceptional manifestation of divine power in certain situations—are very old, and neither one can claim precedence over the other."[13] This observation is in keeping with the OT perspective that Spirit-possession was necessary for prophetic ministry and leadership. Furthermore, Spirit-reception was a programmatic imperative for all of God's people so that they too could experience God's intimate presence, so that they too could

[10] C. H. Dodd, "Jesus as Teacher and Prophet," *Mysterium Christi* (ed. G. K. A. Bell and A. Deissmann; Longmans, 1930) 53–66.

[11] See Dunn, *Jesus and the Spirit,* 82–84.

[12] Ibid., 170–75. For an in-depth overview of the character of early Christian prophecy, see D. E. Aune, *Prophecy in Early Christianity and the Ancient Mediterranean World* (Grand Rapids: Eerdmans, 1983) 189–230.

[13] Aune, *Prophecy,* 200–201.

take part in the mediatorial process (1:8; 5:32), and intercede for others (4:31; Rom 8:26–27).

The Spirit of God and Miracles

From the beginning of Scripture, the biblical worldview is one in which the miraculous can occur through the power and word of God (Gen 1:2; Exod 7:3; Deut 4:34; 6:22; 7:19; 26:8; 29:3; 34:11; Pss 78:43; 105:27; 135:9; Jer 32:20f.). In chapter 2 we surveyed the OT conception whereby the invisible is brought into reality through the spoken word of God, which is then acted upon by the Spirit and brought to fulfillment (cf. Isa 34:16; 55:10–11). The OT is uncompromising on the fact that spoken formulas, repetition, and manipulation are not factors in bringing about the design, word, and will of God. It is only God's word brought about by the Spirit that is effectual and able to supersede natural laws. Signs and portents may point to God's overriding power of nature and history. They often verify his word and legitimize his chosen leaders (Exod 4:1–9; 8:19; 7:8–13). Words spoken by the prophets could come true and be fulfilled when the prophet was commissioned, inspired, motivated, and guided by the Spirit of God.

The NT perspective is generally the same. Miracles occur but are mainly related to the expansion and development of the kingdom of God. The Gospels are in agreement that Jesus performed miracles—exorcisms, healings, and narratives of miraculous provision are frequent in the Gospels. Jesus quotes Isaiah 61:1–2 to indicate that the miraculous results of his preaching are due to the anointing of the Spirit of the Lord (Luke 4:18–19). Jesus is aware that his power comes through the Spirit. Spiritual power is evident in his offensive against evil and demonic possession. "But if I drive out demons by the Spirit of God, then the kingdom of God has come upon you" (Matt 12:28; Luke 11:20). Dunn comments:

> When he spoke or stretched out his hand something happened—the sufferer was relieved, the prisoner freed, the evil departed; this could only be the power of God. Here, we may already conclude, is the source of Jesus' authority—the sense that God's Spirit was ready to act through him, the knowledge that God would use him to heal, to overcome demons when they confronted him.[14]

---

[14] Dunn, *Jesus and the Spirit,* 47. Also see pp. 71–76.

Jesus is anointed by the Spirit who accomplishes the miraculous signs through him. After his ascension, however, Jesus becomes the dispenser of the Spirit to enable the disciples to carry on his ministry on earth. In speaking of salvation wrought by Christ, the writer to the Hebrews says, "God also testified to it by signs, wonders and various miracles, and gifts of the Holy Spirit distributed according to his will" (Heb 2:4; cf. Gal 3:5).

Apostles, prophets, and evangelists experience the miraculous in their ministries (Acts 2:43; 4:30; 5:12–16; 8:6, 13; 14:3; 15:12; 16:16–18; 19:11), a fact to which Paul testifies. "I will not venture to speak of anything except what Christ has accomplished through me in leading the Gentiles to obey God by what I have said and done—by the power of signs and miracles, through the power of the Spirit" (Rom 15:18–19).

Bibliography

Aberbach, M. and B. Grossfeld. *Targum Onkelos to Genesis: A Critical Analysis Together with an English Translation of the Text.* New York: Ktav, 1982.

Abrahams, I. *Studies in Pharisaism and the Gospels.* Cambridge: University Press, 1924.

Ackroyd, P. R. *Exile and Restoration.* OTL. Philadelphia: Westminster, 1968.

________. "*yāḏ.*" *TDOT* (1986). Volume 5, 397–426.

________. "Isaiah 1–12: Presentation of a Prophet." VTSup 29. Leiden: E. J. Brill, 1978.

Albertz, R. *Weltschöpfung und Menschenschöpfung: Untersucht bei Deuterojesaja, Hiob und in den Psalmen.* Stuttgart: Calwer, 1974.

Albertz, R. and C. Westermann. "*rûaḥ, Geist,*" *THAT* (1976). Volume 2, 726ff.

Albrektson, B. *History and the Gods.* Lund: Gleerup, 1967.

Allen, L. C. *The Books of Joel, Obadiah, Jonah and Micah.* NICOT. Grand Rapids: Eerdmans, 1976.

________. *Psalms 101–150.* WBC. Waco: Word, 1983.

Allison, D. C., Jr. "The Baptism of Jesus and a New Dead Sea Scroll." *BARev* 18 (1992) 57ff.

Alter, R. *The Art of Biblical Narrative.* New York: Basic, 1981.

Alter, R. and F. Kermode, eds. *The Literary Guide to the Bible.* Cambridge: Belnap, 1987.

Anderson, B. W. *Creation Versus Chaos.* Philadelphia: Fortress, 1987.

________. "Exodus Typology in Second Isaiah." In *Israel's Prophetic Heritage.* Edited by B. W. Anderson and W. Harrelson. Pages 180ff. New York: Harper and Brothers, 1962.

________. "A Stylistic Study of the Priestly Creation Story." In *Canon and Authority.* Edited by G. W. Coats and B. O. Long. Pages 150ff. Philadelphia: Fortress, 1977.

________, ed. *Creation in the Old Testament.* Philadelphia: Fortress, 1984.

Anderson, B. W., and W. Harrelson, eds. *Israel's Prophetic Heritage.* New York: Harper and Brothers, 1962.

Arichea, D. C., Jr. "Translating Breath and Spirit." *BT* 34 (April, 1983) 209ff.

Auld, A. G. "Prophets and Prophecy in Jeremiah and Kings." *ZAW* 96 (1984) 66–82.

Aune, D. E. *Prophecy in Early Christianity and the Ancient Mediterranean World.* Grand Rapids: Eerdmans, 1983.

Baltzer, K. *The Covenant Formulary.* Philadelphia: Fortress, 1971.

Barr, J. *The Semantics of Biblical Language.* Oxford: University Press, 1961.

Barrett, C. K. *The Holy Spirit and the Gospel Tradition.* London: S.P.C.K., 1947.

________. *A Commentary on the Epistle to the Corinthians.* 2d ed. London: Adam & Charles Black, 1968.

Bell, G. K. A. and A. Deissmann, eds. *Mysterium Christi.* London: Longmans, 1930.

Bergman, J. "*ʾānaph, ʾaph,*" *TDOT* (1974). Volume 1, 348–50.

Bernhardt, K. H. "*bārāʾ,*" *TDOT* (1975). Volume 2, 245ff.

Beuken, W. A. M. "*mišpāṭ:* The First Servant Song in Context." *VT* 22 (1972) 1–30.

Beyerlin, W. "Das Königscharisma Bei Saul." *ZAW* 73 (1962) 186–201.

Bieder, W. "*pneuma, pneumatikos,*" *TDNT* (1968). Volume 6, 368–72.

Birch, B. C. "The Development of the Tradition on the Anointing of Saul in 1 Samuel 9:1–10:16." *JBL* 90 (1971) 55–68.

Blenkinsopp, J. *A History of Prophecy in Israel.* Philadelphia: Westminster, 1983.

________. *Ezra-Nehemiah: A Commentary.* OTL. Philadelphia: Westminster, 1988.

Blocher, H. *In the Beginning: The Opening Chapters of Genesis.* Translated by D. G. Preston. Downers Grove, Ill.: InterVarsity, 1984.

Block, D. I. "The Period of the Judges: Religious Disintegration under Tribal Rule." In *Israel's Apostasy and Restoration: Essays in Honor of R. K. Harrison.* Edited by A. Gileadi. Pages 39–58. Grand Rapids: Baker, 1988.

Boling, R. G. *Judges: Introduction, Translation and Commentary.* AB. Garden City: Doubleday and Co., 1975.

Botterweck, G. J. and H. Ringgren, eds. *Theologisches Worterbuch zum Alten Testament.* Band 1–6, Stuttgart: W. Kohlhammer, 1972–91.

________. *Theological Dictionary of the Old Testament.* 6 vols. Translated by J. T. Willis et al. Grand Rapids: Eerdmans, 1974–91.

Bratcher, R. G. "Biblical Words Describing Man: Breath, Life, Spirit." *BT* 34 (1983) 201–9.

Bratsiotis, N. P. *"bāśār," TDOT* (1975). Volume 2, 317–30.

________. *"ʾîsh," TDOT* (1974). Volume 1, 222–35.

Brenton, L. C. L. *The Septuagint with Apocrypha: Greek and English.* Peabody, Mass.: Hendrickson, 1986.

Briggs, C. A. "The Use of *rûaḥ* in the Old Testament," *JBL* 19 (1900) 132–45.

Bright, J. *A History of Israel.* 3d ed. Philadelphia: Westminster, 1982.

Bromiley, G. W. et al., eds. *The International Standard Bible Encyclopedia.* 4 vols. Rev. ed. Grand Rapids: Eerdmans, 1979–88.

Bronner, L. *The Stories of Elijah and Elisha As Polemics Against Baal Worship.* Leiden: E. J. Brill, 1968.

Brown, F., S. R. Driver, and C. A. Briggs. *The New Brown-Driver-Briggs-Gesenius Hebrew and English Lexicon.* Peabody, Mass.: Hendrickson, 1979.

Brunner, F. D. *A Theology of the Holy Spirit.* Grand Rapids: Eerdmans, 1970.

Budd, P. J. *Numbers.* WBC. Waco: Word, 1984.

Burge, G. M. *The Anointed Community: The Holy Spirit in the Johannine Tradition.* Grand Rapids: Eerdmans, 1987.

Buttrick, G. A., ed. *The Interpreter's Dictionary of the Bible.* 4 vols. and supplement. Nashville: Abingdon Press, 1962–76.

Caquot, A. *"gār," TDOT* (1978). Volume 3, 49–53.

Cassuto, U. *A Commentary on the Book of Genesis.* Volume 1. Translated by I. Abrahams. Jerusalem: Magnes, 1961.

Childs, B. S. *Myth and Reality in the Old Testament.* SBT. London: SCM, 1960.

________. *The Book of Exodus.* OTL. Philadelphia: Westminster, 1974.

________. *Introduction to the Old Testament as Scripture.* Philadelphia: Fortress, 1979.

________. "On Reading the Elijah Narratives." *Int* 34 (1980) 128–37.

Clements, R. E. *God and Temple.* Oxford: Basil Blackwell, 1965.

Clines, D. J. A. *The Theme of the Pentateuch.* Sheffield: JSOT, 1986.

________. "The Image of God in Man." *Tyn Bul* 19 (1968) 53–103.

________. "Cyrus," *ISBE* (1979). Volume 1, 845–49.

________. "The Significance of the 'Sons of God' Episode (Genesis 6:1–4) in the Context of the 'Primeval History' (Genesis 1–11)." *JSOT* 13 (1979) 33–46.

Coats, G. W. and B. O. Long, eds. *Canon and Authority.* Philadelphia: Fortress, 1979.

Coggins, R., A. Phillips, and M. Kribbs, eds. *Israel's Prophetic Tradition.* Cambridge: University Press, 1982.

Cohen, G. G. "*šāʾāl,*" *TWOT* (1980). Volume 2, 891.

Cohn, R. L. "Literary Technique in the Jeroboam Narrative." *ZAW* 97 (1985) 24ff.

Collins, J. J. "The Court-Tales in Daniel and the Development of Apocalyptic." *JBL* 94 (1975) 218–34.

Conrad, J. "*zāqēn,*" *TDOT* (1980). Volume 4, 122–24.

Craghan, J. F. "Mari and Its Prophets: The Contributions of Mari to the Understanding of Biblical Prophecy." *BibTheoBul* 5 (1975) 32–55.

Craigie, P. C. *Psalms 1–50.* WBC. Waco: Word, 1983.

________. "The Comparison of Hebrew Poetry: Psalm 104 in the Light of Egyptian and Ugaritic Poetry." *Semitics* 4 (1974) 10–21.

Crenshaw, J. L. *Prophetic Conflict: Its Effect upon Israelite Religion. BZAW.* New York: Walter de Gruyter, 1971.

Cross, F. M. *Canaanite Myth and Hebrew Epic.* Cambridge: Harvard University, 1973.

________. "The Priestly Houses of Early Israel." In *Canaanite Myth and Hebrew Epic.* Pages 195–215. Cambridge: Harvard University, 1973.

Cross, F. M., and D. N. Freedman. "A Royal Song of Thanksgiving: 2 Samuel 22 and Psalm 18." *JBL* 72 (1953) 15–34.

Cross, F. M., W. E. Lemke, and P. D. Miller, eds. *Magnalia Dei: The Mighty Acts of God: Essays on The Bible and Archaeology in Memory of G. Ernest Wright.* Garden City: Doubleday, 1976.

Davids, P. *Commentary on James.* NIGTC. Grand Rapids: Eerdmans, 1982.

Davidson, A. B. *The Theology of the Old Testament.* Edinburgh: T. & T. Clark, 1904.

Davies, G. H., "Pillar," *IDB,* 3:817.

Day, J. *God's Conflict with the Dragon and the Sea: Echoes of a Canaanite Myth in the Old Testament.* Cambridge: University Press, 1985.

DeVries, S. J. *Prophet Against Prophet: The Role of the Micaiah Narrative (1 Kings 22) in the Development of the Early Prophetic Tradition.* Grand Rapids: Eerdmans, 1978.

Dodd, C. H. "Jesus as Teacher and Prophet." In *Mysterium Christi.* Edited by G. K. A. Bell and A. Deissmann. Pages 53–66. London: Longmans, 1930.

Dozeman, T. B. "The Way of the Man of God From Judah: True and False Prophecy in the Pre-Deuteronomic Legend of 1 Kings 13." *CBQ* 44 (1982) 382–93.

Dumbrell, W. J. *Covenant and Creation.* New York: Thomas Nelson, 1984.

________. *The End of the Beginning.* Homebush West, N.S.W., Australia: Lancer, 1985.

________. *The Faith of Israel.* Grand Rapids: Baker, 1988.

________. "Spirit and Kingdom of God in the Old Testament." *RTR* 33 (1974) 1–10.

________. "The Purpose of the Book of Judges Reconsidered." *JSOT* 25 (1983) 23–33.

Dunn, J. D. G. *Jesus and the Spirit.* Philadelphia: Westminster, 1975.

________. "Spirit, Holy Spirit." *NIDNTT.* Volume 3, 693–707.

Eichrodt, W. *Theology of the Old Testament.* OTL. 2 vols. Translated by J. A. Baker. Philadelphia: Westminster, 1961–77.

________. *Ezekiel: A Commentary.* OTL. Translated by C. Quin. Philadelphia: Westminster, 1970.

Elliger, K. and W. Rudolph, eds. *Biblia Hebraica Stuttgartensia.* Stuttgart: Deutsche Bibelgesellschaft, 1966–77, 1984.

Ellis, E. E. *Pauline Theology: Ministry and Society.* Grand Rapids: Eerdmans, 1989.

Emerton, J. A., ed. *Studies in the Historical Books of the Old Testament.* VTSup. Leiden: E. J. Brill, 1979.

Erickson, M. J. *Christian Theology.* Grand Rapids: Baker, 1983.

Even-Shoshan, A., ed. *A New Concordance of the Old Testament.* Jerusalem: "Kiryat Sepher," 1983.

Fabry, H. J. "*sāʿār,*" *TWAT* (1977). Volume 5, 895ff.

Fee, G. D. *The First Epistle to the Corinthians.* NICNT. Grand Rapids: Eerdmans, 1987.

Fensham, F. C. "A Few Observations on the Polarisation Between Yahweh and Baal in 1 Kings 17–19." *ZAW* 92 (1980) 227–36.

Feinberg, J. S. and P. D. Feinberg, eds. *Tradition and Testament.* Chicago: Moody, 1981.

Fishbane, M. "Biblical Prophecy as a Religious Phenomenon." In *Jewish Spirituality.* Edited by A. Green. Pages 62–81. London: SCM, 1989.

Gage, W. A. *The Gospel of Genesis: Studies in Protology and Eschatology.* Winona Lake, Ind.: Carpenter, 1984.

Gärtner, B. *The Temple and the Community in Qumran and the New Testament*. Cambridge: University Press, 1966.

Gaston, L. *No Stone On Another.* Leiden: E. J. Brill, 1970.

Gesenius, F. W. *Hebrew Grammar.* Rev. ed. by E. Kautzsch. Translated by A. E. Cowley: Oxford: Clarendon, 1910.

Giliadi, A., ed. *Israel's Apostasy and Restoration.* Grand Rapids: Baker, 1988.

Gray, G. B. *Numbers: A Critical and Exegetical Commentary.* ICC. Edinburgh: T. & T. Clark Ltd., 1903.

Gray, J. *1 and 2 Kings: A Commentary.* OTL. Rev. ed. Philadelphia: Westminster, 1970.

Gronbaek, J. H. *Die Geschichte vom Aufstieg Davids: Tradition und Komposition.* Copenhagen: Prostant Apud Munksgaard, 1971.

Gross, W. "Lying Prophet and Disobedient Man of God in 1 Kings 13." *Semeia* 15 (1979) 100ff.

Guillaume, A. *Prophecy and Divination.* London: Hodder and Stoughton, 1938.

Gunkel, H. "The Influence of the Babylonian Mythology Upon the Biblical Creation Story." In *Creation in the Old Testament.* Edited by B. W. Anderson. Pages 33–44. Philadelphia: Fortress, 1984.

Gunn, D. M. "Joshua and Judges." In *The Literary Guide to the Bible.* Edited by R. Alter and F. Kermode. Pages 104–5. Cambridge: Belnap, 1987.

Habel, N. C. *The Book of Job: A Commentary.* OTL. Philadelphia: Westminster, 1985.

Halpern, B. *The Constitution of the Monarchy in Israel.* Chico, Calif.: Scholars, 1981.

Hamilton, V. P. *The Book of Genesis: Chapters 1–17.* NICOT. Grand Rapids: Eerdmans, 1990.

Hanson, P. D. *The Dawn of Apocalyptic.* Philadelphia: Fortress, 1975.

________. *The People Called: The Growth of Community in the Bible.* San Francisco: Harper and Row, 1986

Haran, M. "From Early to Classical Prophecy: Continuity and Change." *VT* 27 (1977) 385–97.

Harris, R. L., G. L. Archer, Jr., and B. K. Waltke, eds. *Theological Wordbook of the Old Testament.* 2 vols. Chicago: Moody, 1980.

Harrison, R. K. *Numbers.* WEC. Chicago: Moody, 1990.

________. *Old Testament Times.* Grand Rapids: Eerdmans, 1970.

Hartley, J. E. *The Book of Job.* NICOT. Grand Rapids: Eerdmans, 1988.

Hasel, G. F. "The Polemic Nature of the Genesis Cosmogony." *EvQ* 46 (1974) 81–102.

________. "Dove," *ISBE* (1979). Volume 1, 987–89.

________. *"nāgîḏ," TWAT* (1975). Volume 4, 204ff.

Hatch, E. and H. A. Redpath. *A Concordance to the Septuagint and the Other Greek Versions of the Old Testament.* 2 vols. Reprint. Grand Rapids: Baker, 1983.

Hehn, J. "Zum Problem des Geistes im Alten Orient und im Alten Testament." *ZAW* 43 (1925) 218–25.

Heidel, A. *The Babylonian Genesis: The Story of Creation.* Chicago: University of Chicago Press, 1942.

Herrmann, S. "Prophetie in Israel und Agypten." VTSup 8. Leiden: E. J. Brill (1963) 53–64.

Hertzberg, H. W. *1 and 2 Samuel: A Commentary.* OTL. Translated by J. S. Bowden. Philadelphia: Westminster, 1964.

Hesse, F. *"chriō," TDNT* (1974). Volume 9, 502ff.

Hildebrandt, W. "An Investigation of *rûaḥ* as the Spirit of God in the Hebrew Canon." Th.M. thesis, Regent College, 1989.

Hill, D. *Greek Words and Hebrew Meanings: Studies in the Semantics of Soteriological Terms.* Cambridge: University Press, 1967.

Hobbs, T. R. "Excursus: On the Term 'Sons of the Prophets.' " In *2 Kings.* WBC. Waco: Word, 1985.

Hoffmeier, J. K. "Egypt as an Arm of Flesh: A Prophetic Response." In *Israel's Apostasy and Restoration: Essays in Honor of R. K. Harrison.* Edited by A. Gileadi. Pages 79–98. Grand Rapids: Baker, 1988.

________. "Moses." *ISBE* (1986). Volume 3, 423ff.

Holstein, J. A. "The Case of *ʾîš hā ʾelōhîm* Reconsidered: Philological Analysis Versus Historical Reconstruction." *HUCA* 49 (1977) 69–81.

Horton, S. M. *What the Bible Says About the Holy Spirit.* Springfield: Gospel, 1976.

Huffmon, H. B. "Prophecy in the Mari Letters." *BA* 31 (1968) 101–24.

________. "The Origins of Prophecy." In *Magnalia Dei: The Mighty Acts of God.* Edited by F. M. Cross et al. Pages 172–86. Garden City: Doubleday, 1976.

Hyers, C. "Biblical Literalism: Constricting the Cosmic Dance." In *Is God a Creationist? The Religious Case Against Creation-Science.* Edited by R. M. Frye. New York: Charles Scribner's Sons, 1983.

Imschoot, P. van, *Theology of the Old Testament.* Vol. l. Translated by K. Sullivan and F. Buck. Rome: Desclee Co., 1954.

Jenni, E. and C. Westermann, eds. *Theologisches Handwörterbuch zum Alten Testament.* 2 vols. Munich: Chr. Kaiser; Zurich Theologischer, 1976.

Jepsen, A. "*ḥāzāh*," *TDOT* (1980). Volume 4, 280–90.

Jeremias, J. *New Testament Theology.* Translated by J. Bowden. London: SCM, 1971.

________. "*nābîʾ*," *THAT* (1976). Volume 2, 7–26.

Jewett, P. K. "God Is Personal Being." In *Church, Word, and Spirit: Historical and Theological Essays in Honor of Geoffrey W. Bromiley.* Edited by J. E. Bradley and R. A. Muller. Pages 273–90. Grand Rapids: Eerdmans, 1987.

Johnson, A. R. *The Vitality of the Individual in the Thought of Ancient Israel.* Cardiff: University of Wales Press, 1949.

________. *The Vitality of the Individual in the Thought of Ancient Israel.* 2d ed. Cardiff: University of Wales Press, 1964.

________. *The One and the Many in the Israelite Conception of God.* Cardiff: University of Wales Press, 1971.

Johnson, B. "*mišpāṭ*," *TWAT* (1977). Volume 5, 102.

Johnson, E. "*ʾānaph, ʾaph*," *TDOT* (1974). Volume 1, 350–360.

Jones, G. H. *1 and 2 Kings.* Vol. 2. NCBC. Grand Rapids: Eerdmans, 1984.

Kaiser, O. *Isaiah 1–12: A Commentary.* OTL. Rev. ed. Translated by J. Bowden. Philadelphia: Westminster, 1974.

________. *Isaiah 13–39: A Commentary.* OTL. Translated by R. A. Wilson. Philadelphia: Westminster, 1974.

Kaiser, W. C., Jr. *Toward an Old Testament Theology.* Grand Rapids: Zondervan, 1978.

________. "The Blessing of David: The Charter for Humanity." In *The Law and the Prophets.* Edited by J. Skilton. Pages 298–318. Philadelphia: Presbyterian and Reformed, 1974.

Kapelrud, A. S. "Die Theologie der Schöpfung im Alten Testament." *ZAW* 91 (1979) 159–70.

Keel, O. *The Symbolism of the Biblical World: Ancient Near Eastern Iconography and the Book of Psalms.* Translated by T. J. Hallet. New York: Crossroad, 1985.

Kilian, R. "Genesis 1:2 und die Urgötter von Hermopolis." *VT* 16 (1966) 420–38.

Kirk, J. A. "The Meaning of Wisdom in James." *NTS* (1969) 25ff.

Kitchen, K. A. "Joseph." *ISBE* (1982). Volume 2, 1127–29.

Kittel, G. and G. Friedrich, eds. *Theological Dictionary of the New Testament.* 10 vols. Translated by G. W. Bromiley. Grand Rapids: Eerdmans, 1964–76.

Kleinknecht, H. "*pneuma, pneumatikos*," *TDNT* (1968). Volume 6, 332–59.

Kline, M. G. *Images of the Spirit.* Grand Rapids: Baker, 1980.

———. "Primal Parousia." *WTJ* 72 (1972) 245ff.

Knierim, R. "Die Messianologie des Ersten Buch Samuel." *EvTh* 30 (1970) 113–33.

Knight, G. A. F. *A Christian Theology of the Old Testament.* London: SCM, 1959.

Koch, K. "Wort und Einheit des Schöpfergottes in Memphis und Jerusalem." *ZTK* 62 (1965) 251–93.

———. "Is Daniel Also Among the Prophets?" In *Interpreting the Prophets.* Edited by J. L. Mays and P. J. Achtemeier. Pages 237–48. Philadelphia: Fortress, 1987.

Kohlenberger, J. R. III, ed. *The NIV Interlinear Hebrew-English Old Testament.* 4 vols. Grand Rapids: Zondervan, 1979–85.

Kohler, L. *Old Testament Theology.* Translated by A. S. Todd. Philadelphia: Westminster, 1957.

Kosmala, H. "*geburah,*" *TDOT* (1975). Volume 2, 367–82.

Kraus, H. J. *Worship in Israel: A Cultic History of the Old Testament.* Translated by G. Buswell. Richmond: John Knox, 1966.

———. *Theologie der Psalmen.* Neukirchener Verlag des Erziehungsvereins GmbH, 1979.

———. *Psalmen: 1–63, Biblischer Kommentar.* 1 Teilband, Neukirchener Verlag des Erziehungsvereins GmbH, 1979.

Kuntz, J. K. *The Self-Revelation of God.* Philadelphia: Westminster, 1967.

Kutsch, E. *Salbung als Rechtsakt: Im Alten Testament und im Alten Orient.* Berlin: Topelman, 1963.

Lacocque, A. *The Book of Daniel.* Translated by D. Pellauer. Atlanta: John Knox, 1979.

Lambdin, T. O. *Introduction to Biblical Hebrew.* New York: Charles Scribner's Sons, 1971.

Lambert, W. G. "A New Look at the Babylonian Background of Genesis." *JTS* 16 (1965) 287–300.

Lamberty-Zielinski, H. "*nišāmāh.*" *TWAT* (1977). Volume 5, 670ff.

LaSor, W. S., D. A. Hubbard, and F. W. Bush. *Old Testament Survey.* Grand Rapids: Eerdmans, 1982.

Lemke, W. E. "The Way of Obedience: 1 Kings 13 and the Structure of the Deuteronomistic History." In *Magnalia Dei: The Mighty Acts of God.* Edited by F. M. Cross et al. Pages 301–26. Garden City: Doubleday, 1976.

———. "Life in the Present and Hope for the Future," *Interpreting the Prophets.* Edited by J. L. Mays and P. J. Achtemeier. Page 200. Philadelphia: Fortress, 1987.

Leupold, H. C. *Exposition of Isaiah.* Grand Rapids: Baker, 1968.

Levenson, J. D. *Theology of the Program of Restoration of Ezekiel 40–48.* HSM 10. Atlanta: Scholars, 1976.

Liddell, H. G. and R. Scott, *A Greek-English Lexicon.* Rev. by H. S. Jones. Oxford: Clarendon, 1978.

Lindars, B. "The Israelite Tribes in Judges." In *Studies in the Historical Books of the Old Testament.* Edited by J. A. Emerton. Pages 95ff. VTSup. Leiden: E. J. Brill, 1979.

Lindblom, J. *Prophecy in Ancient Israel.* Philadelphia: Muhlenberg, 1962; Oxford: Basil Blackwell, 1962.

Lindsey, F. D. "The Career of the Servant in Isaiah 52:13–53:12," *BSac* [139] (1982) 312–29 & *BSac* [140] (1983) 21–39.

________. "The Commission of the Servant in Isaiah 49:1–13," *BSac* [139] (1982) 129–45.

________. "The Commitment of the Servant in Isaiah 50:4–11," *BSac* [139] (1982) 216–29.

________. "Isaiah's Songs of the Servant Part 1: The Call of the Servant in Isaiah 42:1–9." *BSac* 139 (1982) 12–31.

Lindström, F. *God and the Origin of Evil.* ConB 21. Lund: Gleerup, 1983.

Long, B. O. *1 Kings.* FOTL. Grand Rapids: Eerdmans, 1984.

Lys, D. *Ruach: Le Souffle dans l'Ancien Testament.* Paris: Presses Universitaires de France, 1962.

McCarter, P. K. *1 Samuel.* AB. Garden City: Doubleday, 1980.

McCready, W. O. "Priests and Levites." *ISBE* (1986). Volume 3, 965–70.

McCurly, F. R. *Ancient Myths and Biblical Faith: Scriptural Transformations.* Philadelphia: Fortress, 1983.

McKane, W. *Proverbs: A New Approach.* Philadelphia: Westminster, 1970.

McKelvey, R. J. *The New Temple: The Church in the New Testament.* Oxford: University Press, 1969.

Malamat, A. "Charismatic Leadership in the Book of Judges." In *Magnalia Dei: The Mighty Acts of God: Essays on the Bible and Archaeology in Memory of G. Ernest Wright.* Edited by F. M. Cross, et al. Pages 152–68. Garden City: Doubleday, 1976.

________. "Prophetic Revelations in New Documents from Mari and the Bible." VTSup 15. Leiden: E. J. Brill, 1966.

Mann, T. W. "The Pillar of Cloud in the Reed Sea Narrative." *JBL* 90 (1971) 15–30.

________. *Divine Presence and Guidance in Israelite Traditions: The Typology of Exaltation.* Baltimore: Johns Hopkins University Press, 1977.

Mansfield, M. R. *Spirit and Gospel in Mark.* Peabody, Mass.: Hendrickson, 1987.

Marsh, F. E. *Emblems of the Holy Spirit.* Grand Rapids: Kregel, 1957–76.

Matthews, V. H. "Theophanies Cultic and Cosmic." In *Israel's Apostasy and Restoration: Essays in Honor of R. K. Harrison.* Edited by A. Gileadi. Pages 307–18. Grand Rapids: Baker, 1988.

Mays, J. L. *Micah: A Commentary.* OTL. Philadelphia: Fortress, 1976.

Mays, J. L. and P. J. Achtemeier, eds. *Interpreting the Prophets.* Philadelphia: Fortress, 1987.

Mettinger, T. N. D. *King and Messiah: The Civil and Sacral Legitimation of the Israelite Kings.* Lund: Gleerup, 1986.

Miller, J. M. and J. H. Hayes. *A History of Ancient Israel and Judah.* Philadelphia: Westminster, 1986.

Miller, P. D., Jr. *Genesis 1–11: Studies in Structure and Theme.* JSOT 8. Sheffield: University of Sheffield, 1978.

Mitchell, C. W. *The Meaning of BRK 'To Bless' in the Old Testament.* Atlanta: Scholars, 1987.

Moltmann, J. *God in Creation: An Ecological Doctrine of Creation.* Translated by M. Kohl. London: SCM, 1985.

________. *The Spirit of Life: A Universal Affirmation.* Translated by M. Kohl. London: SCM, 1992.

Montague, G. T. *The Holy Spirit: Growth of a Biblical Tradition.* Peabody, Mass.: Hendrickson, 1994.

Moore, G. F. *Judges: A Critical and Exegetical Commentary.* ICC. Edinburgh: T. & T. Clark, 1895.

Moran, W. "New Evidence from Mari on the History of Prophecy." *Bib* 50 (1969) 15–56.

Mowinckel, S. *The Psalms in Israel's Worship.* 2 vols. Translated by D. R. Ap-Thomas. New York: Abingdon, 1962.

________. "The 'Spirit' and the 'Word' in the Pre-exilic Reforming Prophets." *JBL* 53 (1934) 199–227.

Müller, H. P. "*ḥokmāh.*" *TDOT* (1980). Volume 4, 370–85.

Ness, A. W. *The Holy Spirit.* 2 vols. Christian Centre, 1979.

Neve, L. *The Spirit of God in the Old Testament.* Tokyo: Seibunsha, 1972.

Newsome, J. D., Jr. "Toward a New Understanding of the Chronicler and His Purpose." *JBL* 94 (1975) 201–217.

North, C. R. *The Suffering Servant in Deutero-Isaiah.* London: Oxford University Press, 1948.

North, R. "*ḥādā.*" *TDOT* (1980). Volume 4, 225–44.

Oehler, G. F. *Theology of the Old Testament.* Translated by G. E. Day. Grand Rapids: Zondervan, n. d.

Oepke, A. "*nephelē*." *TDNT* (1969). Volume 4, 905.
Oppenheim, A. L. *Ancient Mesopotamia*. Chicago: University of Chicago Press, 1964.
Orlinsky, H. M. "The Plain Meaning of *rûach* in Genesis 1:2." *JQR* 48 (1957–58) 174–82.
________. "The Seer in Ancient Israel." *Oriens Antiquus* 4 (1965) 154ff.
Overholt, T. W. *The Threat of Falsehood*. SBT. London: SCM, 1970.
Payne, J. B. *The Theology of the Older Testament*. Grand Rapids: Zondervan, 1962.
Peters, J. P. "The Wind of God." *JBL* 30 (1911) 44–54.
Petersen, D. L. *The Roles of Israel's Prophets*. Sheffield: JSOT, 1981.
________. *Haggai and Zechariah 1–8: A Commentary*. OTL. Philadelphia: Westminster, 1984.
Pope, M. H. *Job*. AB. 3d ed. Garden City: Doubleday, 1973.
Preuss, H. D. "*nûaḥ*," *TWAT* (1977). Volume 5, 299f.
Pritchard, J. B., ed. *Ancient Near Eastern Texts Relating to the Old Testament*. 3d ed. with supplement. Princeton: University Press, 1969.
Rad, G. von, *Studies in Deuteronomy*. SBT. Translated by D. Stalker. London: SCM, 1961.
________. *Old Testament Theology*. Vol. 2. Translated by D. M. G. Stalker. New York: Harper & Row, 1965.
________. *The Problem of the Hexateuch and Other Essays*. Translated by E. W. Trueman Dicken. London: Oliver & Boyd, 1965.
________. *Genesis: A Commentary*. OTL. Translated by J. H. Marks. 1st ed. 1961; Rev. ed. Philadelphia: Westminster, 1972.
________. *Wisdom in Israel*. Translated by J. D. Martin. Nashville and New York: Abingdon, 1972.
________. "The Levitical Sermon in 1 and 2 Chronicles." In *The Problem of the Hexateuch and Other Essays*. Translated by E. W. Trueman Dicken. Pages 271ff. London: Oliver & Boyd, 1965.
Rea, J. *The Holy Spirit in the Bible: All the Major Passages About the Spirit*. Altamonte Springs, Fl.: Creation House, 1990.
Rendtorff, R. "*prophetes*," *TDNT* (1972). Volume 6, 797.
Richter, W. "Zu den 'Richtern Israels'." *ZAW* 77 (1965) 61–71.
Ringgren, W. "König und Messias." *ZAW* 64 (1952) 120–47.
________. "*bînāh*," *TDOT* (1975). Volume 2, 99–107.
________. "*bᶜr*." *TDOT* (1975). Volume 2, 201–5.
________. "Prophecy in the ancient Near East." In *Israel's Prophetic Tradition*. Edited by R. Coggins et al. Pages 1–11. Cambridge: University Press, 1982.

________. *"ḥōšeḵ,"* *TDOT* (1986). Volume 5, 248–58.

Roberts, J. J. M. "The Hand of Yahweh." *VT* 21 (1971) 244–51.

Robinson, H. W. *Inspiration and Revelation in the Old Testament.* Oxford: Clarendon, 1946.

Ross, J. F. "Prophecy in Hamath, Israel, and Mari." *HTR* 63 (1970) 1–28.

Rowley, H. H. *The Servant of the Lord and Other Essays on the Old Testament.* 2d Rev. ed. Oxford: Basil Blackwell, 1965.

________. "The Nature of Old Testament Prophecy in the Light of Recent Study." In *The Servant of the Lord and Other Essays on the Old Testament.* 2d Rev. ed. Pages 97ff. Oxford: Basil Blackwell, 1965.

Sabourin, L. *The Psalms: Their Origin and Meaning.* New York: Alba House, 1974.

Sailhamer, J. H. "Genesis." *Expositors Bible Commentary* [12 vols.] Grand Rapids: Zondervan, 1990.

Sanders, J. A. *Torah and Canon.* Philadelphia: Fortress, 1972.

________. "Canonical Hermeneutics: True and False Prophecy." In *From Sacred Story to Sacred Text.* Pages 87–105. Philadelphia: Fortress, 1987.

Scharbert, J. " *ʾrr."* *TDOT* (1974). Volume 1, 405–18.

________. *"brk."* *TDOT* (1975). Volume 2, 279–308.

________. *"nepes."* *TWAT* (1977). Volume 5, 538.

Schmidt, W. H. *"dāḇar."* *TDOT* (1978). Volume 3, 94–125.

Schoemaker, W. R. "The Use of *rûaḥ* in the Old Testament and *pneûma* in the New Testament," *JBL* 23 (1904) 13–67.

Schweizer, E. *"pneuma."* *TDNT* (1972). Volume 6, 332–455.

Seybold, K. *"māšaḥ."TWAT* (1977). Volume 5, 51ff.

Shepperd, G. T. "Wisdom." *ISBE* (1988). Volume 4:1076ff.

Simon, U. "1 Kings 12: A Prophetic Sign—Denial and Persistence." *HUCA* 47 (1976) 81ff.

Skilton, J., ed. *The Law and the Prophets.* Philadelphia: Presbyterian and Reformed, 1974.

Sklba, R. J. "'Until the Spirit from on High Is Poured out on Us' (Isa 32:15): Reflections on the Role of the Spirit in the Exile." *CBQ* 46 (1984) 1–17.

Smith, J. M. P. "The Syntax and Meaning of Genesis 1:1–13." *AJSL* 44 (1927–28) 108–15.

________. "The Use of Divine Names as Superlatives." *AJSL* 45 (1928–29) 212–13.

________. "A Semotactical Approach to the Meaning of the term *rûaḥ ʾᵉlōhîm* in Genesis 1:2." *JNWSL* 81 (1920) 99–104.

Snaith, N. H. *The Distinctive Ideas of the Old Testament.* New York: Schocken, 1964.

Soggin, J. A. *Judges: A Commentary.* OTL. Translated by J. Bowden. Philadelphia: Westminster, 1981.

Speiser, E. A. *Genesis: A Commentary.* AB. Garden City: Doubleday, 1986.

Steck, O. H. *Der Schöpfungsbericht der Priesterschrift: Studien zur literarkritischen und uberlieferungsgeschichtlichen Problematik von Genesis 1,1–2,* 4a. Göttingen: Vandenhöeck & Ruprecht, 1975.

Stronstad, R. *The Charismatic Theology of St. Luke.* Peabody, Mass.: Hendrickson, 1984.

Sturdy, J. "The Original Meaning of 'Is Saul Also Among the Prophets? (1 Samuel 10:11, 12; 19:24)' " *VT* 20 (1970) 206–13.

Tengstrom, S. "*rûaḥ.*" *TWAT* (1990). Volume 6, 385–418.

Thomas, D. W. "A Consideration of Some Unusual Ways of Expressing the Superlative in Hebrew." *VT* 3 (1953) 209–24.

Thompson, J. A. *Deuteronomy: An Introduction and Commentary.* Tyndale OT Commentaries. Downers Grove, Ill.: InterVarsity, 1974.

Thompson, W. R. "The Epistle of James—A Document on Heavenly Wisdom," *WTJ* 13 (1978) 7–12.

VanGemeren, W. A. "The Spirit of Restoration." *WTJ* 50 (1988) 81–102.

Vaux, R. de, *Ancient Israel.* 2 vols. Translated by J. McHugh. New York: McGraw-Hill, 1965.

Verhoef, P. A. *The Books of Haggai and Malachi.* NICOT. Grand Rapids: Eerdmans, 1987.

Vetter, D. "*rʾh, sehen.*" *THAT* (1976). Volume 2, 694–702.

Volz, P. *Der Geist Gottes.* Tübingen: J. B. C. Mohr, 1910.

Wakeman, M. K. *God's Battle with the Monster.* Leiden: E. J. Brill, 1973.

Waltke, B. K. "The Creation Account in Genesis 1:1–3. Five Parts. *BSac* 132–33 (1975–76).

________. "Joshua," *ISBE* (1982). Volume 2:1133f.

________. "The Phenomenon of Conditionality Within Unconditional Covenants." In *Israel's Apostasy and Restoration: Essays in Honor of R. K. Harrison.* Edited by A. Gileadi. Pages 123–39. Grand Rapids: Baker, 1988.

________. "The Literary Genre of Genesis, Chapter One." *Crux* 27 (1991) 2–10.

Watts, J. D. W. *Isaiah 34–66.* WBC. Waco: Word, 1987.

Weiser, A. *The Psalms: A Commentary.* OTL. Translated by H. Hartwell. Philadelphia: Westminster, 1962.

Weisman, Z. "Charismatic Leaders in the Era of the Judges." *ZAW* 89 (1977) 399–411.

________. "The Personal Spirit as Imparting Authority." *ZAW* 93 (1981) 225–34.

Wenham, G. J. *Genesis 1–15.* WBC. Waco: Word, 1987.

Westerholm, S. "Tabernacle." *ISBE* (1988). Volume 4, 703ff.

Westermann, C. *Isaiah 40–66: A Commentary.* OTL. Translated by D. M. G. Stalker. Philadelphia: Westminster, 1969.

________. *Genesis 1–11: A Commentary.* Translated by J. J. Scullion. Minneapolis: Augsburg, 1984.

________. "*tᵉhôm.*" *THAT* (1976). Volume 2, 1030–31.

________, ed. *Studien zum Pentateuch.* Vienna: Herder, 1977.

Westfall, M. R. "The Scope of the Term 'Spirit of God' in the Old Testament." *IJT* 26 (1977) 29–43.

White, W. "*rōʾêh.*" *TWOT* (1980). Volume 2, 823.

Whybray, R. N. *The Heavenly Counsellor in Isaiah 40:13–14.* Cambridge: University Press, 1971.

________. *Isaiah 40–66.* Greenwood, S.C.: Attic, 1975; NCBC. Grand Rapids: Eerdmans, 1981.

Williams, J. G. "The Prophetic 'Father:' A Brief Explanation of the Term 'Sons of the Prophets'." *JBL* 85 (1966) 344–48.

Wilson, J. A. *The Culture of Ancient Egypt.* Chicago: University of Chicago Press, 1951.

________. "The Prophecy of Nefer-rohu." In *ANET,* 444–46.

Wilson, R. R. "The Journey of Wen Amon to Phoenicia." Pages 25–29. *ANET,* 1955.

________. "Early Israelite Prophecy." *Int* 32 (1978) 10f.

________. "Prophecy and Ecstasy: A Reexamination." *JBL* 98 (1979) 321–37.

________. "Prophecy in Crisis: The Call of Ezekiel." In *Interpreting the Prophets.* Edited by J. L. Mays and P. J. Achtemeier. Pages 167–68. Philadelphia: Fortress, 1987.

Wolff, H. W. *Anthropology of the Old Testament.* Translated by M. Kohl. Philadelphia: Fortress, 1974.

________. *Hosea: A Commentary.* Translated by G. Stansell. Philadelphia: Fortress, 1974.

________. *Joel and Amos.* Hermeneia. Translated by W. Janzen et al. Philadelphia: Fortress, 1977.

________. *Haggai: A Commentary.* Translated by M. Kohl. Minneapolis: Augsburg, 1988.

Wolff, H. "The Transcendent Nature of Covenant Curse Reversals." In *Israel's Apostasy and Restoration: Essays in Honor of R. K. Harrison.* Edited by A. Gileadi. Pages 319–25. Grand Rapids: Baker, 1988.

Wood, L. J. *The Holy Spirit in the Old Testament.* Grand Rapids: Zondervan, 1976.

Woude, A. S. van der, "Micah in Dispute with the Pseudo-Prophets." *VT* 19 (1969) 244–60.

Yates, J. E. *The Spirit and the Kingdom.* London: S.P.C.K., 1963.

Young, E. J. "The Interpretation of Genesis 1:2." *WTJ* 23 (1960–61) 151–78.

Zimmerli, W. *Ezekiel 1: A Commentary on the Book of the Prophet Ezekiel Chapters 1–24.* Hermeneia. Translated by R. E. Clements. Philadelphia: Fortress, 1979.

________. *Ezekiel 2: A Commentary on the Book of the Prophet Ezekiel Chapters 25–28.* Hermeneia. Translated by J. D. Martin. Philadelphia: Fortress, 1983.

________. *"pais theou." TDNT* (1970). Volume 5, 654ff.

________. "Der Prophet im Pentateuch." In *Studien zum Pentateuch.* Edited by C. Westermann. Pages 197–211. Vienna: Herder, 1977.

Zlotowitz, M. *Bereishis: Genesis—A Translation with a Commentary Anthologized from Talmudic, Midrashic, and Rabbinic Sources.* Brooklyn, N.Y.: Mesorah, 1986.

Index of Subjects

Mediate, 107, 129, 152, 155–56, 158, 173, 181–82, 207
Messiah, 24, 27, 62, 66, 90, 92, 124, 127, 129, 135–36, 149, 152, 197, 200, 202
Miracles, 23, 62, 88, 108–9, 139–40, 174–75, 178, 197, 202, 207–8
Mission, 75, 113, 131, 199, 206
Monarchy, 25, 27, 76f., 84, 92, 121, 127, 130, 135, 137, 139, 183–84
Motivation, 22, 26–27, 93, 96, 99, 115, 117, 121, 129, 137, 149, 168, 180, 188–89, 202, 205
Mountain, 47, 49, 64, 71, 80, 159

Nation, 24–25, 29, 31, 39, 46, 67–69, 80, 85, 96–97, 103, 109, 112, 121, 131, 149, 159, 167, 201

Official, 22, 111, 113, 130
Oil, 2, 101, 104, 107, 122–25, 133
Order, 31, 43, 132–33, 201

Paradigmatic, 107, 110, 157–58
People of God, 29, 64, 67ff., 71, 86, 102, 107, 129, 198
Pillar, 72ff., 100
Plan, 27, 41, 81, 89, 108, 137, 147, 149, 158, 167, 173, 181–82, 194–95
Pneumatology, 1, 3, 44, 91, 193
Power, 24, 30, 37, 41, 45, 54, 56, 61, 64, 68–69, 71, 77, 81–82, 84, 87–89, 93, 95, 97, 100, 108–10, 114, 116–17, 121–22, 126, 129, 131, 133–34, 139–40, 142, 147, 158, 161, 163, 166ff., 175–76, 178, 188, 192, 196, 199, 200, 206–8
Prayer, 51, 66, 78, 82–83, 97, 117, 119, 156, 173, 201, 202–3
Presence of God, 21–23, 32, 35, 42, 46–51, 53–54, 76, 82–87, 89, 97–101, 107, 125, 148, 166–68, 171, 194
Preservation, 21, 28, 55, 58, 67, 76–80, 82, 105, 145
Priest, 27, 65, 96, 98, 105ff., 122–24, 145ff., 154, 159, 173, 185, 191, 204
Programmatic, 22, 86, 98, 110, 116, 157–58, 206
Promise, 86, 94, 97, 101, 128–29, 136, 167, 185
Prophecy, 23–24, 26, 74, 92, 97, 99–101, 110, 120–21, 138, 142, 146, 151ff., 169–71, 180, 191, 205
Prophecy: False, 10, 17, 156, 163, 182ff., 204; True, 182ff., 187
Prophet, 17–19, 21, 24–25, 49, 68, 72, 74, 96, 98, 105ff., 123–24, 143, 151ff., 177, 180, 191
Prosperity, 60–61, 78, 95, 125
Protection, 22, 73, 75–76, 80, 82, 87, 124, 134, 147–48, 171, 175
Punishment, 9, 14, 20–21, 23, 121, 128, 131, 141, 184, 188
Purification, 62, 64–65, 86–87, 96, 200
Purpose, 27, 136–37, 149, 166, 181

Redemption, 39, 68
Remnant, 17, 21, 25, 99–101, 139, 176
Renewal, 55–56, 62, 65–66, 82, 91–93, 102, 148, 197, 200–201
Repentance, 21, 99, 199–200, 204, 206
Rest, 23, 48, 55, 88, 100–102, 113, 128
Restoration, 2, 21–22, 24, 27, 49, 62–67, 87–88, 91–96, 101–3, 133, 136, 147, 200–201
Revelation, 22, 47, 72, 74–75, 90, 106–7, 138, 151, 155–58, 161, 164, 168, 173, 184–85, 195
Righteousness, 24, 92, 128–29, 132, 135, 138
Rule, 24, 48–49, 55–56, 59–62, 92, 108, 113, 119, 122–23, 125, 127–28, 135, 138–39, 145, 172

Salvation, 52, 61, 63, 68, 79, 93, 97, 118, 129, 131–32, 134, 154, 201
Sanctifies, 51, 127, 201

Index of Modern Authors

Index of Hebrew and Greek Words

Index of Scripture References

Old Testament

New Testament